Miss Ella

OF

COMMANDER'S PALACE

Miss Ella
== OF ==
COMMANDER'S PALACE

‖ "I DON'T WANT A RESTAURANT WHERE A
JAZZ BAND CAN'T COME MARCHING THROUGH" ‖

ELLA BRENNAN & TI ADELAIDE MARTIN

GIBBS SMITH
TO ENRICH AND INSPIRE HUMANKIND

Published by
Gibbs Smith
P.O. Box 667
Layton, Utah 84041

1.800.835.4993 orders
www.gibbs-smith.com

Jacket designed by Michel Vrana
Interiors designed by Renee Bond
Printed and bound in the United States of America
Gibbs Smith books are printed on either recycled, 100% post-consumer waste,
FSC-certified papers or on paper produced from sustainable PEFC-certified
forest/controlled wood source. Learn more at www.pefc.org.

Library of Congress Cataloging-in-Publication Data
Names: Brennan, Ella, author. | Martin, Ti Adelaide, author.
Title: Miss Ella of Commander's Palace / Ella Brennan with Ti Adelaide Martin.
Description: First edition. | Layton, Utah : Gibbs Smith, [2016]
Identifiers: LCCN 2016003385 | ISBN 9781423642558 (hardcover)
Subjects: LCSH: Brennan, Ella. | Restaurateurs—United States—Biography. |
Commander's Palace (Restaurant) | Cooking, American—Louisiana style.
Classification: LCC TX910.5.B685 A3 2016 | DDC 647.95092—dc23
LC record available at http://lccn.loc.gov/2016003385

TO MY SISTER DOTTIE (AND MY AUNT), WHO IS THE MOST KIND, GENEROUS, STRONG, UNSELFISH PERSON WE KNOW. SHE HAS BEEN THE CORE AND THE BACKBONE OF THE BRENNAN FAMILY FROM THE BEGINNING.

ELLA BRENNAN
TI ADELAIDE MARTIN

Contents

Acknowledgments

The most special thanks to Judith Weber, who pushed, encouraged and needled me to do this book for years, even though the subject wanted nothing to do with it. Her honest assessment, as well as cheerleading along the way, was my guiding light.

My entire life is one big collaboration. This book was no exception. Restauranting is a team sport. Writing *Miss Ella* was too. Thank you to dear Jerry Shriver, who interviewed, researched, organized, edited and wrote much of *Miss Ella*. Jerry got incredibly good at taking our long and winding interviews and notes and fashioning them into organized, coherent passages and chapters whilst channeling Mom in a scary spot-on way. And to Deb Shriver, who said, "When are you going to do the book on Ella? And you need to do a documentary, too." And to Leslie Iwerks, who did the amazing documentary and allowed us to share in all her interviews. To Darla Fisackerly, who keeps me sane and typed the entire book from my handwritten notes and made good suggestions along the way. To Lally Brennan and Sam Fritz, who helped pull it all together. And to the amazing teams that never let the standards drop in our restaurants and allowed me the time to work on *Miss Ella*: my cousin Brad Brennan, Steve Woodruff, Tory McPhail, Don Strunk, Chris Barbato, Tom Robey, Dan Davis, Arlene Nesser, Lelia Lambert, Juan Carlos Gonzalez and Meg Bickford. And Reginelli's leaders, Darryl Reginelli and Lisa Millet.

Thanks to our wonderful good friend Cokie Roberts, who feels like family, for a charming, warm foreword. And to the amazing list of dear friends who agreed to be interviewed for the book and helped us find old photographs and articles: Daniel Boulud, Gene Bourg, Alex Brennan Martin, Dickie Brennan, Dottie Brennan, Lally Brennan, Ralph Brennan, Frank Brigtsen, Leah Chase, Tom Fitzmorris, Joe Henican, Emeril Lagasse, Kate Lindquist, Maggie McCabe, Danny Meyer, Drew Nieporent, Emily Oppenheimer, Chris Owens, John Pope, Julia Reed, Melvin Rodrigue, Jack Robinson, Jerry Siegel, Ron Thompson, Poppy Tooker, Jeremiah Tower, Hal Williamson, Donn Young, and Tim and Nina Zagat.

And to Gibbs Smith and delightful editors Madge Baird and Kerry McShane and designer Renee Bond.

—TI ADELAIDE MARTIN

Foreword

HAPPILY FOR ME, I've known Ella Brennan all my life. (If I'm off by
a year or two, meaning my parents probably didn't bring me to Breakfast at
Brennan's until I was a toddler, there's no one around who's going to correct me.)
I've known her to be a smart, funny, generous person who's wonderfully entertaining to be around and is a great contributor to the city she loves. And I always
knew, despite appearances to the contrary, that she worked unbelievably hard to
make her restaurants as fabulous as they are. But I didn't know, until I read this
book, what an assiduous student Ella has been of the world of food and wine,
and what a phenomenal teacher she's become in the world of business. No one
should think about opening a restaurant without first reading this book.

This is, in essence, a history of fine dining in America, written by one of the
people universally recognized in the world of restaurateurs who brought about
the revolution that taught many in this country what good food and service is
all about. It's fair to say that Ella Brennan changed the way Americans relate to
food as much as Julia Child did. They were (fortunately Ella still is) women who
understood that people just needed to know how delicious food could be, and
in Ella's case, how perfect a dining-out experience could be, and how it could
change their lives. Ella has run restaurants that have won every award the industry can confer, but more important, she has genuinely enjoyed doing it and made
it enjoyable for all of us who are lucky enough to partake of her hospitality. I'm
always mesmerized when I have the chance to listen to Ella, especially when I
can convince her to talk about the family or tell funny incidents like how Bananas
Foster came to be, and thankfully her voice comes through loud and clear in

this book. As I read her words, I can hear her speaking them, and I sit here with a smile as her impossible-not-to-share laugh tickles my imagination. Great characters from politics and show business and the arts have come through her restaurants and come through these pages, not to mention the chefs that Ella recruited and nurtured until they became household names. She writes about her months-long interviewing of Emeril Lagasse, a story I have heard from him as well, until she felt ready to bring the young man from Massachusetts to the demanding diners of New Orleans, where he famously succeeded under Ella's careful guidance.

That guidance and care extends to every person who works with Ella Brennan, contributing mightily, along with the to-die-for food, to the atmosphere that makes Commander's Palace and other Brennan restaurants places you want to return to again and again. And having learned from the master—mistress?—the next generation of the family continues to give personal attention to employee and patron alike. I didn't know until I read this book that there's a restaurant rule: BOD, or Brennan on Duty, meaning there's always a family member there making sure all is as it should be. I might not have known the rule, but I certainly experienced it over these many decades, including during the 1992 Republican National Convention in Houston, when Ella relocated there for the duration to make sure that Brennan's outpost, run by her son Alex, lived up to the name. (A died-in-the-wool Democrat, Ella put the business first but was awfully happy when we journalists took our tables among the conventioneers.) One personally rewarding benefit of the BOD rule: it allowed me to meet and then get to know Ella's remarkable daughter Ti Adelaide Martin, now a true friend.

And that's as it should be, because my mother, Lindy Boggs, counted Ella Brennan as one of the most important people in her life. Mamma and Ella had a grand time together, and it was special for me when I supped alongside them, soaking in their stories, lapping up their laughter and wondering at their wisdom. In these pages, you'll find much of that wisdom and many of those stories. I suspect you'll share the laughter as well. If not, you don't deserve to join us in the Saloon in the Sky, but I personally have great hopes of ending up there with Ella and everyone she loves.

Introduction

BY TI ADELAIDE MARTIN

"IF YOU STAND AT THE DOOR of a good restaurant in New Orleans, you'll eventually meet everybody," says my mom, Ella Brennan. I never met anyone more interesting than she.

Whether she was grooming young managers and great chefs at Commander's Palace, entertaining celebrities at Brennan's, celebrating Mardi Gras in grand style, pushing politicians to do the right thing, or coming to my horse shows or my brother Alex's football games, she was—and remains in her tenth decade—the ultimate motivator.

This New Orleans–born child of the Great Depression stands just five foot five and possesses no formal training other than her own hard-won knowledge gleaned from working at her brother Owen's saloon and restaurant on Bourbon Street when she was still in her teens. Yet she became a force of nature (who knows how many times she has been called "Hurricane Ella" out of earshot?) in the restaurant world.

I have watched her change people's lives in a single conversation. She has a way of talking to you and making you feel capable of things you never dreamed of. More than that, she makes you feel you'd be letting yourself down if you didn't give your very best to accomplishing those things. No athletic coach has anything on her. Push, push, push to get you ready and then cheer like hell when you do it. Her pat on your back and her look into your eyes make it feel like the whole world's applauding you.

And yet she always makes sure that you understand your proper place in that world. When I was a kid, I came into the office at Commander's Palace to photocopy some papers for a school project. Mom was standing there with the general manager, and she asked me what I was doing. When I explained, Mom said, "Well, you better talk to Carl about that because his paper costs are going to be up and he's going to be in trouble." So I understood right away that she respected her employees and that the boss's kid was not allowed to do whatever she wanted. Years later, upon hearing that story, Mom reaffirmed the lesson: "The whole idea was that you had to respect the people who were there. They were doing their jobs and this was not a playground."

Indeed, the kitchens in the restaurants that Mom led, most notably Commander's Palace, took on the air of a classroom, where young managers and chefs, including Paul Prudhomme, Emeril Lagasse, Jamie Shannon and Tory McPhail, could build leadership skills and acquire deep knowledge of the art of service. In turn, many of those who have passed through this training ground have gone on to elevate the level of hospitality throughout New Orleans, and America.

Yet despite her love and natural affinity for the restaurant business, Mom discouraged me from following her path. Truth is, it's hard: hard work, hard hours, hard to make a lot of money. She wanted my brother Alex and me to be prepared to take care of ourselves. Never was I taught to be a nice young lady who would let a man take care of me. That certainly hadn't panned out for Mom, and she wanted us to make it on our own. Alex and several of my cousins were sent off to language school in France and then learned the business by working at restaurants in Europe, New York and San Francisco. Somehow I missed that gig. I was pushed to get my MBA and to learn about finance and marketing. My first job out of graduate school was working in Houston for a real-estate syndication firm.

But one day in 1985, I got a call from my Aunt Dottie alerting me that Mom was having heart bypass surgery the next day and would be absent from overseeing Commander's Palace for a while. I drove home right away. On the way to New Orleans, I asked myself what I was trying to prove and what I truly wanted out of life. I started helping out at the restaurant and soon found the answer. Mom recovered, and I have been working alongside her ever since.

I don't know what other girls talk to their mothers about. Mom and I talk about business—our business and other businesses that could give us some insight. We talk about food, marketing, motivating people. We talk about restaurants. A lot.

The life lessons that were imparted to her by her parents and siblings and later passed on to my brother and me are as much a part of my family's legacy as Breakfast at Brennan's and 25-cent martinis at Commander's Palace. The seriousness of purpose, the drive to succeed, the strong work ethic, the attention paid to the needs of family, guests, and those less fortunate—all of Ella's values were shaped while she was growing up in a family of six children in the Roaring Twenties in New Orleans' ragtag Irish Channel neighborhood. She was fresh out of high school and trying to stave off boredom in a secretarial school when her brother Owen, fifteen years her senior, put her to work in his legendary French Quarter saloon, the Old Absinthe House, and later at a Bourbon Street restaurant called the Vieux Carré.

Besides learning by the seat of her pants the skills she would need to succeed in the restaurant business, Ella also learned to embrace all of the sensory pleasures that New Orleans and its French Quarter had to offer. Drinking and conversing with the community of artists, writers, politicians and businessmen who held forth after hours at her favorite watering hole, Café Lafitte, fed her intellectual curiosity, deepened her love of this one-of-a-kind city and undoubtedly prepared her to host the glamorous throngs who would flock to Brennan's on Royal Street, and later to Commander's Palace.

Ella wants everyone to have a good time and to live life to the fullest. The people of New Orleans are not ones to go to their graves with too many regrets about fun times that were missed.

Those values absorbed in her formative years also helped her to deal with the tragedies and hardships in her life—the death of Owen six months before the opening of Brennan's; her divorce from my father, Paul Martin; the tensions that led her and her siblings to depart Brennan's and achieve even greater rewards at Commander's Palace; the premature deaths, from cancer, of her sister Adelaide and one of her favorite chefs, Jamie Shannon; and Hurricane Katrina, which severely damaged our restaurant and her city and nearly broke her heart.

Through it all, Ella has remained a pillar of strength who met those challenges as they arrived, dealt with them intelligently and compassionately—and moved on.

The story of this rich and fulfilling life begs to be told to a wider audience, yet Mom has always resisted. As a young girl she was shy by nature and came of age as part of that World War II "Greatest Generation" that performed their duties honorably without expecting to be recognized. Her focus has always been on improving the lot of other people or entities, be it her chefs, Haute Creole cuisine, the family's restaurants or her beloved city of New Orleans—never her own.

For my whole life, though, people have told my mother and me that we should write a book. We'd both created/written several cookbooks and cocktail books in which we offered tidbits of our philosophy of food and life. But we knew that was not what people meant. They wanted more—a more complete history laced with the stories. Most of all, they wanted insight into how Ella became Ella.

Ella was not interested. "Who cares?" she'd say. "I don't have any secrets, anyway. They've all been printed in the pages of the *Times-Picayune.*"

I can vouch for the fact that she has kept very little in the way of mementos or awards. There was never an office with photos of her with celebrities. The office was full of books, magazines and menus—all of which she gave away nonstop. If it was good, she wanted you to read it—right now—and tell her what you thought within a few days.

Her whole thought process is about what she can learn or do—she's an original thinker. She wants to learn from the recounting of *your* past. She reads biographies and autobiographies all the time. But the recounting of her own history is boring to her. So whenever the subject came up, she would shrug, scrunch up her nose like a kid being forced to eat something she didn't like—and rule it out.

But now, as she approaches the final chapter of her life and watches with pleasure as a new generation of Brennans tests the waters of the restaurant biz, Mom concedes that some of the lessons and stories she has gleaned might be of use to others, especially her wonderful gaggle of grandchildren, her grandnieces or nephews, and the people in our company. And that's why she has graciously, though a bit reluctantly, agreed to let me tell her story in her own words. A few of her friends, family members and colleagues will also chime in to testify how she changed their lives.

Modesty prevents her, however, from telling the story of what might have been the moment in her career of which she is most proud, a moment that exemplifies her approach to life and her career and the people who enriched both. That privilege falls to me, her daughter, business partner and biggest fan.

In 1992 the James Beard Foundation in New York added to its annual awards program a category that would recognize restaurants that provided outstanding service. These industry awards had become known as the "Oscars of the food world," and Mom's friend Danny Meyer, the highly regarded New York restaurateur, won the Outstanding Service award in its inaugural year for his Union Square Cafe. Commander's Palace had been among the nominees and was nominated again the following year.

As we sat in the audience at the awards ceremony at the Marriott Marquis hotel in New York, I found myself wondering if Mom had thought of something to say in case Commander's was declared the big winner. Sometimes the recipients make poignant, eloquent acceptance speeches, but more often the remarks are too long and a bit disappointing—kind of like the film Oscars in that regard.

Suddenly, the presenters announced our category: "And the winner is . . . Commander's Palace!" Hot damn!

Mom slowly made her way to the stage. After seeing so many trembling young people accept their awards, her presence and mastery of the circumstances were a welcome contrast. Thundering applause made clear that she was a crowd favorite. Mom stood before the podium and delivered this speech in its entirety: "I accept this award for every damn captain and waiter in the country." The entire auditorium rose to its feet for a standing ovation as my mother endeared herself to anyone who has ever set a table or taken an order.

Though it hardly seems possible, my admiration for her has only grown since that night more than twenty years ago. She continues to be my guiding light, my confidant, my hero—my mother. Now that we've gotten that straightened out, it's your turn, Mom.

1

Scrambled Eggs, Sautéed Bananas and One Unshakeable Family (1925–1943)

"YOUR BROTHERS AND SISTERS ARE SPECIAL IN YOUR LIFE. I'M NOT RAISING CATS AND DOGS—YOU ARE BROTHERS AND SISTERS. NOW BEHAVE YOURSELF!"
—NELLIE VALENTINE BRENNAN

My mother had magic in her hands. Nellie was an extraordinarily good cook who didn't rely on recipes or precise measurements or any kind of training when she bustled into the kitchen. She just did it. And did it well. In many ways, that was the same approach she took to managing and caring for our bursting-at-the-seams household in New Orleans during the Great Depression. She just did it. No complaints—at least none she shared with my siblings and me. And as I would come to realize, her ability to figure things out, meet the challenge, cope with the disappointments and get on with life was the greatest gift she passed on to me. That, and her breakfasts.

My earliest food memory is of her scrambled eggs and sautéed bananas. I just loved them. Nellie stirred the eggs a little in a bowl, poured them into a pan sizzling with butter, stirred them again gently and slid them out while they were still very soft. Perfection! Then she'd put a little brown sugar and cinnamon on bananas sliced lengthwise into quarters, turn them over in hot butter until they were caramelized—imagine what our kitchen smelled like!—and serve them with the fluffy eggs. This was way, way, way back, but to this day I beg my sister Dottie to make me some of Nellie's eggs and bananas. Dottie's are almost as good, and they transport me back to that little kitchen every time.

Years later at the Brennan's restaurant on Royal Street, we featured elaborate egg dishes at our famous breakfasts, and we served Bananas Foster for dessert, of course. But we also had Filet Mignon Stanley and Chopped Steak Stanley that were topped with a sauce of creamed horseradish and sautéed bananas. Big, bold flavors inspired by a recipe from an old French cookbook. I promise you they were magnificent. Nellie never could have imagined what her handiwork in our home kitchen would lead to, but let's just say that eggs and bananas have been very good to our family.

We lived in a couple of houses when I was growing up, very near where Dottie and I live now, in the Garden District. They were also near where my mother had been raised, in the Irish Channel, though the borders were different then. My father's family lived a little farther downtown, at Constance and Jackson, in a big, old, charming two-story house. They always seemed to have much more than my mother's family had.

The house where we six kids spent most of our growing-up time was on Eleonore Street. It had a nice kitchen where my mother eventually installed a big, red Chambers stove. She treasured that stove. A wonderful black woman named Leona Nichols worked for us, and she and my mother would trade off cooking and cleaning that six-bedroom house. Leona was lovable—you wanted to sit and laugh with her, hug her and just be around her. She was family. The only time I didn't like her so much was when some of us had to go to church with her every now and then. Leona didn't have any children, so we were her kids on those Sundays. The church had a good gospel choir, but we just didn't like sitting there through everything else. We went because that's what our mother said we had to do and there was no argument. We were raised Catholic and Nellie insisted we go to mass regularly. My father didn't go to church, but he made sure everyone got up and got ready to go. Over the years, I kind of dropped away from the church; by the time I was out of high school, I was finished. Dottie now says we're "recovering Catholics." Those beliefs stay with you though. I always figured that God and I were OK and that He understood I had to work Sunday brunch.

If Leona was washing and cleaning one day, my mother would cook, and the next day they'd switch. When they cleaned the house, the only thing they couldn't do was put the furniture back in place to my older sister Adelaide's satisfaction. So Adelaide's job was to go around and reposition every damn thing in the house. If there was an ashtray, it had to be *here*, not over *there*.

Evening meals were at six o'clock, and that's when our big Irish family would gather. There was my father, Owen Patrick Brennan, who was a supervisor of shipbuilding at Johnson Iron Works. He was tall and good-looking, always well dressed. Every day of his business life—*every day*—he'd leave the house in a white shirt that my mother or Leona had ironed, a blue suit from Hart Schaffner & Marx, and one of the seven pairs of perfectly shined shoes that he kept in his closet and rotated daily. He always carried a package, precisely wrapped in brown paper and tied with a string, that contained his khaki shirt, khaki pants, socks and probably underwear. He'd change into those clothes at the shipyard, then change back into his suit at the end of the day and head home.

Also at the table was my oldest sibling, whom I followed around like a puppy dog, Owen Edward, fifteen years older than me. Adelaide was next, then John. I came along on November 27, 1925, followed by Dick and the youngest, Dottie, who was twenty-three years younger than Owen. We were far apart in age, but we would always eat together. Our family rarely ate out because we didn't have any money to eat out. And the restaurants then couldn't touch what we had at home anyway. Even after he got married, Owen and his wife, Maude, would eat with us to save expenses, so there would be at least six or eight at the kitchen table on most nights, and often more than that when we'd bring our friends home.

Somehow, my mother and father parceled out their love and attention to all of us in equal measure so that my siblings and I never felt neglected nor favored over one another. Perhaps that was because they freely shared so many of their passions with us. Dad loved sports—we kids would take turns going with him to Tulane University football games and to see the Pelicans, a minor league baseball team. He especially liked going to the racetrack on Sunday afternoons. My mother didn't like the track or anything to do with it, so he'd go alone. I never knew whether he won any money or not, but often he'd bring home a "peace-maker" for Nellie—a fried-oyster po' boy fully dressed.

Nellie loved, loved, loved to entertain, every bit as much as she liked to sing and sew and dance and grow pink roses. My father enjoyed gardening too—I can just see them out there clipping and tending to those flowers. But he didn't like to dance, so at home Nellie would dance with Owen or John, or even Adelaide or Dottie—Dick and I had declared ourselves to be tone deaf so that we wouldn't have to get involved. There would be music either on the phonograph or from my mother's cousin, who visited frequently and played the piano beautifully. My father would sing "My Wild Irish Rose" to my mother and get carried away, but it was great fun.

The real entertainment, even though we didn't think of it as such, was the meals, which took on aspects of a performance. Nellie would stand at that stove next to the kitchen table and cook fried oysters and french-fried potatoes in two cast-iron skillets. She'd cook for the first person and then serve that person. Then she'd cook for the next person. No more than two people at a time. She didn't cook anything ahead of time because she didn't want her oysters to be too well done. I remember those oysters to this day. I wish I had some right now.

I don't know where she ever got her cooking talent. Her parents died when she was about thirteen, so it must have come from her sisters. But you know the thing that I found most amazing about her? She was a clean cook. By the time she was finished doing her basic preparation and getting it in the oven, the kitchen was clean. I don't remember ever seeing a mess. And we were taught that if you used something, you cleaned it. You *did not* leave anything in the sink. Nothing. But in spite of her attention to detail and discipline, Nellie was a happy person who cooked to the music on the radio. And she listened to the news. Had to hear the news.

Our meals were exciting, rich and varied even though money was tight. Nellie had three brothers, and they would hunt and fish and bring her whatever they had. Game. Venison. Ducks, ducks, ducks! If it flew, they'd shoot it and bring it home. They'd always bring in these big redfish, which they'd clean, and then Nellie would immediately start cooking. As soon as my father walked in the door from work, we'd sit down to a fabulous redfish courtboullion, a light, spicy stew made with a little tomato paste from a tiny, red Contadina can.

On Mondays, in keeping with New Orleans tradition, Nellie or Leona would often cook red beans and rice; only ours was usually made with sweet pickled pork instead of sausage. On another day Nellie would make baked sweet potatoes and roasted pork loin—I've never known anybody who could make it so moist. She'd season the meat very well and cook it in its fat in a pot with celery and green onions. Then she'd strain out the vegetables, leaving only the gravy. She also made wonderful rabbit, and veal roasts stuffed with oyster dressing. We ate veal often—roasts, chops, panéed cutlets—all of it delicious.

And the vegetables! Nellie would say, "Eat your carrots. Good for the eyes!" She was always talking about vegetables being good for you. Cabbage with pickled pork instead of corned beef. Fabulous stuffed eggplant or stuffed peppers to go with the meat. About three times a week for most of my early life, a man named Tony would bring us vegetables from the farm stands at the French Market in the French Quarter—cauliflower, broccoli, potatoes, you name it. The French Market was a big deal then, and the raw products were extraordinary. At first, Tony would pull up in a horse-drawn cart, and later a truck. He'd come in and have a cup of coffee with my mother, and sometimes he'd drive Adelaide to high school even though it was only four blocks away. My sister felt it was her due.

Nellie usually would go to a neighborhood fish market herself to buy things such as oysters, and she'd use those oysters to make dressing so good that I don't think anybody's ever duplicated it. *Anybody.* When she'd make it, she'd tell us, "Whenever you think you have enough oysters, double it, double it, double it!" My mother loved all kinds of seafood dishes—deep-fried fish, pan-fried fish, shrimp. And oh my god—gumbos!—stuffed with seafood usually. She'd always have soups in the wintertime, made with what she called the "soup meat"— whatever was left over. Her oyster stew with milk was to die for, and she also made a clear version using the oyster water and chopped vegetables. If Nellie was going out on a Saturday—Leona was off on Saturdays and Sundays—she'd make a big casserole of potato salad to go with the soup so that any of us who came in later in the day could feed ourselves.

For dessert there would be custards, bread pudding and several kinds of cakes. During fruit season, when the peaches and strawberries came in, Nellie would get out the ice cream maker and we'd have to turn the crank while squatting on a little porch off the kitchen. "I need help," she'd say. "I'm not going to sit there and do it by myself." So we'd promise to pitch in. Oh, would we promise, because then she'd say, "OK, you did the most work? You get to lick the paddle."

My mother could walk into the kitchen and say, "I'm going to make an apple pie," and poof!—the pie was in the oven. It was miraculous how adept she was with things like crusts, which so many people can't get right. She was just good at it. It was a chore, sure, but she never let you think it was a chore. Nellie enjoyed seeing people eat her food, and we could always bring our friends. If they ate up all of the pie, she'd say, "That's OK. I'll make another one before your daddy gets home." And if she didn't have dessert to give him, he'd say, "Poor, poor me," and would go get the sugar bowl and have a teaspoon of sugar. To her, that was the biggest insult!

We usually ate in the kitchen because there was a big table there and that's where the cooking was going on. But if we spilled into the dining room, then we'd eat in shifts. Our whole family life revolved around food. Dick played basketball at St. Aloysius High School and was later recruited by Adolph Rupp to play at Kentucky. But he said, "No, no, no! I am going to go to Tulane." Why? He didn't want to leave home because my mother treated him like a prince! He was a Sigma Chi, but he didn't eat at the Sigma Chi house. He came home, and he'd often bring three or four teammates with him.

Nobody missed a meal, and I loved it all.

But all of this meant that I never did learn how to cook. Today, I know a lot about cooking. I can tell you what's right with it, I can tell you what's wrong with it, and all that stuff, but I can never actually cook it. Why? Well, I never tried. When I was a kid, my mother and Leona were in the kitchen, and they didn't need kids around. It wasn't that I wasn't allowed in there, it's just that my mother never said, "Come here and let me teach you how to cook." They didn't do that. We kids were playing and doing something else, and the next thing you know we're off to grammar school and high school. I did teach myself to make bologna sandwiches, however, using garlic bologna, mayo and good bread from the deli on Freret Street. Still crave them today.

Most of the pleasures of my youth were simple things that didn't cost much. My family gave me a two-wheeled bike when I reached fourth grade, and my great joy was the freedom that it gave me. My friends and I would ride from our house to Audubon Park, and then up and down a big slope called Monkey Hill, which was built by the WPA (though only a New Orleanian would consider it a hill). At least once a week we'd ride along St. Charles Avenue to Lee Circle and careen down the slanted steps leading to the monument. You were proving how old you were when you did that.

I remember the day my mom handed me some money and let me go downtown to pay the bills. That was a big deal for me because exploring New Orleans was always great fun. My friends and I liked to sit by the Mississippi River and play ball nearby, and it didn't cost a thing. Part of the soundtrack of my youth was the stately foghorns on the cargo ships and the rude whistle blasts from the trains that ran along the riverbank. Sometimes we'd walk to the corner where you could see the ships cruising slowly above you. We were down on the land, below the water level and protected by the levees, and we'd have to look up to see the traffic on the river. Absolutely amazing. The Mighty Mississippi fascinates me to this day.

Nellie was a steady presence in our lives, levelheaded, industrious—and prudent. She would usually give me 25 cents a day—the streetcar cost 7 cents each way, so it would be 14 cents for transportation and 11 cents for lunch. If I wanted to save up money to see a movie, I'd ride my bike during the week instead of spending it on the streetcar fare.

We loved, loved, loved going to the movies at the big theaters along Canal Street. Tickets for kids at the Saenger and Loew's cost about 25 cents, and Adelaide and I would go three or four times a month. I especially loved Clark Gable and Judy Garland. I remember going to church one Sunday and the priest said, "Don't go see that movie with Jane Russell." It was *The Outlaw*, and I promise you we went right out and saw it. Everybody had been talking about it—Jane Russell and her boobs. I met her later in life and told her that story and she loved it.

Reading was another passion of mine, so I was forever going to the public library near Lee Circle, where the K&B building now stands. I started reading very young, and my dad put a basket on my bike so I could carry books back and forth. I read everything that was around. We had *Life, Look* and *Time* magazines at the house, and the schools were very good about putting together reading lists and letting you borrow from their library.

Looking back I can see that all of this emphasis on simple pleasures, from reading to making ice cream and eating together as a family, helped shield us kids from the fact that even before the war there was a depression going on. We didn't know times were tough. My dad kept his job, but I'm certain some of my parents' acquaintances didn't. I probably internalized some things, but my impressions of my childhood are extraordinarily satisfying. The relationships between my siblings and me were secure, and even though my mother could be stern, her bond with Daddy and us was unshakeable. We weren't a huggy-kissy family; we were just close.

Part of the reason for that solidarity, I think, is that my mother and my father agreed never to argue at the same time. She did most of the arguing anyway, so my father would just wander around the house saying, "Poor me, poor me." With us kids, she was a strict disciplinarian but adorably sweet. She'd say to us, "I'm not raising cats and dogs. You are brothers and sisters. Now behave yourself!" And she instilled in us a family feeling. If we got into an argument, she'd say, "Your brothers and sisters are special in your life and you don't talk to them like that. And you don't sell things to them—you give them something. They are the only people in the world with the same blood as you." While that wasn't necessarily true medically, the idea made an impression on me. It was always family, family, family.

Just as important, my parents taught us to always make sure that others were taken care of and to keep up our standards. I remember vaguely Nellie bringing someone in off the street and feeding him in the kitchen, then fixing him up with something to take with him before sending him on his way. We had tenants in our double house, and my parents let them go without paying the rent for three or four years. My mother would urge my dad, who hired men at the shipyard, to "find a place for so-and-so. He stopped by today and needs a job." Nellie had a crippled brother, Paddy, who lived about a mile away; she would fix him meals and send me off on my bike to deliver them. And it was common at the time for people to at least paint the front of their house even if they couldn't afford to paint the entire thing. Just as a matter of pride. And if they needed help painting, there was always someone to lend a hand. None of these things seemed odd to me—it was simply the way life was. But those memories never go away.

By the time I hit my mid-teen years, I was becoming much more aware of what was going on far from the banks of the Mississippi, and life became a lot more unsettling. One of my most vivid memories is of a day I was pushing the lawn mower in the backyard. My brother Owen was telling me how to mow— always the superintendent—and that's when they announced on the radio that Pearl Harbor had been attacked. Nellie came running out to give us the news— one of the few times I saw her flustered. So much changed after that. So many of the men in our city soon left to join the military, including my brother John, who served in the Navy as a pilot. Owen didn't serve (he was married with two sons at that time), but he worked for a while at Higgins Industries, a company that made amphibious landing craft for the military. It's hard to explain now what it was like to have this big, scary world war going on and family and friends swept up in it. John couldn't even tell us where he was stationed. We all agreed to write him once a week so he'd at least get mail. (In the mid-1950s, my brother Dick, and Owen's oldest son, Pip, both served stateside in the Army.)

While the conflicts raged far away, I plugged away at my studies and tried to figure out who I really was. My sister Dottie likes to say that I was a "good girl" who was stubborn and opinionated, but I always thought of myself as shy. I was an average student at McMain High, which was a public school, and I loved the teachers there. They were all women, and those were the days when teachers weren't allowed to be married. High school was tough in the sense that you were expected to do your best and nothing less was acceptable. The teachers were there to help if you needed help, but they weren't going to do the work for you. It was a rigorous curriculum, comparable to that of today's best private schools. I liked that it was a structured environment where you knew what was expected. No playing around. I always loved American history and current events—I never did like ancient history—and English classes. I wasn't a straight-A student, but I certainly worked hard.

When I graduated from high school in January 1943, I didn't have a clear direction in mind. All of us needed to have a job, though, so I enrolled in a local business school where they tried to teach me secretarial skills such as typing and filing and all of that boring stuff. I lasted maybe four months before I quit. I wasn't going to type for any man. That wasn't in my DNA (which I didn't even know I had in those days). Years later, I would counsel my daughter Ti to never learn how to type or practice stenography, because then she'd be viewed as a secretary, not the boss. That advice has worked out pretty well in her case.

While I was looking for something else to do, my brother Owen asked me to help out doing clerical work and banking at a bar he owned on Bourbon Street called the Old Absinthe House. My mother didn't like it because it was in the French Quarter, and she thought everything about the place was bad. Me hanging out in that part of the city, where people caroused all night and visited the burlesque houses, was a horrible, horrible situation as far as she was concerned. She wouldn't even let me walk on Bourbon Street, so I had to walk on Royal Street, one block closer to the river. But Owen convinced her that he would look after me. I later figured out that he desperately wanted me to take care of things in the daytime so that he could sleep late. He and my sister Adelaide would become legendary afternoon risers, but I never had that option.

But just like that, I was helping to run a bar that was at the center of café society. In the "horrible, horrible" and incredibly alluring French Quarter no less. I was eighteen and didn't know a thing.

2

"Your Restaurant Stinks!" (1944–1954)

"WELL, GO FIX IT, SMARTY PANTS."
—OWEN BRENNAN

When you walked into the Old Absinthe House on the corner of Bourbon and Bienville, you'd hear ghosts murmuring even before you downed the first Sazerac at the polished wood-topped bar. That was probably true even in its early days during the Jean Lafitte/Andrew Jackson era in the early 1800s, and it became even more true over the years when Mark Twain, P. T. Barnum, Enrico Caruso and Jenny Lind were said to have knocked back a few there. When Owen bought the bar in 1943, he was determined to make it prominent again as a gathering place for New Orleans society—and give those ghosts fresh material to whisper about.

He'd been looking for a business that all of us could be in together and that would allow us to take care of Mom and Dad. They were approaching retirement age, though few people in those days had pensions or any money saved up for their later years. Owen had bought a service station and a drug store up near City Park, and he helped run the Court of Two Sisters restaurant in the French Quarter while the owner was serving in World War II. So he had made a little money but was looking to make more. Owen also had been doing business with a liquor wholesaler, who loaned him $15,000 to buy the Old Absinthe House. It was a money machine, but Owen soon took it to another level of sophistication. He reasoned that if you drew a higher-class crowd and charged more for drinks, your income would go up. Very smart move.

One of the first things he did was hire a great black piano player and jazz singer, Walter "Fats" Pichon, and create a stage for him in the back room, which was like a nightclub within the bar. The room was usually crowded but in an intimate way, and I can still hear the clinking ice in the highballs and see the candles flickering on the tables. Fats wore a tuxedo and played in front of a giant mirror with a spotlight on him and would dazzle the patrons with the pop and jazz standards of the day, everything from "Don't Get Around Much Anymore" to "Night and Day" to "Life is Just a Bowl of Cherries," which became my favorite. Fats's showmanship took the crowd to giddy heights and glided back down so as to not interrupt the conversation too much.

Boy, I'd give anything to hear him do his act again, his way with that piano, his joy in it. My musical tastes have always run to the American songbook, the early New Orleans jazz repertoire, and show tunes (especially when sung by Judy Garland, the greatest performer of all time; Ti always touts Barbra Streisand, but she's dead wrong!). Fats was a virtuoso with nearly any genre.

The place had two stories and a mezzanine level, with an office and a small guest room on the second floor, where Louis Armstrong once stayed to get around the segregation laws that governed hotels. Robert Mitchum stayed there too. Owen had met him when Mitchum was hitchhiking after his stint on a Georgia chain gang—busted for loitering, of all things! In that era, not having a job could lead to such harsh treatment. Owen brought Mitchum home that night for dinner, and they become good friends. He was a love, and we all adopted him.

Daddy would come in sometimes after work at the shipyard and help with the seating—the small tables in back had red-and-white tablecloths and candles, and everybody wanted a good view of Fats. Our clientele was either going to dinner nearby or coming from dinner, or sometimes they'd drop by before *and* after. Everyone dressed up—the women competed for the fanciest cocktail dress, and the men wore coats and ties no matter whether they were going to Galatoire's,

Antoine's or Arnaud's, the dominant old-guard restaurants. It was smashing! Like Rick's Café Américain in *Casablanca*. Owen knew how to set a stage.

Owen was the host and knew everybody and talked to everybody. If there was something interesting going on, he was probably involved. Some people have referred to him as the "impresario of the French Quarter," and it was true. One night he stood in the middle of Bourbon Street and said to anyone who would listen, "If you can't sell New Orleans, you can't sell anything! This has got to be the best tourist town in America." He believed it would be the easiest thing in the world to promote the city if we got our act together. (And the city did, eventually, though it took a while for other large, high-end hotels to be built that would give the Roosevelt, with its famous Blue Room and Sazerac Bar, a run for its money.)

Owen just knew what it took to make people happy. It was an instinct. He understood hospitality and he understood service, and he taught them to us all. He was the first Brennan to go into that type of business, and it was a great choice because the bar brought in money steadily and gave him a chance to work his natural charisma—and sleep late. I'll never forget the day World War II ended. Somebody must have awakened Owen and told him the news, and he immediately said, "Close those big doors on the outside! Close it up until I can get there." He was so afraid the bar would be mobbed, and people did go crazy on Bourbon Street, as you can imagine, but his goldmine came through unscathed except for the (temporarily) depleted liquor supplies. He owned the place until the day he died.

I don't remember much about Owen before he got married (I was four), but as a kid I always wanted to be near him. Whenever he and Maude (we called her Maudie) would get ready to go home after eating dinner at our house, I'd want to go with him, and they'd frequently take me. Spending so much time in their company gave me an early window into the exotic (to my eyes) world of adults and shaped my views in ways that I'm still discovering. At the time, I'm certain that I thought, "Well, if this is what grown-ups do, if this is how they live their lives, then let's get cracking!"

And boy did Owen enjoy life to the fullest. He took flying lessons (until he walked away from a crash, which dampened his enthusiasm), drove a nice Lincoln and wore a Patek Philippe wristwatch. In the summer it was white linen suits; in the winter, black silk. His style was classic and debonair, and he carried himself well. He wasn't materialistic, but he appreciated fine things and would save his pennies to afford them. As glamorous as our sister Adelaide and he were, I always said they could stretch a dollar further than anyone I knew—they just knew what to spend it on. Most often it was on classic, stylish things and not silly, wasteful stuff. His life was all about balance—he was foremost a night person, so he'd spend the afternoon at home with his family, then come down to the Quarter.

Owen's reputation as a savvy and charismatic entrepreneur reaped enormous benefits for our businesses, and for the city as well. Owen met Maggie Ettinger, a famous Hollywood publicist and the cousin of entertainment columnist Louella Parsons, during one of her trips to New Orleans. She was another one of those wonderful people that just adopted us. Since Owen seemed to know everybody, people would often come to him to see if he could arrange celebrities to attend or speak at their fundraising events, which would prompt Owen to ask Maggie to help him out. One time Maggie sent Hedda Hopper and another time, Gracie Allen. I stayed in touch with Maggie and even managed to see her during a business trip I made to Los Angeles when she was dying of cancer. She was a grand gal.

Sometimes Owen was just playing around—he was a world-class practical joker. The famous ventriloquist Edgar Bergen was often in New Orleans doing his act at the Blue Room in the Roosevelt Hotel, and naturally Owen ended up befriending him. One time, Edgar's wonderful wife, Frances, an actress and model, was going to perform at the Swan Room at the Monteleone Hotel, though Edgar wasn't able to join her. So he called Owen and told him to please take good care of Frances. Owen had her to dinner, where they became instant friends.

Owen had an idea to surprise Frances at her show with some famous "audience members." He'd created something called the Secret Room at the Old Absinthe House, where he had installed these life-sized papier-mâché characters from the history of New Orleans, such as Andrew Jackson and the pirate Jean Lafitte. Owen had concocted all sorts of stories about the general and the pirate having secret meetings to plan the battle of New Orleans and all sorts of non-sense. People would pay a nickel to go up into the Secret Room where there was a wonderful man who played the banjo and told the stories. It was a bit like the wax museums of today.

WHEN SATCHMO CAME TO TOWN

One of my favorite memories is of Louis Armstrong coming back to his hometown in February 1955 to perform on *The Colgate Comedy Hour* TV show, which was being broadcast live from Mardi Gras. The show was originally planned to be staged elsewhere, but somehow Owen got wind of that and finessed the situation. The next thing you know, it's being broadcast on national television right in front of our little business. When youngsters today think some people are just lucky, I think about that incident. You can make your own luck if you're always pushing yourself. A little fancy footwork doesn't hurt.

When Louis's segment was done, he stood in the intersection and played "Way Down Yonder in New Orleans" while we watched from the balcony. It was like he was the Pied Piper. People were coming out of every place and gathering in the street just to be near him. This man, our Louis, kept playing. I don't think there was a dry eye around. We couldn't help it, because we all knew what was going on with segregation at that time. Here was our beloved, homegrown genius who no doubt knew better than anyone what it means to miss New Orleans. I was in awe and weak in the knees with sadness for him and for my fellow citizens. Shame on all of us. Why didn't we fix it sooner? It was so damn wrong. We love you, Louis . . . and we're sorry.

Anyway, on the night of Frances's show, Owen had Andrew Jackson and Jean Lafitte carted over to the front row of the theater, hoping Frances would spot them and fall out laughing. She did, as did everyone else. Frances stayed in touch with me for years, calling whenever she was headed to town. I was always happy to see what a great success their daughter, Candace, became.

By the time Owen asked me to come to work at the Old Absinthe House in late 1943, he had turned it into something special. Our brother John was still in the military and Owen needed someone to do the daytime grunt work, mostly clerical duties and banking, and to help collect rent for his real estate business. I was mostly confined to the office upstairs, but it was something to do after I had quit secretarial school, and I began to take to it, even though it was a learn-on-the-job situation. It kept me in movie money, I was more or less my own boss, and it gave me entrée to what Mom continued to call the "nasty old French Quarter." It also didn't hurt that Owen had bought me my first car, a used blue Ford convertible with whitewall tires. How's that for a big brother? I look back and wonder how he managed to do things like that. Times were tough. As the oldest of six, he felt the weight of being responsible for all of us as well as his own family, which would grow to include three sons. That sense of love of and duty to family was something that was always there for all of us—unspoken but strong. I adored him.

Owen was enjoying his success, and my job was working out well for me, but he was always looking for more opportunities. At one point his friend "Count" Arnaud of Arnaud's restaurant laid down a good-natured challenge, saying something along the lines of, "I doubt that a dumb Irishman could ever run a successful restaurant." Naturally, Owen set out to prove him wrong. He had a hunch that the owner of a nondescript family-dining place across the street from the Old Absinthe House, called the Vieux Carré, might be putting the business up for sale. So one night he gave the owner's son a ride home and said, "I hear your family is planning to sell the Vieux Carré." The son was stunned. "How did you know that? We just talked about it last night."

The truth was, Owen *didn't* know. He was just fishing, but he ended up reeling in a potentially lucrative business opportunity. Thinking, aiming for a goal, making his own luck . . . again. Owen and Daddy bought the business in 1946, and about six months later they asked me to help manage the place. Owen planned to have Adelaide come on board soon after to handle the business side of things, but he needed somebody to oversee the day-to-day right away.

"You can do it, kid," said the big brother, though I was saying to myself, "What the *hell* are you thinking?!"

So much for getting comfy!

I was just shy of twenty-one, and once again I was thrust into a situation that I didn't know the first damn thing about—I'd only worked in Owen's bar, never a restaurant—and would have to figure it out for myself. I'd like to think that Owen saw some brains and energy in his little sister, or maybe he just needed someone in a pinch so that he could focus on his bar. I don't know. What I did know is that the Vieux Carré wasn't a very good restaurant. In fact, it stank. The place had thirty-one tables and a few more seats at the bar, all on the street level, and four big windows covered with curtains. The interior just looked and felt tired. Even the chandeliers were way too small given the tall ceiling. Just blah.

Our family rarely dined out, and even though I had gotten to know a few people who ran restaurants, I had no experience in that world. Thanks to Mom and Leona, however, I did know great home cooking, and I eventually realized how good theirs was. That was one of my big concerns with Vieux Carré: the menu was boring and skimpy. They had about five entrées—trout meuniere, some kind of chicken, roasted veal or leg of lamb with mint jelly out of the jar, that kind of thing. Awful. No one thought in terms of "regional cuisine" back then, but they did serve gumbo, and shrimp remoulade, which consisted of four teeny-tiny shrimp, maybe the size of my fingernail, that arrived on a bed of shredded lettuce and were dabbed with the remoulade. For dessert there was bread pudding and ice cream. Heck, I had eaten better food every day of my life at home, and here customers were paying good money for this inferior stuff.

I kept bitching and moaning to Owen—"Your restaurant stinks! It just stinks!"—until he'd finally had enough and said, "You think you're so smart? Well, go fix it, smarty pants." And so my career as a restaurateur was launched.

I was scared to death and very insecure about being in an environment with grown-up people who seemed to know what they were doing. But we got right to work fixing the operation.

At the beginning we were losing money hand over fist. One day I was in the ladies room getting ready to leave when Owen barged in. Without knocking. I was putting on my lipstick and he was bitching at me about how we had to start making some money. "Don't you see this statement here?" he said, thrusting some papers at me. "I'm going broke!"

"I don't know what else to do. How can you make money off of a place like this?" (I never was much good at diplomacy.)

He grabbed the lipstick out of my hand and wrote "40%" on the mirror in fire engine red.

"Owen, that's my favorite lipstick! What the hell is this?"

"Forget the damn lipstick. You go take the food inventory and work on that menu until the food cost is forty percent. Not a percentage higher."

We were probably doing fifty percent on food costs, but who knew?

"I hate taking inventory."

"Well, take it until you get it right or until you're smart enough to get someone else to take it for you. Otherwise, you're fired."

Owen fired me at least three times that I recall, but Mom always made him hire me back. It was like a bad comedy.

We were making customers happy, but we didn't know how to turn a profit, like some of our nearby competitors did. We'd be getting ready for dinner and I'd walk out our back door and look at the front door of Arnaud's, where there was a line of people. Then I'd walk out the front and see the line at Galatoire's up the street. We never had a line out the door, I promise you that.

One day, a guy from Antoine's came to our kitchen and handed us one of their menus and asked if he could have one of ours. "Well," I thought, "that's a classy way to do it." Nowadays I suppose that might be called price fixing. It wasn't price fixing then; it was simply the way we worked. You see my prices, I see your prices and we go on from there. I'll never forget that as long as I live.

Eventually Adelaide joined us and John came home from the service and started buying the supplies. Daddy quit the shipping business and became a mature presence in the front of the house, handling reservations and seating. He was bringing in people he knew from the shipyard to dine, and Owen was sending us customers from his bar across the street, so things slowly picked up. (I'm not sure if I ever got food costs down to 40%, but I was trying.)

At first we were making it up as we went along, everyone falling all over one another. Masters of improvisation, we were. But things began to stabilize and that allowed me to tackle the kitchen, where I had the great good fortune to be taken under the wings of two fine cooks, Paul Blangé and Jack Eames, whom Owen had convinced to stay on when he bought the restaurant.

It's not much of an exaggeration to say that I lived in that kitchen, which was dinky by today's standards and had a cement floor. One of the most exciting times in my life was sitting on a barstool watching Jack and Paul take a haunch of meat and break it down or take a whole fish and use every scrap of it to make something. At that point I didn't know beef from lamb from pork in the raw stage, and I became fascinated by the whole process. These were serious cooks who yearned to do more and better things with their skills, and they taught me everything. Jack came in early in the morning and did the prep and the ordering, and Paul would arrive early afternoon and take over the cooking.

It was a wonderful education and I was thrilled, especially when it got to the point where I could begin writing the menus. I read everything I could find about food and cooking (and about running a business, too), though the sources were meager and the cookbook boom in this country was still decades away. Photocopiers hadn't been invented, so you had to bring the book over from the library or wherever you had scrounged it up and sit there taking notes.

I finally got my hands on *The Escoffier Cookbook: A Guide to the Fine Art of Cookery*, the bible for all things French, and right there, in the first 160 or so pages, were the primary sauces of cooking. When I started to understand the basics, the rest of French cooking began to make sense. (I even began to see some similarities to what cooks were doing in New Orleans.) I had been trying to come up with these dishes, but I didn't know how to get there. Paul and Jack knew enough that they could take what I was trying to do and move with it. They had felt handcuffed and uninspired by the limited menu and were happy to shake things up. I give them all the credit in the world.

To begin with, we did away with French titles on the menu—Coq au Vin, Boeuf Bourguignon or what have you—and translated them into English so our customers could better understand them. Sacrilege! I believe we were the first fine-dining restaurant in New Orleans to do that, strangely enough. Then we added dishes that weren't on other menus: chicken Pontalba; Paul's trout with a gumbo-like seafood sauce that was definitely Creole, but unique; stuffed flounder; redfish courtbouillon; pheasant, duck and venison like we had grown up on; soups and stews like Nellie made; and baked oysters on the half shell with different sauces. The menu was still French, but we Americanized it with Creole touches.

Right away Paul added more and bigger shrimp to the remoulade—food costs be damned!—and he replaced the tame French remoulade with one using Creole mustard that became quite good after it marinated a bit in the large ceramic crock on the counter. On the dessert menu, flaming Bananas Foster—another nod to my upbringing—became an instant hit. We also began serving breakfast and lunch on Sundays and added egg dishes to the repertoire, a concept we would greatly expand a few years later at Brennan's on Royal Street. We opened at 10 a.m. because we wanted to offer a breakfast for people who had been out all night; then we'd go right into lunch.

It wasn't just I who was doing the learning. John would normally get up at 6 a.m. to do the buying, but some nights Daddy would come home late and wake him up to tell him the steaks hadn't been good that night. Well, that's how the steaks got better: John was tired of Daddy waking him up! Next thing you know, he became an authority on steaks and got to know the men at the meatpacking house.

Once we started getting the food under control, we turned our attention to improving the service, which was making me very unhappy. In those days the servers came in from the bayou country, and I swear half of them didn't wear shoes. Antoine's and Galatoire's were about the only places where waiting on tables was a profession, and I wanted us to move in that direction. I hired a few seasoned waiters, service team captains and a maître d', and they helped me assemble a crew and whip them into shape. I would go home at night, and if I'd spotted someone with a dirty uniform, I'd call the offender and tell them that if they didn't have a clean one, they couldn't come to work the next day. Then we had to teach them everything that was on the menu. We'd gather them together and have one of the cooks come out to talk to them—standard practice today, but rare then.

At the same time, I wanted to teach the staff about wine, so I had to study it myself. I learned how it was made and got out the maps to learn where it came from. We mostly served French wine because it went well with the food and our customers were used to it. (We didn't have much American wine back then. At the bottom of the menu it said, "California wine, $4.50 and $2.50"—no producers' names or anything.) It was a learning process, trying to teach wine and proper service to these little boys from the bayou. But all of these lessons were the origin of what we now call the twice-daily pre-meal meeting, where we teach and motivate the staff—a central component of our modern restaurant culture.

Besides teaching the nuts and bolts of the job, I began to cultivate personnel skills: you spend time with one guy at a time, you relate to him as a human being and you make him want to come work for you. And you start with mutual trust and respect. That one-on-one conversation where you tell them you want to earn their trust and respect is how it all starts. You learn about an employee as a person and commit to helping them. People work for a person, not a company. And as Owen would say, "You train animals, but you teach people." This idea has become a hallmark of our business. I work to earn your trust and respect, and you work to earn mine.

That was one of my most gratifying early successes: getting the waiters to respect their jobs. Teaching just sort of came naturally to me. I had enough sense to know right from wrong. But to teach them and get them to listen to me and understand that I meant business—remember, it's the 1940s and I'm a woman in my very early twenties—took awhile.

I never did reach some folks. We had a guy who every night would go into the cooler just before closing. He had this belt under his uniform where he'd put a brick of butter and some steaks for his meal at home. I just thought he was fat, but it was the steaks. John, who was ordering supplies, noticed this and told him, "You know you don't have to do that. We'll gladly give you stuff to take home, but don't steal it because we want to keep track of it. Write it down so we know where everything went." The guy said, "Oh, no, I'd rather keep doing it this way. I don't want to get out of practice." True story.

Then there was this French guy, Angel, who was a really good cook. One weekend morning he was carrying on in the kitchen acting crazy and causing all kinds of turmoil. I went in there and said, "That's not acceptable, now let's calm down." I walked back to my desk, and he came at me with a butcher knife. I got him simmered down and he went away, but I had to fire him. "You're finished; go get your things. I'm writing your check now."

I called Owen and told him what happened. He said, "You fired him? He's one of the best cooks in New Orleans! I've been trying to get that guy to come work for you forever. You can't fire him."

"Too late. He's fired. Out the door." Imagine—my brother taking the side of a guy who'd threatened to knife me, because he didn't want to lose a good cook!

Even though I was making headway and learning a lot about everything—including self-defense—I can't say that I had had an epiphany about my career at that point. All I knew was that I would get up every day and go to work, then go home when I couldn't stand up anymore. And do it again the next day.

After about five years—and a name change to Brennan's Vieux Carré—the restaurant had come together. We got some great help from our interior designer and dear friend Charlie Gresham, who worked with Adelaide to rescue the disaster area that was the second floor and add seating that doubled our capacity. (We even cadged a beautiful old rug that the Monteleone Hotel had tossed out to the sidewalk and hauled it over to our place for one of the new upstairs dining rooms!) Adelaide also called upon her businessman friend Clay Shaw, who was deeply involved in French Quarter preservation. He convinced her to add wallpaper, which was a very big deal then, and to do something about the four big windows that fronted Bourbon and Bienville streets.

"You're on one of busiest corners of the city," he pointed out, "so why don't you get rid of the silly curtains and put candles on the table?"

That was a big step for us. None of the other restaurants had a view from the street, and soon people began to stop in front of our place just to see who was in there. A simple idea, but ingenious.

Finally we started making money. We weren't drawing salaries, but we could pay for everything and start doing some traveling. Owen and Daddy believed strongly that in order for our restaurant, and New Orleans restaurants in general, to succeed, we had to see how the best places in Europe and America operated and what the trends were. That's how I wound up observing the operation at '21' in New York and getting to know the city's restaurant scene.

Owen had made friends with the Kreindler and Berns families that ran '21,' and they graciously taught me how their whole operation worked. Every time Owen or Adelaide or I went there, Jerry Berns or Jack Kreindler would introduce us to practically everybody in the place. I don't care if it was Humphrey Bogart and Lauren Bacall sitting two tables away, he'd say, "These are our 'cousins' from New Orleans," and introduce us.

During my visits, which were almost like an internship, I suppose, I'd spend a few days at a time hanging out in the kitchen and the dining rooms and everywhere else they'd let me, including the wine cellar. I was particularly fascinated by the way they handled the guests as they arrived. The Kreindlers had five family members that ran the place, and before the restaurant opened they'd read the reservation sheet to see who was coming in. Then they'd hang around the front door, and when somebody arrived, they'd attack and make that person feel like the most beloved human on earth—a long-lost brother or sister. They treated me the same way they treated the heads of AT&T and CBS who worked nearby. To me, that level of hospitality was extraordinary, but it was natural to my brother Owen. He was always saying to us, "You've got to make these people feel that you're happy to have them. You've got to make them *feel,* and you just don't show, you *feel.*" That was a big word—feel. And the Kreindlers instilled that sense of joy, graciousness and camaraderie in everyone who dined and drank with them, which, it being New York, was practically the entire world.

I think New York is the best food city in the world—I thought that then and I reaffirm that belief every time I visit. From the first day, it blew me away. It's where I went to really learn the restaurant business—in the early days I could always go right into the kitchen—and to meet the people in the trade. James Beard took me into the kitchen at the Four Seasons, which couldn't have been more exciting for this little girl from New Orleans. I went to Lidia Bastianich's first restaurant when her kids were young. Her son and business partner, Joe, is now a major New York restaurateur and owns wineries in Italy. Later, I met Danny Meyer when he opened his first restaurant and mingled with a young Drew Nieporent and upcoming chefs such as Daniel Boulud at culinary events. Such a thrill and an education.

For one of my first visits to New York, Owen had asked his friend, the author Robert Ruark, to show me around. He took me to Toots Shor's on W. 51st Street for lunch, and there were all these baseball players and coaches and actors sitting around. "That looks pretty impressive, doesn't it?" he asked. I nodded.

"Now, I'm going to walk you to '21' on the next block and introduce you to the people who these people work for."

Startling, perhaps, but true: at '21' you had the owner of the team or the company or the theater. Different sides of the same coin; different people, both fabulous. Robert was teaching me about New York.

When I started visiting Europe, I didn't know anybody. I would sit there and look at the menu, but I didn't speak or read French, so I would have the captain choose food for me. This was classic French food, way before *nouvelle*. Compared to what I was used to, the food was subtle, maybe cooked in stock or topped with a little sauce. My favorite place was Lasserre. They greeted you at the elevator and took you up to the next floor. The service couldn't have been more formal, but it wasn't cold. When you were sitting there, they'd open the ceiling and white doves would fly out. I'd never been to a place that could even begin to touch it.

My eyes were popping all through Paris. The food in the bistros was great, and I loved the art galleries and the museums. We always had a great hotel . . . we'd walk the neighborhoods . . . those grand cafés on Saint-Germain . . . God, I love Paris!

Italy was a different story. Goodness knows I love the place and right now would love to go and stay, but at that time they didn't have a lot of real restaurants. The best food was in the homes, and you knew what the food was. Though I haven't been to Italy in nearly twenty years, I know from my reading that they now have many, many very good restaurants.

Along with our regular visits to New York and Paris, Adelaide and I spent time in San Francisco, Chicago, London, Bordeaux, and Provence, hitting every notable place we could find—sometimes more than a dozen in a day. We didn't necessarily eat in all these restaurants—though if you look at me now, you'll see we didn't go hungry. (I joke with my colleagues that I donated my body to the hospitality industry a long time ago.) But we would go in and look around, ask to see the kitchen, check out the ladies room, maybe talk to the manager about the ordering system, ask questions about the basics—and maybe make a friend. All of the people seemed happy to welcome us except the French, so I had to keep working on them. I can't tell you how many times those connections paid off, especially when it came time to send my son, Alex, and my nephews to other cities to learn the business.

All those scouting trips taught us what good food is all about and made us realize that, in general, the established restaurants in New Orleans weren't as good as they should be—including ours.

Our customers, however, seemed to disagree. A lot of them came from fine families, where the parents may have traveled abroad but the children didn't because of the war. Now they were starting to visit Europe again, and they'd come back and tell us, "Listen, you've got it made. New Orleans food is better, better, better than what we had in Paris. Their food is sophisticated, but they don't season it right, the way we do here. We enjoyed ourselves, but we'd rather eat in New Orleans."

So even though I secretly disagreed, we got excited that people appreciated our more highly seasoned food than France's subtle fare. And we didn't just season food. We liked to say "We season food with food, not just spices." It's all in the technique. We were finally able to say, "OK, we're not so bad, we learned and got better."

Toward the end of our stay on Bourbon Street, we began to be noticed by some of the national press. Kate Titus, a public relations lady from New York, came down one day and walked into the restaurant. She told me she was bringing down food editors from New York City, five at a time. They'd come into town for a night and then she'd take them down to the Tabasco estate on Avery Island, which was picking up the tab. So she started bringing them to our restaurant about three or four times a year. Then they'd go home and write about the restaurants of New Orleans. A simple strategy, really. That was also part of the beginning of my love affair with writers, from Robert Ruark to the *New York Times'* Johnny Apple. I just love their minds and being around them.

Well, Kate was going to put those writers up in a guesthouse on Royal Street, but she came to me and said it's filthy dirty. I asked what we could do to help, and she replied that we needed to find some cleaners. I don't know how it all got put together, but I got a couple of cleaners and we went down with buckets and mops and cleaned it the best we could. This is when I'm first meeting her—and I'm leaving the restaurant to go help clean the toilets in this rooming house! But I'll tell you what, when we were first starting out, that lady did more to help our restaurant become known than anyone. When people ask me about making contacts, I have often said, "First you make a friend."

Our financial success and the positive feedback we were getting gave us the confidence to face our next challenge head-on: we would be losing our lease at the end of May 1956 and would have to find a new home if we wanted to stay in business. And we very much did. In fact, Owen had envisioned a classy, high-end restaurant that would put New Orleans on the map for good. He felt that the opportunities were extraordinary and that, if we did it right, we could set a new standard for what a New Orleans restaurant should look and be like.

In 1954, about two years before we would have to move, Owen took out a lease on a building where he planned on making that dream a reality: 417 Royal Street.

THE SCOOP ON BANANAS FOSTER

Here's how the most famous dessert from our early days came into being in 1951:

Owen waltzes into the kitchen one morning.

"Hey, Kid, we're having a dinner honoring our friend Richard. He's just been appointed the chairman of the new vice commission, and I would like to honor him with a newly created dessert named for him. And I need it for tonight."

"Owen, I don't have the time for that. I have to order all the liquor today, and I'm working on that new breakfast menu."

"Kid—an exciting new dessert. By tonight. For Richard. Got it?"

"Damn you, Owen . . ."

Our maître d', Frank Bertucci, walks in as I'm fussing and banging stuff around in the kitchen.

"Whatcha doing?"

"My stupid brother wants us to come up with a dish by tonight for this big dinner honoring the chairman of the new vice commission."

"What happened to the old vice commission?

"Too much vice."

"Gotcha. What do you have in mind?"

"I don't know—I'm looking at all these bananas. They're cheap and everybody loves them. Let me show you kind of what Mama does at home. She sautés 'em with a little butter and brown sugar. Mama's bananas. Let's try that. All anybody ever serves in this town is ice cream or cake."

"Except the baked Alaska at Antoine's."

"Everybody loves that damn dessert and there's nothing to it. A little cake and they put some meringue on top. Geeze!"

"Folks love it, though, because they flame it."

"So let's flame ours. Grab some rum, or maybe banana liqueur. Hell, let's do both."

"If we flame it in the dining room, the whole place will smell good. And if you toss some cinnamon into that fire, it'll sparkle, especially if we dim the lights."

"Sounds good to me, but something's missing. Let's serve the bananas over ice cream."

"Perfect! The vanilla-bean flavor will bring everything together."

That night at the dinner, Owen summons me to the head table. "Ella, would you show Richard what we created to honor him?"

"Absolutely. Mr. Foster, here's our new dessert."

3

'Some Girls Went to Finishing School. I Went to Café Lafitte.'

"DRINK SCOTCH AND WATER—IT'LL GROW ON YOU AND YOU'LL LOOK MORE SOPHISTICATED."
—JOHN BRENNAN TO HIS SISTER ELLA

Now let me tell you about my *real* education. Working behind the scenes in a French Quarter saloon and restaurant was an invaluable introduction to the world of hospitality, don't get me wrong, but it wasn't the most formative experience of my career. Not by a long shot. That came after hours, at a place down the street at 941 Bourbon Street. Café Lafitte (also called Lafitte's Blacksmith Shop at various times in its long history) was a charming gathering place for everyone and everything that was New Orleans after the war. It wasn't a gay bar, but many gay people were among the fascinating crowd that gathered there. You'd find directors of the ballet and symphony and the editors and publishers of both of the city's newspapers. Tennessee Williams and Noel Coward were known to have dropped by.

Owen would take people to Café Lafitte late at night. He'd start out the evening by meeting somebody at the Old Absinthe House, and maybe Count Arnaud would come over, and they'd all walk down Bourbon to a cozy candlelit bar with a piano and a courtyard. For a moment in time it *was* New Orleans café society—just late at night and with drinks.

Café Lafitte was housed in a stone building dating back to the 1700s. According to local lore, it may have been connected to the smuggling operation of famed pirate brothers Jean and Pierre Lafitte. Somewhere along the line it became a bar, and by the time I was old enough to go there, it had become *the* after-hours place to see and be seen in the French Quarter.

I'd hear people talking about whom they knew and whom they saw, so I'd pester Owen: "You've *got* to take me and my friends to Lafitte's. I really, *really* want to go. I *need* to go. I *have* to go."

"Mama will kill me if I bring you down Bourbon. She'll kill me."

But I kept after him and reminded him that I was old enough to go wherever I wanted. So he finally gave in, and every now and then he'd come get me and we'd go there together.

We'd walk down past the strip joints and nod to the barkers who were jawing at people to get them in the door. If you were lucky, you might encounter a "battle of the bands." On most nights you could hear Al Hirt and Pete Fountain in their own clubs, or other top-flight jazz musicians at places like the Famous Door, and occasionally the bands would spill out into the streets and square off against one another musically. The restaurants would empty out, and the bands would get everybody going. And then someone would say, "The bar's open!" and they'd all march into the restaurant. The clubs staggered their set times so that you could hear different groups at multiple venues. So there was always something going on along Bourbon Street, and whatever it was, it was not to be missed.

Eventually we'd get to Café Lafitte and we'd see everybody, like it was a neighborhood within a neighborhood. If there was someone I didn't know, Owen would introduce me.

I would sit in on these conversations, and I was so excited I didn't know what to do. It was like going to a party. You didn't have to sit at a table; you could wander around and talk to anyone about anything—art, movies, politics, who'd been seen canoodling in the back streets. With all of the reading I was doing—a couple of newspapers a day, tons of magazines and books—I felt as though I could hold my own. When the ballet was in town, the dancers would end up there. If there was a play at the Civic Theater—there were always shows on the road in those days—the performers would all want to go to Lafitte's. Bill Clinton would have been there had he been around. Somebody might sit down at the piano and start a sing-along. I loved every minute because it made me feel as though I were taking part in a slightly naughtier version of the famous round table at the Algonquin in New York.

On several occasions in the late 1950s, we met up with a then-little-known politician named Hubert Humphrey, who had been the mayor of Minneapolis. I was dating Paul Martin (a recent arrival to New Orleans whom I would later marry), who had known and worked with Hubert in Minneapolis. We used to call Hubert a "snow digger" to tease him, because we knew that whenever it started snowing up there, he'd find a reason to have to come to New Orleans. He was a wonderful man, and we all sensed he would go on to do great things. He did.

I always said that some girls went to finishing school, but I went to Café Lafitte. (Lately, people keep giving me notecards and shirts with that saying on it.) That was where I learned how and what to drink. One night I went down to Lafitte's and my brother John was there, home on leave from the Navy. He looked at what I was ordering, which was probably a variety of sugary concoctions, shook his head and said, "You've got to learn how to drink. You can't drink all this stuff, all these cocktails. If you're gonna drink, drink Scotch and water, and you'll look more sophisticated."

"Well, I don't like the way it tastes."

"It'll grow on you and you'll look more sophisticated."

So I started to drink Scotch and water—and it grew on me. He chose that because he thought it was a drinking-man's drink. His view was that if you're going to stay out and drink and have two or three, don't drink gin and tonics and Sazeracs and whiskey sours. Definitely don't drink all of those together. "And don't mix the grain and the grape," he'd say. "Just drink Scotch." I don't remember what the brand was in those days, but eventually it became Ballantine's, which was what they served at '21' in New York. Later on, wine, especially French wine, became my drink of choice. John also introduced me to stingers, a combination of crème de menthe and cognac, which were perfect for after a meal. John and all of his fellow Navy flyboys drank them.

Despite all my experimentation, my memories of Café Lafitte remain very strong and very good. They had this crazy guy, a short Italian man with a wooden leg who was the caretaker and the watchman and the cleanup guy, and he lived up in the attic of the place. When he came in, you knew it was late and probably time to go. As I'd prepare to leave, Owen would usually say, "OK, Slim"—I was only allowed to use two cab drivers, and Slim was my favorite—"take her home!"

On one of those nights, as we were all leaving, the vegetable deliveryman came across the street. We piled into the back of his wagon and we rode up Royal to the Monteleone Hotel, where we'd parked our cars. In those days, you could do crazy, spontaneous things like that. It was a thrilling time. People in New Orleans always knew how to have fun, even if it was a Tuesday night, if you know what I mean.

Tommy Caplinger leased the place. He was a highly intelligent businessman, and how he wound up in this venture, I don't know. He was a bon vivant of the highest order. But a friend of Owen's was a friend of mine. When I was at the Old Absinthe House, Owen would mention that someone from Lafitte's was going to come in to pick up a couple cases of liquor. I was to let him take what he wanted off the shelf and then put it in the book. The guy would come in, but he didn't have any money because half of the people at Lafitte's didn't pay. It wasn't that they didn't want to pay, but nobody was giving them a check. So I asked Owen, "Why are you sending these people this whiskey out of our inventory?" And he said, "If you go to Lafitte's tonight and they don't have any booze, it's going to be terrible." That was his only explanation. And for years that went on.

Tommy died in 1957, and it was the end of an era. When it came time to settle the estate, it seemed that no one had paid rent for a long time, and it wasn't clear who held the title, so all of a sudden Tommy's partners got this huge bill. They were going to be evicted, so they rented a place up the block and named it Café Lafitte in Exile, which today is a bar that's popular with the gay community. To raise some cash for the bill, someone staged an auction of a notorious sculpture called *The Lovers*, by local artist Ricky Alferez. It depicted a nude couple in a very close embrace and had been on display at a public building but was removed on the grounds of indecency. Enough money was raised to pay the back rent and taxes, and then the club was sold to someone who revived the name Lafitte's

Blacksmith Shop, which is why we have both Lafitte's Blacksmith Shop and Café Lafitte in Exile on the same block to this day. I'm telling you, it was crazy.

Today, Lafitte's is more of a ramshackle bar with a jukebox. It's popular with tourists, which is fine, but completely different from what it was in (what I think of as) its golden era after the war. Today, if you visit it during one of the big festival weekends, you're likely to see crowds spilling out into the street, a tour guide performing a voodoo demonstration in the courtyard, or patrons hanging their heads out the window singing "Sweet Caroline."

Good times, perhaps, but surely not as good as the ones I remember.

4

A Vision on Royal Street (1955–1969)

"THERE WASN'T ANY PLACE YOU COULD LOOK WHERE IT WASN'T PRETTY."

—DOTTIE BRENNAN

Life truly can be a bowl of cherries, as Fats Pichon would often remind me, but first you have to grow the fruit. And then you have to spit out the pits.

Our family had grown confident at our place on Bourbon Street, based on what we were hearing from our well-traveled customers, but a tidal wave of unexpected challenges smacked us as we prepared to launch the first Brennan restaurant to be created from scratch.

We had only a vague notion of how difficult it might be to develop a new restaurant while running an existing place and trying to maintain its standards. Owen was ambitious and a successful entrepreneur, and I had acquired nearly a decade of management experience, but this grand project was something else entirely. It would have been nice if we'd had a template to guide us, but that template didn't yet exist, at least not in New Orleans. This was long before the days of franchises and upscale restaurant "concepts" or "collections," so once again we began to figure things out for ourselves.

After months of scouring the French Quarter, Owen thought he had found the right building: a capacious two-story structure on Royal Street that had been built in the late 1700s by the great-grandfather of artist Edgar Degas. Beginning in the early 1800s, it housed the Banque de la Louisiane. Over the decades it had served many other purposes: it had been a rooming house for guys in the Navy during the war; the residence of world chess champion Paul Morphy; and most recently a party space called the Patio Royale, which hosted debutante balls. At one time, the Patio Royale had been a nice place, but you could never quite figure out what it was because it had been put to so many different uses, and it was starting to fall apart. Tulane University, which had inherited the building from a wealthy philanthropist, was willing to lease it to Owen for a hefty sum (the exact amount has been lost to history).

He went to our banker and jawed with him until the banker finally agreed to finance the deal. But some of us were scared to death because the location was two blocks farther away from Canal Street (which was the border with the business district that supplied much of our customer base) and a block closer to the river, on a stretch that was quiet and dark and a little scary at night. We would be making people walk all that way from the business district in the New Orleans heat. "No way," I thought, "we can't do it."

"We're going to do it," Owen insisted, and so the deal was done, with the intention of opening at the end of May 1956, when our Bourbon Street restaurant lease expired. What did I know?

It was obvious that 417 Royal had been unbelievably mistreated: the carriageway was all trimmed in neon, the restrooms were revolting, and the décor was tacky. Daddy planned to strip that building because he wanted to inspect it closely. He took down everything that was on the wall, wherever there was a nail, and he came back and declared, "This is one of the best buildings in the French Quarter. The bones are extraordinary. It's going to work."

So we started to get excited.

I say "we," but I had nothing to do with it. I wasn't qualified to design a restaurant. I was capable of running one—that was my job. But I didn't have the natural instincts of design and imagination. Adelaide had that. Our interior designer and dear friend Charlie Gresham had that. And Daddy knew the building was solid, even though people had abused it. "We've got something pretty fantastic here," he'd say.

Owen brought in the restoration architects Koch & Wilson, and everyone came up with all these wonderful ideas. My father did the kitchen drawings using drafting skills he had learned at the shipyard, and Sam Wilson and the architects decided to build the restaurant around the patio. Adelaide worked with Charlie and got that going. At the time, we were just going to operate the downstairs because the money wasn't there to open the upstairs, where there was a series of beautifully proportioned rooms that initially would be used for storage and offices.

Owen had the vision and was a big part of the planning, but as tasks presented themselves he would say, "I don't know how to do that—*you* do that." Everybody was saying, "Just do what you do best." And finally, somehow, our family's dream in the French Quarter began to materialize.

One night Owen asked me to walk with him down Royal Street, where all of the antiques stores were located. The Royal Orleans Hotel wasn't there yet, and the street was dark. Store owners would turn out their lights at night and go home, making the street seem uninviting and a little dangerous. "We've got to do something about this," he said, "something mutually beneficial." Soon we went door-to-door and asked all the shop owners to "please keep your lights on when you leave"—and they did! Every single shop. That whole stretch became inviting. It was just wonderful the way the community wrapped us in their arms. We were so fortunate.

Until one day we weren't.

• • •

I was overseeing breakfast service at Bourbon Street around 10:30 a.m. on November 4, 1955, when I got a call from Owen's wife, Maudie.

"Owen's dead."

"What? What are you talking about?"

"Owen's dead," she sobbed. "He had a massive heart attack this morning."

None of us had any idea this was coming; we'd only known that he always had Rolaids in his pocket. I knew that he had dined at Antoine's the night before (much, much later that fact became a source of amusement between our family and the Alciatores of Antoine's). At first I had a difficult time processing the news—Owen was just 45, had three children (Pip, 21, Jimmy, 14, and Teddy, 7), and was living a life most people could only dream of. It didn't make sense.

I ran out and got in a taxicab and told the driver, "Owen is dead—take me out to his house, quick!" So he started speeding and a policeman stopped us. I said, "Look, my brother Owen Brennan just died and I gotta get there, I gotta get there, West End Boulevard, out toward Lake Pontchartrain! I gotta get there!"

"Come on, I'll take you." And the officer spent the rest of the day doing whatever he could for the family. The situation was terrible. I mean absolutely, totally terrible. When I got there, Owen was still in the bed. John and Adelaide soon arrived and took care of everything while my parents consoled Maudie and their sons.

I knew I was loved and supported by an unbelievably strong family, but at that moment I was crushed. The man I had followed around like a puppy dog— the big brother who always called me "Kid" and "Toots" and goaded me to attempt things I never thought possible—was gone. I miss him still, though he has been present in spirit at every venture I've attempted.

The next day the newspapers ran headlines on the front page in the same type size they had used to announce the end of World War II: "Owen Brennan, dead at 45." It seemed that half of the city was at his wake, including everybody from the French Quarter in his or her strange attire. Everybody was there.

While that was comforting, we were absolutely miserable souls.

People have asked me over the years how we got through it, and I tell them we didn't have a choice but to get through it. Owen died on a Friday morning, and we were back to work on Monday. We had to. We had a restaurant to run and another in the pipeline.

Personal tragedy haunted us over the next few years. I lost both of my parents, Mom in late 1957 and Daddy in early 1959. Boy, did he miss her—if she had lived a few more months, they would have celebrated fifty years of marriage. We lost an infant nephew named Johnny, who had been born to John and his wife, Claire, and then our close family friend Ralph Alexis, who had become a mentor to me after Owen died. I don't remember any of us not being able to cope. I guess these losses made us realize that life is short and precious and that we all needed each other. We had to exercise discipline because we had to make this thing go. At this point, Adelaide became the great voice of reason within the family, a role she would maintain the rest of her life. I have to say I have always felt safe and secure. We would handle whatever—divorce, cancer, death—as a family.

Soldiering on through our grief over my brother wasn't simply a matter of summoning willpower and toughing it out emotionally. We immediately faced stone-cold, hard-nosed business challenges. Within a matter of days of Owen's death, the bank pulled their financing for the project. Gone! Even though we were just six months away from opening and had already invested substantial resources. I don't remember how we got the message but what we heard was that they weren't going to back a project headed by a woman (I hadn't yet developed my Hurricane Ella reputation). Eventually, the hospitality industry would become an excellent place for women to climb the ranks and make a good living, but in the mid-1950s that was practically unheard of. I took the affront personally, but no amount of pleading could sway the moneymen, even though our family had a solid reputation.

What to do, what to do, what to do?

Very quickly we found out who our friends were and recognized the strength of our family bond. Daddy and I gathered everyone and plotted how to get the money that would get us across the finish line. We mortgaged all of our houses (about ten places, as I recall), and we got loans from John's in-laws (the Lallys) and Dick's in-laws (the Trists). It came out to about $1 million, enough to allow us to open. In the mid-1950s, spending that enormous amount of money to open a restaurant was absolutely unheard of. But the project was in motion. The train had left the station as they say. It was open or bust.

During this time, Ralph Alexis stepped in to help us. He was a tax consultant and took over mapping the financial end of the project. "Don't worry about it," he said. "We're going to get there. Just get it ready. Go. Do. Don't think about the money. We can handle that." Turned out he was right.

Even the contractor, Gaston Gardebled, and the architects said, "Let's just get the restaurant open and we will go from there. You can pay for it as we go." They never asked us to sign anything, never charged us interest. They became part of our team. Can you imagine that happening today?

And so we forged ahead. Dick and Pip were still in the Army, and Dottie was recently married and living in San Francisco, but the rest of us pitched in. Daddy went to the site nearly every day to see that things continued on schedule, John helped with some of the mechanical stuff, and Adelaide worked on the décor with Charlie Gresham, a marvelous interior designer who had been a decorator at the D. H. Holmes department store. Charlie was one of the most elegant gentlemen you'd ever meet—well educated, well traveled, well groomed—an extremely fun guy who adopted all of us.

"We're not going to decorate, we're going to accentuate the features of this building," was his assessment. It already had a beautiful patio with a great big magnolia tree in the middle, so he said to simply paint the patio walls white and then we could do whatever we wanted. Charlie ordered a beautiful green rug to "bring the outside in" and mirrors to reflect the outdoors.

Adelaide had always been on Owen's back about how the place should look because she had more style than he ever had, and she was in agreement with Charlie. Those two, and Dottie, who would call in regularly to consult, made it look right. They loved the details. Charlie added woodwork in certain areas, but he didn't take anything away from the building. We were putting the kitchen up front, so they decided to install showcase windows along the front of the building facing Royal Street. In the dining rooms they added just a few very basic, but quite lovely, things—coffee pots and cups, some framed menus and several pieces of furniture.

Charlie went to an art dealer, got a dozen beautiful paintings of all different sizes and put them in what we were calling the Red Room. He told us to send the dealer a check for $25 each month. Many years later the dealer called us and said, "Look, you gotta stop sending that check. Those are your paintings now, not mine." The payment had gone out automatically from our account, and it just kept going.

From the outside, the effect was simple. But you walked in and you'd say "Wow!" The front of the building had been painted a very pale peach color, which Charlie said to freshen up but not change. The pink color of later years was not our doing. It was peach—a soft Caribbean color. Never pink. As a final touch, he added a brass replica of a Brennan's signature to the right of the front door.

Leading up to the opening day, I would go over and sit in front of these big windows on the second floor over the patio and just observe. Maybe I wasn't working, but I was learning all the time. We may have been the only people in the world who had a restaurant with a patio and liked when it rained. We decided then that all the seating would be inside; how could we plan otherwise? It's a good thing we did that, because for the first thirty days we were open, it rained at lunchtime. Every. Single. Day. It hadn't rained in months. And it didn't rain at 2 p.m. or at 7 a.m.—it rained at lunch. Our stretch of Royal Street would be flooded because the city had done a lousy job with the drainage system, and people would be carrying their shoes in their hands. Walking into our place barefoot at lunch became the most exciting thing to happen to New Orleans! (I guess I owe an apology to all of those "barefoot boys from the bayou" I used to grouse about.)

We had to leave our Bourbon Street restaurant by May 31 so that we could open on Royal Street on June 1, but we served dinner right up until the very end. We were afraid that if we closed up for a few days, nobody would come to the new place. After we fired up our last meal, Daddy and John helped move the stoves in a couple of borrowed pick-up trucks—that's how tight we were on the scheduling.

Early the next morning, dozens of friends and regular customers arrived and we launched a jazz parade to our new home. As it went down, a photographer from *Life* magazine captured the silliness from a balcony. These people were carrying crazy things like pots and pans over their heads and under their arms and dancing, oh my Lord they were dancing. And the band was wonderful. (I'm not sure if they played "Life is Just a Bowl of Cherries," but if not, they should have. Let's just say they did.)

The band went right into the restaurant, and we set everybody up with a lavish spread of turtle soup, gumbo and shrimp remoulade, and drinks, drinks, drinks! Everybody toasted Owen, who'd died just six months earlier. But thanks to his foresight, *Life* covered the event, and Jerry Berns from '21' came down from New York to join us. It was a great, great day, hysterically incorrect, if you know what I mean. Nobody was sitting down and eating lunch. Nobody was behaving. Everybody was carrying on.

We had arrived—with old stoves and pots and pans and memories and hard lessons learned, but with a new, stronger appetite for life.

LIKE A HOLLYWOOD SET

My sister Dottie, who lived in San Francisco while her husband was in the military and had given birth to her daughter Brenne right before the opening, wasn't able to visit or cut the ribbon on the place to which she had contributed so much via phone. But finally seeing the finished product in all its splendor made the first impression that much more memorable.

"The whole family took me and my husband down there at night, and it was like a Hollywood set—so much prettier than I thought it was going to be, because I had last seen the building in its deteriorated state. I was speechless. It was absolutely the loveliest restaurant I had ever been in, and I had been in many, in New York, San Francisco, Paris and elsewhere.

"I stood outside the big glass doors—the planning commission later made us change those—and looking in it was like they weren't there. The carriageway had red stripes on its awning and looked like it went on forever, and the patio had been replanted and was all so lush.

"And then we walked in and I saw the main dining room and the bar. The lighting was perfect, with candles giving everything a beautiful glow. In the stairway were a gigantic mirror and a marvelous chandelier, hanging from above when you looked up. They kept the interior doors to the upstairs that I'd told Daddy to preserve. The doors had curved glass in them because that was the way they fit into the walls when they were opened. There wasn't any place you could look where it wasn't pretty.

"The ladies' room was maybe the best of all. All the department stores on Canal Street begged Louise, the woman who ran the ladies room, to carry their makeup and grooming products, so she had perfumes, lipsticks, stockings—anything a woman could want—on the dressing tables. Guests would walk in and give *her* a hug. Louise was petite and elegant, and Adelaide always bought her beautiful outfits to wear. Louise's uniforms were pink or gray silk with a white silk apron. Whenever we ordered one, it would arrive in a gift package addressed to Louise from Bergdorf's in New York City. She was a lady. It was all done in such good taste. You felt very much like you were a lady when you walked into Brennan's on Royal Street."

Brennan's was an instant success, and it never let up for the eighteen years that my siblings and I were there. In the restaurant business in the United States of America, this new upstart was the No. 1 thing everybody talked and wrote about for the entire year of 1956. All those people Owen had met at the Old Absinthe House came, and every major general interest magazine—*The Saturday Evening Post, Collier's, McCall's, Holiday* and more—ventured to New Orleans to write stories about us. *Look* even gave us a double-page photo spread. I was thrilled beyond belief.

America was coming to appreciate dining as entertainment, and all of the newspapers were just beginning to have columns about food, so many of them sent their writers to take a look. While they were here, they took notice of New Orleans as a swell place to visit, and that gave a boost to tourism, just as Owen had predicted. We had only about five notable hotels at that time, so the real launching of the city as a must-visit destination was still on the horizon. But we were on our way. After the opening hoopla, the restaurant and the city continued to get tremendous publicity, and I believe we helped generate some of that. I recently found a letter Conrad Hilton had written in response to a letter Owen had written him pushing to get a Hilton Hotel in the city.

For as long as I can remember, we'd been trying to get the city to get its marketing organized—convincing out-of-town hoteliers to open outlets, figuring out how to get conventions to town, etc. Along the way there was a "convention bureau" or a "tourist commission" run out of the New Orleans Chamber of Commerce, but few of us in the hospitality industry thought this was going well. We needed an organization to be more independent. So one day Glenn Douthit, our close friend who was doing public relations in Mayor Chep Morrison's office, and my husband, Paul, and I decided we would send telegrams to the chamber and to lots of people involved, telling them that we would still be dues-paying members but that we were going to form our own commission to work on tourism. Plenty of people would not be happy about this, but Chep backed us and gave an office in the courthouse to Glenn, our one employee.

One night we sat on the porch of our house on Eleonore Street, scared to death as we talked about our plan. When people have control of something, they don't often like to give it up. No exception here. The members of the chamber were our customers and friends, but we knew we were doing the right thing. We may have had a few extra stingers that night as we contemplated sending those telegrams the next day. But our message succeeded in bringing about a separate commission. The courthouse was directly across the street from Brennan's, and Glenn would come in and out of our kitchen talking things through and figuring out our next steps.

Thanks to a lot of planning, stingers and guts, what became known as the Tourist Commission (now the New Orleans Metropolitan Convention & Visitors Bureau) was formed on the porch of our house.

• • •

Settling in at our new digs on Royal Street seemed natural this time. My job was the same as always—I had to get the menu going and organize the cooks and kitchen. Daddy was magnificent at the front of the house—he dressed and spoke beautifully and people just adored him. He was always "Mr. Brennan." He oversaw about twenty-eight tables downstairs (given the success of the opening, we immediately began working to open the second floor) as well as the bar patio, which was open year-round, with waiters in crisp uniforms—red in the winter and green in the summer. Adelaide looked after the accounting and business side of things, and when Dick got out of the Army during our first year, he became the daily go-to guy. No titles, just everyone doing what they did best.

But there were a few gaps. At first, we didn't know how to take reservations. Our system is perfection now, but then . . . We had a gentleman named Aymore Dore standing in the carriageway entrance and our regular guests simply knew that he would take care of them. Some would call or stop by ahead of time, but most of our guests just showed up. It was unbelievable. People would arrive at 7 p.m. and head to the bar, and two or three hours later, they'd still be drinking there, waiting for a table. And because this was New Orleans, nobody seemed to mind. It was the place to be. (Within a year or two we opened the second floor, which increased our capacity by two-and-a-half times and alleviated most of the logjam downstairs.) We had a little black book for reservations, but it was not a sophisticated system. It took us years to get better at that. There is an art to it. It amazes me how little attention some restaurants pay to this when it can so dramatically affect your sales. My son, Alex, invented something called Maitre D'ata that was way ahead of the pack in using computers to take better care of our guests. It enables us to coordinate reservations so that we can accommodate more guests when they want to come, rather than when we have availability.

About four months after we opened, Dottie and her husband, Ben, were finally able to travel from San Francisco to see the restaurant, and we eventually enlisted her help in handling reservations. Dottie and her family moved home in August 1965, after Ben got out of the service. Things were so chaotic that one night she asked me, "Do you know the ropes they use to keep people in line at the theater? Do you think I could get one and string it across the carriageway? Because people are getting past me before I get their names, and it's just mass confusion."

"I don't care what you do," I said, "just make it work." So she got some green velvet ropes, a nice lectern and a book to take down names, and that brought some sense of order that everyone appreciated.

I consider Brennan's to have been the city's first glamorous restaurant. I don't think there was really any competition—we vied for French Quarter customers with Antoine's, Arnaud's and Galatoire's, and uptown there was Pascal's Manale, but all of them had been open for years and were very traditional. None of them had a chef, and New Orleans didn't seem to want one. Some of the restaurants had good cooks but nobody directed them. They were free to stand outside smoking cigarettes, and they did what they wanted to do, betting on horses, flirting with the waitresses and what have you.

We brought Paul Blangé over from Bourbon Street and put him in charge, but he wasn't a chef in the way we think of chefs today. Still, people thought we served the best food in New Orleans. I'd be lying if I said I knew what he and I were thinking when it came to the opening menu. I'm almost positive we copied the menu we already had from our Bourbon Street place, including the egg dishes at breakfast, and then shortly after opening we began adding and dropping things and figuring out what our customers really wanted. At Brennan's Vieux Carré, Owen and I had been taking our cue from '21,' where they didn't worry so much about the food and just offered what people wanted to eat. You'd go there and eat something like chicken hash, but God knows it was a popular restaurant.

On Royal Street, rather than be daring, we tried to improve upon the dishes that New Orleanians craved. We had a tremendous amount of fish available to us, including pompano, trout and flounder, plus oysters, shrimp and crabmeat, so we tried to serve them in a fashion that was not routine and make it the best seafood a person had ever put into his or her mouth. Our guests just wanted something good to eat while they soaked up the atmosphere.

One thing that was a no-brainer was to continue serving breakfast for people who had been out all night—a practice we had started on Bourbon Street when nobody else was doing it, except for maybe a few hotels. There, we had opened at 10 a.m. On Royal Street we opened at 8:30, but only because we had to—people were standing out front, waiting to get in from the very beginning. We couldn't believe our luck!

Most of our guests were locals who had followed us from Bourbon Street: lawyers, doctors, business owners, the heads of the major department stores on Canal Street—and their sales ladies. We were a very cosmopolitan sort of place. But because of all the publicity we were getting nationally, we quickly became known to many of the Hollywood stars and other entertainers who came through town. TV was still in its infancy, so celebs would tour the country to promote their films and shows via local radio station shows, including Jill Jackson's *Let's Join Jill*, which was broadcast five nights a week from Brennan's on the 50,000-watt clear-channel WWL. It could be heard as far away as Chicago (the promotion was so successful for us that we named a salad after Jill). New Orleans was a big cultural center, particularly for music (I loved opera, ballet, classical music and musical theater), so when these performers hit New Orleans, they often wound up at our restaurant, and sometimes at our homes after dinner. And we were still working the connections Owen had made with Hollywood publicists.

Over the years we became close to some of these high-profile guests, including Raymond Burr (Ti and Alex would call him Uncle Raymond), Danny

EGGS OVER BIG EASY

Everybody has a version of how "Breakfast at Brennan's" came about, but I happened to have lived this one, OK?

By the late 1940s we were just beginning to get things going on Bourbon Street, but we weren't packing them in like they were at some other places. Adding to our challenge was the fact that Frances Parkinson Keyes, a novelist who set many of her books in southern Louisiana, had just published a popular murder-mystery titled *Dinner at Antoine's*, which brought a lot of attention—and business—to our French Quarter neighbor.

One day, Owen came in (one of the rare times he visited before sunset) and was fuming about this public relations coup with his friend Lucius Beebe, who was visiting from San Francisco. Lucius was a delightful, wealthy and very eccentric bon vivant who wrote for the *New Yorker*, *Gourmet* and other magazines. He sometimes traveled in a private railroad car, which came complete with a wine cellar, a Turkish bath and a gigantic Saint Bernard named T-Bone Towzer.

"Here I am, trying to get this restaurant up and running and that damn Keyes writes this book about having dinner at Antoine's," Owen said. "We have to do something like that."

"Well, you know," Lucius said, "I have grown to enjoy eating in the daytime. I am older now, and I don't want to be eating late at night and carousing the way I used to."

They started brainstorming and Owen noted that there was a nationally syndicated morning radio show hosted by Tom Breneman called *Breakfast in Hollywood* that was quite popular. "Why don't we do a 'Breakfast at Brennan's?' Get those people who stay out all night or who want to get a jump on the day."

Lucius said, "That's it! Breakfast at Brennan's!"

At his suggestion I traveled to London and Paris to see how the elite hotels did their breakfasts. In Paris they'd just serve you a croissant and coffee and send you on your way, so that wasn't much help, and in London they offered what they thought was fabulous, elaborate food, but it would never fly in New Orleans.

Then Lucius had me meet him in San Francisco at the Palace Hotel, which had a reputation for serving the best breakfast in town. It was absolutely lovely, and a nice step up from the continental breakfasts that were served all over Europe, but it still wasn't right or uniquely suited to New Orleans.

When I returned, I explained all of this to Paul Blangé: "What are we going to do to make Breakfast at Brennan's something special, and not a repeat of these other restaurants?"

He went to his bookshelf and pulled out some old French and British cookbooks that had big sections on egg dishes, and that generated some ideas that we could adapt to a New Orleans style. Eggs Benedict was already popular in many places, and Antoine's had invented Eggs Sardou (poached eggs over English muffins with hollandaise, artichokes and creamed spinach), so we started doing versions of those. Along the way we added such items as Eggs Hussarde (poached eggs with English muffins, hollandaise, Canadian bacon and marchand de vin sauce), Eggs a la Turk (with chicken livers), grits and grillades, omelets, corned duck hash, and Steak Stanley (topped with a sauce of horseradish and bananas).

Because this was so new, people didn't quite know how to order, so we taught them by presenting breakfast as an elaborate meal. We said New Orleanians always need an "eye-opener," so we started them off with drinks that were designed for the daytime, such as the Ramos Gin Fizz, the Absinthe Frappe and champagne cocktails. We did some experimenting and found that white Alsatian wines went particularly well with the main dishes, so we added them. Next came a little pastry with Creole cream cheese, or something fruity, like grapefruit grilled with kirschwasser (a refined cherry brandy), and then an onion soup that was a lot creamier than the classic French version. Then you'd have your egg or meat dish, and we'd finish if all off with a flaming dessert made right at the table—Bananas Foster, Crepes Fitzgerald (strawberries, kirschwasser and strawberry liqueur) or Crepes Suzette. Our breakfast was over the top and loads of fun—just like New Orleans.

We even enjoyed a little synergy from something we hadn't thought of: our rooster logo. Long before these breakfasts began, we had hired the Kottwitz Agency to do our advertising. One of their graphic artists, Bill McHugh, created a logo featuring a rooster that the French referred to as "Chanteclair," which can symbolize hospitality, among other things. We just liked the big, bold colors, but later everyone thought we were clever to use the rooster to signify breakfast. That wasn't our intent; it was all one happy coincidence.

Those breakfasts caught on quickly and became a nice profit center for us (Ti and Alex say that eggs paid for their college education). And when we began serving them in our stylish new home on Royal Street, they quickly became one of the "must-do" things in the city.

Kaye, Jack Benny, Gary Cooper, Rowan & Martin, Phil Harris, Phyllis Diller (she joked that she was the only person who could get Adelaide to rise before noon), Rock Hudson (Ti says he was the first person ever to tell her about eating Lean Cuisine frozen dinners to stay slim), Eva Gardner, Joan Crawford, Barbara Stanwyck and her husband, Robert Taylor, and Isaac Stern (a master of traveling salesman jokes).

I don't think we were starstruck—most of these folks were simply interesting people who would drop by now and again when they were in town—but I have to admit that hosting them was a heck of a way to make a living. (Ti still teases me about the time, years later, when I came home after work and told her that a "Mike Jagger somebody" had been in for dinner. He and his mates asked to eat in the wine cellar and Dick said, "I think they were smoking something funny." The kids love that tale.)

One of my favorite stories involves the actor Van Johnson, who was starring in a production at a local dinner playhouse. Several of us were sitting at the bar after the play was over, and the man who was running the place brought Van over and introduced him to us. Among our group was a very attractive lady named Martha, who was exotic looking and did lots of things to attract attention. She had long fingernails, glued-on eyelashes out to here, a lo-o-o-ng silver cigarette holder, and a very deep voice. Van was being very kind and talking to everybody, and when he got to Martha, the whole room got quiet at that particular moment for some reason. He told her that he "liked her drag," and everyone just gasped! Martha couldn't believe it—she thought she was so feminine, but he thought that *she* was a *he* in drag! Somehow, we got through the rest of that evening.

One of our earliest acquaintances was the handsome Metropolitan Opera star Robert Merrill. When he was in town to perform, he'd come to our house and practice singing while his wife played our piano. During one of his visits (back when we were still at the Vieux Carré Restaurant), we got a request from a national magazine—I think it was *Holiday*—to do a photo shoot in one of the old buildings on Bourbon Street. Robert agreed to appear in it, but he didn't have a tuxedo with him. Owen said, "I'll loan you mine," but the size difference was hysterical since Robert was rather trim in stature and Owen was not. Robert was a good enough friend by then that he let me pin him up practically head to toe to take up the slack. Then we sat him at a table for the photo shoot so that the alterations would be less visible and paired him with a beautiful young lady from New Orleans, Elena Lyons, to further shift the focus. The result was a wonderful picture that they put in the centerfold of the magazine.

Another sweet tale involves the actress Claudette Colbert, who came to dinner at Adelaide's one night with the playwrights Lillian Hellman and Peter Feibleman, who was a very dear friend. Claudette didn't have a date, so Adelaide said, "That's all right, I'll call my friend Rector Wooten and ask him to come over." Well, Rector came and he was delighted to meet her. "Rector" is simply his first name, but Claudette didn't know that. They were hitting it off, so finally she got around to asking him, "And you are the rector of what?" She assumed he was from a church or a university or something. Everybody cracked up as we set her straight, and they got along wonderfully.

A far bigger faux pas—a colossal one, in fact—was committed by yours truly, and involved the actress and singer Dorothy Lamour, who was famous for her *On the Road to . . .* movies with Bob Hope and Bing Crosby. On this occasion I was laid out on my bed taking a nap "between shows"—lunch and dinner. The phone rang—Ti tells me I am incapable of not answering a ringing phone—and the person on the line said, "Hello, Ella, this is Dorothy." Now, Dorothy was a New Orleans girl and a good friend, but I had another friend who had developed the silly habit of pretending to be a different celebrity every time she called, just as a prank. Silly fun between friends.

Maybe I was half asleep or getting tired of the game, I don't know. But as soon as "Dorothy" shared that she was in town to perform at the opening of the Superdome, I decided that I wasn't going to be fooled by the prankster this time. "Oh, Dorothy," I said, "You wouldn't dare show up to perform on that stage with that giant video screen that they have. As fat as you've gotten? You'll look like a blimp."

Complete silence on the other end of the phone. Oh my god, it really *was* Dorothy Lamour! If I ever wanted the earth to open up and just swallow me, this was the time. I begged for her forgiveness and for her to come over to the house that very night for cocktails and so she could kick me. I also reminded her that I was the one who was fat. (Well, I am.)

That night, Dorothy arrived and I was waiting to answer the door. When she knocked, I opened the door and immediately turned around and bent over to reveal a huge sign on my derriere that read "Kick here!" I turned around, and we laughed and hugged. Whew! We went on to have a fun night eating and drinking and carrying on, and Dorothy, of course, performed beautifully at the Superdome. Friendship saved.

My all-time favorite evening during this phase of my life, however, involved notable people of a different stripe—the royalty of the American restaurant world. In the late 1950s, *Holiday* published its annual list of the Top 100 restaurants in America. The publisher had been a close friend of Owen's, so the year that we first made the list, he sent a marketing man to ask us if we would let them do a party at Brennan's and invite the restaurateurs and chefs from the top restaurants.

I said, "Yes, of course, but we'll give the party." At some point I got a little nervous because you don't want to throw a party where nobody comes, right? So we talked to our friend Mac Kriendler of '21' Brands, who regularly traveled the country and visited the top restaurants that were selling their line of alcohol. He was getting ready to make his rounds of major cities and agreed to stop in at the places on the *Holiday* list and see if they would come to the party. He called me halfway through his tour and said, "Go ahead and throw the party—everybody's coming!" This was decades before the creation of the James Beard Awards ceremony in New York, where schmoozing with your peers from around the country became an annual ritual. There were no groups or associations at all where operators of fine-dining restaurants gathered to get to know one another, learn from one another and commiserate.

We threw the bash and it was unbelievable! About ninety-five of the one hundred restaurants were represented by their chefs or restaurateurs, most of whom brought their spouses. A couple of the French restaurants in New York were the only ones that didn't participate, but from St. Louis, Omaha, Los Angeles, Chicago, San Francisco, Phoenix—everywhere—they came to New Orleans.

We arranged for police escorts from and to the airport, which blew them away. (That gesture came on the advice of Raymond Burr, who said, "They always pick you up at the airport, but no one ever takes you back.") In the daytime we staged a couple of events with our local friends as hosts so that everyone could get to know one another. The result was that many of these people in the business became lifelong friends, with each other and with us.

All of this led up to the big Sunday-night gala at our restaurant, which turned out to be fabulous. Paul's food was fantastic, the champagne flowed, the restaurant looked the best it ever had, and everybody was dressed to the nines and singing and dancing. I don't think the American restaurant world had ever seen anything quite like it.

As far as we were concerned, the party was over once we got everybody back to the airport Monday morning. But I came down to the restaurant Wednesday morning, and all the San Francisco people were still there, sitting at a table having breakfast! Even though they lived in the same city, they had just gotten to know each other, and they became the fastest of friends. After a couple more days, we told them the party was really over, they had to go. None of us wanted it to end.

Later, they called and said they would host the gala the following year (most places assumed they'd still be on the next year's list) and they wanted every member of the Brennan family involved with the restaurant to attend. OK!

What's the date? About ten of us went out and we were welcomed with a red carpet, bouquets of roses, champagne and music on the runway! We had a ball that year, and the next thing we knew, we got a phone call that Los Angeles wanted to do the next party. Then came Chicago. The New Yorkers finally came aboard and said, "OK, I guess we have to stand up and host a party." And it went on and on—Cincinnati, Miami—everyone in the business just having fun once a year and marking another small step in the country's dining revolution.

My time at Brennan's encompassed so many other milestones, both for me personally and for the world. In 1957, I married Paul Martin, a public relations executive and political consultant. Our son, Alex, was born in 1958, and our daughter, Ti Adelaide, in 1960. I recall that I had to skip one of my engagement parties because I was busy entertaining a food writer who had unexpectedly shown up at the restaurant. And Paul and I delayed our honeymoon to Mexico City because, well, it was an especially busy time at the restaurant. It took a few years, but we finally enjoyed a wonderful trip to Europe, where some of the finest hotels opened their suites to us. I had met the manager of Paris's George V Hotel when he ended up in New Orleans on Thanksgiving one year. What do Europeans know of Thanksgiving? Of course I brought him home with me for the holiday and then showed him all around New Orleans. Well, when Paul and I showed up at the George V, Louis met us at the door and showed us to Broadway lyricist/librettist Alan Lerner's (*My Fair Lady*) suite. Five rooms, five balconies and a piano. Let's just say the eyes of this little girl from New Orleans were popping out of my head. It was magnificent. The five views were all over Paris. And Louis took us to Lasserre—elegance defined.

The trip was magical. One of the truly amazing things was that Paul could stand on each of the five balconies and tell me where everything was—and he had never been to Paris before. He had the map of Paris memorized. In some neighborhoods he knew the name of the bakery and the name of the owner and her son. And he spoke fluent French. It was surreal.

Paul had been chosen for a special assignment during the war (no doubt because of his very high IQ) for which he was given six months of immersion in everything about France. Fortunately, the war ended and he never went on the assignment. Like most men of his generation, he didn't talk much about his military experiences. He had also served in the South Pacific under General MacArthur. In later years, I have come to think the wartime experience affected him much more than I ever realized.

When I think of milestones, I remember exactly where I was when I heard that JFK had been assassinated. I was standing in the carriageway of the restaurant and somebody came running in and said, "Did you hear?" At that same moment, a waiter who had worked for us for years came out of the coat-check room and said, "Well, he got what he deserved." Can you imagine? It just hit me: how could anybody say that about anyone, and especially the President of the United States? You could hate John Kennedy all you wanted, but you had to respect that he was President. (That waiter wasn't with us for much longer.)

Some five years later, Jim Garrison, the district attorney for New Orleans, prosecuted a local businessman and dear friend of ours, Clay Shaw, for being part of a conspiracy to murder Kennedy. Garrison was a publicity seeker who cared not one whit that all of this "evidence" was manufactured. He targeted a gay man because he could. After his relentless whisper campaign against Clay and a full-blown trial that attracted worldwide media attention to New Orleans, jurors swiftly dismissed the charges. But it ruined Clay's life. I was beside myself that all of this was happening to this sophisticated bon vivant and French Quarter resident and preservationist. So the day after his acquittal, I invited Clay to dine with us and rolled out a red carpet for his arrival on Royal Street. Critics be damned. I remember our friend and reporter Rosemary James saying on TV, "Clay Shaw is a builder, not a destroyer." She was so right.

In contrast to the political and social turmoil of the 1960s and early 1970s, a period when the whole world was simply going crazy, I felt truly fulfilled in my career for the first time. Our hard work had paid off. Within about eighteen months after opening Brennan's, we repaid the loans to all of those who had stuck with us and began to take some salaries for ourselves. I had established myself in a male-dominated field and, thanks in part to the *Holiday* gatherings, was accepted by my peers.

Dick, Dottie, Adelaide and Pip were now working in the restaurant, so there was less pressure on me, and I was able to relax a little more. I was saying to myself, "OK, you've got it figured out. Let's enjoy it." Paul and I had two beautiful young children, we were traveling to interesting places, and I was enjoying work—where I was still learning something every day. I love learning. You never go a day in this business without something wonderful happening, and you get to enjoy it, whether it be discovering a new wine or watching a new hire begin to blossom.

Perhaps we were still in a bit of shock that this restaurant was so successful, but at that time our dream was to maintain a restaurant that would thrive forever, like Antoine's. Our goal was to have a business that would sustain the family, and we didn't expect business to ever go down. We were at the top of our game in New Orleans and were prepared to meet any challenge.

Except for the ones that would come from within the family.

Tom Fitzmorris has chronicled the New Orleans food scene in minute detail for more than forty years via his New Orleans Menu newsletter/blog and The Food Show, his weekday radio show on WWL. Here, he pinpoints what people yearned for when they visited Brennan's and Commander's Palace—and why they continue to return again and again.

"People do not come to perform some sort of religious rite over the sacred food that was passed down to us from the French people. Brennan's and Commander's were places where you were gonna come and have fun. And if you were laughing up a storm, and drinking a little too much, and running into people you knew, and somebody would knock over a glass of wine—all of that was normal and laughable, and everybody loved it. There was always something going on at Brennan's/Commander's. And it's still that way to this day. Everybody is part of this party."

5

There's Just No Stopping Mardi Gras Memories

"SHE IS LIKE THIS PIZZAZZ AMBASSADOR FOR NEW ORLEANS."

—WRITER AND NEIGHBOR JULIA REED

Few things capture the spirited "only in New Orleans" aspect of my life better than our family's annual Mardi Gras festivities. In the days leading up to Lent, the whole region is swept up in a whirlwind of timeless pageantry, endless parades, bacchanalian parties and decadent, devil-may-care behavior—all fueled by a brassy, jazzy soundtrack. That's my kind of celebration.

All my life I've lived near the main parade route of St. Charles Avenue. My mother always picked out a good spot where we kids could catch beads and trinkets near the corner of Third Street, and that's still where we view the floats and marching bands to this day. When my siblings and I were dating or getting married, the girlfriends and wives who weren't working at the restaurant would make costumes for everyone, from hats to shoe covers, with the newborns getting the most special treatment. Every year it was a different theme—Dalmatians, Eskimos, cowboys and cowgirls, you name it. And our friends did the same, so we'd be a crew of about forty people in crazy gear. (One year I invited the

National Restaurant Association board of directors to the city and everybody dressed as chefs.) It was great fun for all.

The parades were spread out over a week or so, so we'd meet at a house nearby that had a big yard and enjoy an all-day buffet. Our neighbors and family members took turns hosting, and when it was Adelaide's or Dick and Lynne's turn, we'd enjoy a post-parade spread of jambalaya topped with shrimp creole, along with a green salad, garlic bread and wine, with everybody sitting on the floor and the stairs or spilling out into the yard. Every night was a party.

When my kids were finishing grade school, the Royal Sonesta Hotel in the French Quarter had just opened, and we started renting a two-bedroom suite with a balcony so the kids could toss beads to the crowds on Bourbon Street. Back then there wasn't nearly as much of that gross "show us what you got" behavior as there is today, but it was still pretty crazy.

AN UNFORGETTABLE VIEW FROM ABOVE

The Bourbon Street club that entertainer Chris Owens still owns and performs in was sometimes on Ella's itinerary on Mardi Gras day in the 1960s and 1970s. Here, the famed dancer recalls those heady celebrations:

"I always invited Ella and her friends to come to my building because I have a balcony that overlooks Bourbon Street, and you could soak up all of the sights and the sounds from there. Our friend Pete Fountain, the jazz clarinetist, always had his parade and would stop in front of my balcony and we would toast. And when the jazz trumpeter Al Hirt closed his club and needed a spot to play, he came to my club for, I guess, four years before he passed away. But he would always go up on the balcony and they would have a duel. Pete would play his clarinet, I'd play my maracas, and Al would play his trumpet. Back and forth, back and forth, trading licks. Dueling horns on Mardi Gras day. Unforgettable.

During Chep Morrison's terms as mayor of New Orleans in the 1950s, the Cuban government was trying to drum up tourism, and we went many times. One year they asked Chep to "bring Mardi Gras to Cuba." So off we went. There were two planeloads of New Orleanians and Mardi Gras floats that our friend Glenn Douthit shipped down there. As it happened, the day after we got to Havana was May Day, a big holiday for them. When we woke up that day at the Hotel Nacional, there was literally no help in the hotel, so no food, no nothing. Well, we're restaurateurs, so we found our way to the kitchen and cooked up a good breakfast. Then next thing you know, some of the group were putting on a parade and my husband Paul was riding on a float. I wandered off with Bill Reed from WWL and Bill Monroe from WDSU (two of our local TV stations), exploring the streets of Havana and the nuances of a good daiquiri (invented on the island of course.) We thought Cuba was magical. It was so sad to watch it change not long after all the kicks we had there.

In 1968, my nephew Pip, brother Dick and some other businessmen got together and decided that the New Orleans Carnival season was losing its luster and needed to be shaken up. The traditions were growing tired and the whole thing wasn't attracting enough tourists or involving the entire city. The men decided that the vehicle for change would be the Krewe (a krewe is a Mardi Gras club that stages parades and balls) of Bacchus, an organization my brother Owen had founded in the late 1940s. Back then, the major Mardi Gras celebrations were mostly staged for New Orleans society, with their debutantes and royalty and so forth. Owen wanted to open things up for everyone, especially the tourists he was courting. The Bacchus Krewe staged a couple of balls for the general public before Owen's death, but they were discontinued.

So Pip and Dick and the others came up with the idea of staging a super-sized parade and ball on the Sunday night before Mardi Gras—a real break with tradition—and to have the entire thing led by a celebrity king. And that's how, in February 1969, Danny Kaye found himself presiding over the inaugural version of what would soon become the season's biggest and gaudiest celebration. In later years, Raymond Burr, Bob Hope, Phil Harris and Jim Nabors, among others, would follow suit. The Bacchus members claim they toss more than a million bead necklaces and hundreds of thousands of doubloons from their satirical-themed floats each year. The crowds they draw are enormous—and their bawdy exploits are legendary.

In the years since, other krewes have come along and added more parades and public events to the mix, bringing Carnival closer to the vision that Owen and his masked Bacchus mates had in mind.

I didn't belong to a krewe, but I'd often get asked to ride on a float. One day a woman who was in one of the krewes came to Commander's and told Ti that we had to make sure to come to the parade the next day. "We're doing the 'Great Women of New Orleans in History' as the theme, and your mother is a float!" We were watching the next day and Ti asked me what I thought. "I don't know if I want to be a float," I said. "Other than me and Lindy Boggs and Chris Owens, THEY'RE ALL DEAD!"

In 1979, there was a police strike that forced the mayor, very reluctantly, to cancel the Mardi Gras parades at the last minute. This was not well received by New Orleanians, so some of us improvised. We had our usual Mardi Gras–day party at Dick and Lynne's house. She threw a great bash and always had us organized in theme costumes. (Her daughter Lauren, who loves a parade more than anyone I know, keeps up the tradition now.) Talk about all dressed up and nowhere to go. There we were, all in costumes and eating and drinking but no parades, no nothing. Just a city basically closed down.

Somehow, we got the idea to have our own parade. Our friend Alvin Alcorn was playing with his jazz band at one of the downtown men's Mardi Gras clubs, so he agreed to bring everybody up to Dick and Lynne's as soon as their gig was finished. Now we needed a king float. We were in luck: there was the ski boat in Dick's yard that the kids used in Mississippi to water ski and go fishing and crabbing. Lynne and Lauren had it decorated within an hour.

The next missing element was a high-struttin' drum major. No problem. Our dear friend Carol Dienes was at the party. She had been a dancer in her younger years and still had loads of enthusiasm, style and high kicks. Best of all, in the trunk of her car she had a supply of umbrellas and parasols that could be wielded by the parade marchers.

We still lacked a proper king, but our luck continued. As we headed out, there was a man walking down the street dressed as a king. We asked to borrow his

WHERE ARE MY SUBJECTS?

Ella's longtime friend and neighbor Hal Williamson shares one of his favorite Mardi Gras moments, when a Commander's Palace bash upstaged his big night:

"During Mardi Gras season a number of years ago, I had been named King of Saturn, my Carnival organization, and I was looking forward to riding down St. Charles Avenue on my float. My partner, Dale, was giving a huge dinner party inside Commander's for about forty friends and family, and I was expecting them to come out and greet me as my float passed the intersection at Washington Avenue near the restaurant. But when I arrived, none of my friends were there! A waiter came running down the street from Commander's with a bottle of champagne from Miss Ella, and he said, 'Miss Ella says to have a toast and enjoy your night, but they're all staying inside. They're having too great a time!'

"That memory always makes me laugh."

services and he agreed! Turns out he was one of the brothers who taught at the Catholic high schools.

Off we went down St. Charles Avenue with no police to stop us. We were the most ragtag parade there ever was, and that is saying something in New Orleans. There had long been a tradition of the king floats of certain krewes stopping the parade in front of the houses of past kings and queens to toast them. We discovered that all of New Orleans was doing the same thing we were. Still having their parties, just kind of down about the lack of parades.

When we hit the street with our irreverent mock parade and our neighbors heard our jazz band, everyone ran out to see the only parade they were going to see that day. And in grand New Orleans style, many of them fell into what's known in New Orleans as a "second line." (A second line is a jazz funeral tradition of following second in line behind the band after the funeral and doing a little strut. Today, they occur on many occasions, especially during Mardi Gras, and you'll even find them springing up spontaneously at weekend jazz brunches at Commander's Palace.)

People toasted us all along the route, and of course, we had beads to throw from the "float." (Some people say the reason why parts of the city are below sea level is because of the weight of all those Mardi Gras beads that we store in our attics.)

Oh my God, it was fun. You can cancel the Mardi Gras parades, but for New Orleanians Mardi Gras is a feeling. And you can't cancel that.

ABOVE: *Ella talking to guests at Vieux Carré, Owen standing at the far right (photograph by Jack Robinson, The Jack Robinson Archive, LLC; www.robinsonarchive.com).* BELOW, LEFT: *Ella in her yard in the Irish Channel.* BELOW, CENTER: *Ella and her friend Pat Fitzgerald.* BELOW, RIGHT: *Leona and Pip Brennan.*

ABOVE, LEFT: *Ned Reed, Ella Brennan, Al Hirt (standing), and Paul Martin.*
ABOVE, RIGHT: *Ella and Paul Martin.* BELOW: *Ralph Alexis and Ella standing in the door of Vieux Carré Restaurant (photograph by Jack Robinson, The Jack Robinson Archive, LLC; www.robinsonarchive.com).*

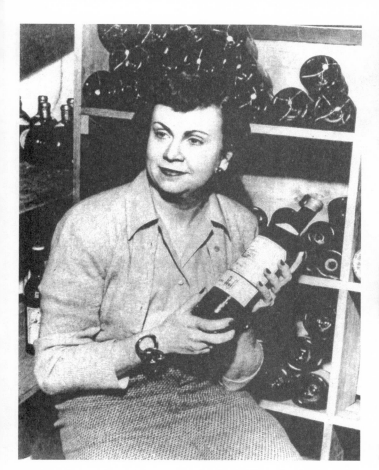

ABOVE, LEFT: *Ella in the wine cellar of Vieux Carré.* ABOVE, UPPER RIGHT: *Ella.*
ABOVE, LOWER RIGHT: *Ella.* BELOW, LEFT: *Ralph Alexis, Paul Martin, Ella Brennan,
and Adelaide Brennan at Paul and Ella's wedding.* BELOW, RIGHT: *Ella and Paul in Paris.*

ABOVE: *Ella and Paul Blangé (right of Ella) in the kitchen of Vieux Carré (photograph by Jack Robinson, The Jack Robinson Archive, LLC; www.robinsonarchive.com).* BELOW, LEFT: *Ella and Paul Blangé in kitchen of Vieux Carré.* BELOW, RIGHT: *Ella and Paul Martin with Alex Brennan-Martin.*

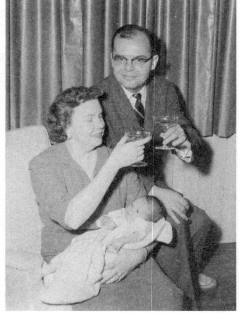

ABOVE: *Ella Brennan float during Mardi Gras parade.* BELOW: *Brennan family in costume for Mardi Gras.*

6

Divisions (1970–1973)

"STOP CRYING! GET UP! GET DRESSED! GO TO WORK!"

—DOTTIE BRENNAN

Accomplished restaurateurs will tell you that creating a successful and respected establishment is incredibly daunting, and yet it's only half the battle. The greater challenge is sustaining and managing that success over time. And when family is involved, the pathway is even trickier but can lead to incomparable rewards—or excruciating heartbreak. I experienced both during my time at Brennan's.

By the late 1960s and early 1970s, Brennan's was still a roaring success night after night, and its national reputation was well established. So my siblings and I began looking at how to grow the business to accommodate the ambitions of the next generation.

Owen and Maudie's son Pip was already working at Brennan's, and his brothers, Jimmy and Ted, would follow. My son, Alex, began learning the ropes there during the summer as a teen, and we would soon send him to Europe and New York for further training. Dick's son, Dickie, was finishing up college and would be looking to join the business, and John's son Ralph, who first worked as a

CPA, would join us in the decade ahead. (Ti, and John's daughter Lally, were very young then, and we had no inkling that they would become restaurateurs.) Even though everyone was doing quite well with the income from Brennan's, the next generation would eventually need work to support their own families.

My siblings and I came up with a plan to open branches of Brennan's in Houston, Dallas and Atlanta, three cities where our name was pretty well known and that were somewhat connected to New Orleans. Potential backers were literally offering to pay the bills to get us to come. If a family member were to run the restaurant in each of those places, it would be good for everybody and be a key to each new restaurant's success. That was the plan, anyway.

We took the plunge in all three cities in the early 1970s and did quite well, particularly in Houston. But there was a flaw in our thinking: none of the family members wanted to move from New Orleans to run these outposts. They wouldn't go. Absolutely would not go. They would open the restaurant but refused to move there full time. In a way, it was hard to blame them, given the allure of New Orleans. In 1964, we had acquired a casual seafood restaurant called The Friendship House, located an hour away on the Mississippi Gulf Coast. Right behind it was a small hotel made up of cabins with a large picnic area in between, and the place next door had a pool that they let the kids use. It was a Gulf Coast paradise. Each family took a cabin and we spent holidays and any summer weeks we could fishing, crabbing, sailing, water skiing, playing softball and volleyball, and telling ghost stories at night. Dick and his brother-in-law Nick Trist loved to tease and scare the kids to death. The family bonds that formed there are still strong and were a big factor in everyone's reluctance to leave the region for another city. (Alas, the restaurant was severely damaged in hurricane Betsy, and we eventually sold it. I think there's an Olive Garden on the site now.)

Back then—and I'm certain it's still true today—it was very hard to find management for a family-held business such as a restaurant. We had to rely on outsiders to run things, which meant that Dick, Adelaide and I were constantly on airplanes to oversee the various branches. Adelaide did move to Houston for several years and spent lots of time in Dallas and Atlanta as well. The money was coming in, but the operations were wearing us out, as were some of the circumstances.

One day soon after we had opened Brennan's of Dallas, we were all putting our feet up for a few minutes and talking through the usual nightmares of opening a restaurant. We were at the lovely Adolphus Hotel in the two-bedroom suite that Adelaide had managed to have beautifully redecorated.

Suddenly, two men appeared at the door. I was catching a catnap in the bedroom when John came in and said these two rough-looking men had come in and told us they wanted to buy our restaurant. John and Dick told them that it was just two days old and not for sale. But these men—I won't say gentlemen—were insistent and bullying. John excused himself and came into the bedroom and told me what was going on. He decided to call some of our guest acquaintances back in New Orleans. Well, he got "Joe," a bigwig in the New Orleans mob family, on the phone and explained the situation. Our New Orleans "friend" asked John to put one of the Dallas men on the phone. John did. Words were said. The men left. We never heard from any of them again. Yep, that's all I know.

Meanwhile, other painful problems were coming to a head. My husband Paul continued to struggle with alcoholism, and the situation at home was becoming intolerable. At one point he and I considered moving our family to Atlanta, where we were getting ready to open a Brennan's. If he and I were to run it, it would give that restaurant its best chance to succeed, and it could be a fresh start for us. But neither that plan, nor our marriage, worked out in the end. Our early years together had been fulfilling in so many ways—the births of our children and some memorable trips to France and New York, in particular—but after thirteen years of marriage, we divorced in 1970.

I would never again engage in a serious romance, and instead became fond of saying, "I'm married to the hospitality industry." I often joked that I gave up men for Lent one year and never took them up again. The truth is, I really loved Paul. I was so attracted to his mind. He was a wonderful conversationalist, and we were both so endlessly interested in the world. He taught me so much. When we wed, I knew he might have a drinking problem, but I naively thought I could change him. Oh, how I tried, but it only got worse. Dear friends like Bryan Bell, Clay Shaw, and Bill Monroe and, of course, my sisters tried to help. I knew I had to protect the children and my sanity. The night I finally asked him to leave, he had fallen all the way down the stairs in front of Ti and Alex as they clung to me. There were many, many incidents like that. It was very hard for this little Catholic girl who believes so strongly in family. After all that, I never wanted to be responsible for another adult's behavior again.

At the same time, tensions were building behind the scenes at the restaurant in New Orleans; my siblings and I frequently butted heads with Maudie, Owen's widow, who had raised her sons to believe that they should be in control of Brennan's. With my father's death and the distribution of his shares in the business among the family members, Maudie and her sons controlled 52 percent of the business, while the rest of us combined controlled 48 percent. Everything that we wanted to do, including the expansions, had to be negotiated with Maudie and her children.

The family had taken care of them after Owen's death, but the sons were only twenty-one, fourteen and seven when he passed, and Maudie had never worked. Even though the business was successful beyond all expectations and being run by a dedicated and experienced management team, Maudie wanted to be the boss. She wanted her kids to own the restaurants. We had created Brennan's on Royal Street, as Owen sadly had died before the restaurant even opened, and we knew we couldn't run a business under those conditions.

Clearly, something was going to give at some point. As a precautionary measure in 1969, Adelaide and I worked out a deal to buy the venerable Commander's Palace restaurant, which had been a fixture in the Garden District since the late 1800s. Adelaide had always had her eye on that place. She lived nearby and loved going there, loved the architecture, the restaurant's storied past, and its romantic location at Washington Street and Coliseum, across from the crumbling glory of Lafayette Cemetery No. 1, a walled necropolis of above-ground crypts and tombs.

Adelaide had let Elinor Moran, the owner with her husband Frank since the mid-1940s, know that if she ever decided to sell, she wanted to be the first to hear about it. Meanwhile, I had made a separate overture to her, saying, "There are a lot of Brennans, Elinor, and we're going to need another restaurant."

So one day she came into Brennan's for lunch and asked to speak to me after the meal. She got right to the point: "I've decided to retire, Ella. I'm ready to sell."

I quickly said, "Well, we'd love to buy. My attorney knows your attorney. Let's have them get together."

The deal was done in a matter of weeks, with us using the sale of several parcels of real estate that came with the business to fund the purchase. (I guess you could say that it was a form of leveraged buyout.) We sent longtime purchasers/managers Jill Rouse and Aymor Dore to run things until we got our feet on the ground.

(Ti loves to tell the story about how I took her to Commander's as a special treat for her ninth birthday on August 29, 1969. We were sitting there enjoying ourselves when I leaned over to her and said, "Guess what? We have quite a birthday present for you. We bought this restaurant today!" By coincidence, the deal had closed on her birthday, but ever since then, she has said the restaurant "is on my list of Top Ten presents.")

That transaction proved to be fortuitous, because our relationship with Maudie and her sons continued to deteriorate. Finally, one day in late 1973 after yet another contentious family meeting, I was relieved of my management duties at Brennan's by Maudie's family. Fired and shown the door. I couldn't believe it. My siblings joined me in walking out, and I didn't set foot in our beautiful creation for another forty years.

I don't like to use the word "split." I like to say that we got together and decided that the family had gotten too big and that we needed to get these young people into restaurants so they could do their own thing, which was true. But it was definitely a split. It was terrible. There were some bitter, bitter people involved. But we never said anything about it to anybody outside the family. There continue to be millions of stories going around, but we have never addressed them.

Both sides met with an attorney to divide the assets. Maudie and her sons wanted Brennan's, and the rest of us were given control of the three out-of-town branches, the Friendship House near Biloxi, and Commander's Palace. That shows you how phenomenally successful Brennan's was at the time: its value approximately equaled the value of our five other restaurants.

The personal fallout for me was devastating. I cried, I cried, I cried—and cried some more. Nearly twenty years' worth of hard work, creativity and financial success were ripped away from us. I'd spent the best years of my life there building a successful brand, and all of a sudden it was gone. Maudie's family continued to run Brennan's for nearly forty years until it collapsed into bankruptcy in 2013. (Happily, in 2014, my nephew Ralph and a partner gloriously re-opened it).

The kids and I had moved into Adelaide's lovely home on Prytania Street following the divorce a few years earlier, and that's where I holed up to lick my wounds and reassess my life. I was forty-nine years old and had reached what I thought was the peak of my career—and now I would be starting over again. And, as always, there was a large family to support.

My siblings, bless them, left me alone for a while, but finally Dottie strode into my room late one morning and said: "What you're doing to yourself is unacceptable. Shape up! Stop crying! Get up! Get dressed! Go to work!"

So I did.

MAKING A GO OF IT ELSEWHERE

Alex Brennan was in his mid-teens and already learning the ropes at Brennan's when the family's business interests were divided.

"Leaving Brennan's was a real life-changing time for Mom. She sat Ti and me down and said, 'Look, we are not going to be down at Brennan's anymore. We are going to have to make a go of it up here at Commander's.' That was really an amazing time. Mom, I am sure, was scared to death, and she let us know that it was going to be a scary time, but she took it on as a challenge and never, ever looked back. And I have always admired that about her, how she handled that life-altering setback. To be fired from a project you have worked on for half your life—by family members, no less. And the way she handled that has given me inspiration throughout my life. There is no such thing as, 'you can't do it.' It's just, 'this is something we have got to do.'"

7

Big Sister, Larger than Life

"ADELAIDE WAS LIKE OUR LOCAL MOVIE STAR."
—ADVERTISING EXECUTIVE AND
FAMILY FRIEND RON THOMPSON

She was one of New Orleans' original beauties—accent on "original." A red-headed, green-eyed, pale-skinned fount of elegance, style, wit—and outrageous fun. The most independent soul on God's green earth—and the glue that bound a family during troubling times.

She was my big sister, Adelaide. The No. 1 person in my life.

If a person is fortunate enough to have an older sibling who develops into a mentor, protector, confidant and friend, well, that's a blessing beyond all words. In my case, I was doubly blessed.

I've tried to convey the tremendous influence that my brother Owen had on my career, as he used his entrepreneurial skills and outgoing personality to make a better life for our family and for New Orleans. He sensed something inside of me, coaxed me into the business and taught me so much about hospitality, promotion, work ethic, forging relationships and running a business.

There were many other aspects of me, however, that were just as raw and in need of shaping and sharpening as my business acumen: my creativity, femininity, intellectual curiosity and unquenchable desire to show others a good time. That is where Adelaide came in. Nellie and Daddy gave me a moral compass and a sturdy, commonsense foundation, and my older siblings took it from there.

Adelaide was, and remains, the stuff of legend (even her exact age is something of a family secret; let's just say that she was born between Owen and me), and people invariably portray her as being charming and giving and reading *Vogue* magazine at age fifteen and never rising before noon. All true. But beyond that, she was the smartest person in our family and the mentor of all five of her siblings in many areas. Adelaide gave a tremendous amount of time to our well-being and was full of practical knowledge. She knew, even from a young age, that there was a better life beyond the Irish Channel and that it was something to which we could aspire.

Adelaide was good at math and finance. She didn't have a degree in those subjects—much of her learning was drilled into her by the German nuns at Redemptorist High School—but she understood the way the world worked. A lover of language, she knew how to express herself clearly and deftly. Adelaide insisted that we use proper grammar, and she would often pause in a conversation to say, "There has to be a better word for that . . . " When one of us needed to write a letter, we'd bring it to her. She might say she was busy at the moment but invariably added, "Tell me what you need." Later that day she'd hand you your letter and it would be perfect, fashioned with exquisite penmanship.

Her obvious beauty and the manner in which she carried herself notwithstanding, Adelaide was so much more than a feminine lady. In fact, she always said, "I want to be a man! I want to be a man!" because men in those days had so many more advantages. (Some people have said that the Stella character in Tennessee Williams's *A Streetcar Named Desire* was partially based on Adelaide, who knew the writer casually; I can tell you she would *not* have liked that.)

She was just a fabulous human being, and very, very generous, someone who did very well with a dollar and saved up for nice things—a beautiful home, stunning wardrobe and trips abroad—but shared everything.

When I entered my awkward teen years, I remember Owen telling me, "Take off the saddle Oxfords and the bobby socks and put on some high heels." That's when Adelaide took over and launched a makeover. I wasn't very cooperative, but she steered me along. I had long hair in plaits, and she finally got me to the hairdresser and got my hair cut. That kind of stuff. Adelaide would play a similar role in her littlest sister's life as well. Dottie says that, because of the age differences, she felt as though she had three mothers: Nellie, Adelaide and me.

Later, when Adelaide, Dottie and I worked at the French Quarter restaurants, we'd join Maudie and Claire, John's wife, to go shopping nearly every Thursday at the Gus Mayer department store on Canal Street, and they'd help me pick out my wardrobe as we sipped cocktails during the fittings. When Lally was old enough, she'd tag along and sit observing us in the corner. I didn't care much about fashion, but they did and always gave me impeccable advice (and I steered them to the right beverages). Afterwards, we'd walk over and have dinner at Brennan's, where John was working.

Being in the restaurant business wasn't Adelaide's preference—very few women sought professions back then—but she did it for the family. She really did. Beginning with the Vieux Carré Restaurant and continuing through her time at Commander's, she saw what was needed and pitched in—overseeing the books, making decisions on design and décor, and promoting our restaurants to the public. She was a natural. During our time at Brennan's, we would visit New York, San Francisco, Paris and other places in France once or twice a year. I couldn't have asked for a better traveling buddy.

One of our jaunts took us to New York, where we dined at Sirio Maccioni's flagship restaurant Le Cirque. Seated next to us was a party of six, including actor Ben Gazzara and director John Cassavetes with his wife, Gena Rowlands. John came over to our table and politely inquired of Adelaide if he could ask her something. She said, "Of course." So he knelt down and explained that he was making a movie in the city and that he would love for her to be in it. She smiled and thanked him but said, "No, no, no." He kept asking her and finally she said, "I just couldn't do that. Y'all get up so early in the morning. I just couldn't do that." He couldn't believe it, but we all knew Adelaide, and we believed it.

Adelaide was her normal glamorous self that night, wearing one of her elegant beaded tops. After a little while, the director came back over and told her, "I hope you'll pardon me again but we are making a bet at our table on how much your top cost." Adelaide laughed and winked, and of course, being a Southern lady, refused to tell.

In keeping with her persona, Adelaide's romantic life was somewhat unconventional and mysterious. Her true love was our family friend Ralph Alexis, who had helped us open Brennan's in the wake of Owen's death. He was eighteen years older than she, and he was in her life from the day she was born until the day he died. A wonderful man, but he was married and he was Catholic. Coming out of the Great Depression, he had made some money, but he wasn't in a position to get a divorce and marry Adelaide. In addition, my family couldn't handle it—all were against it. So Adelaide and Ralph had a sweet, quiet affair for the rest of his life. And when he was dying, Daddy invited him to live with us—a big step for him (and for mankind, for that matter).

Later, there were plenty of suitors, and she married a guy named Jack, whom she had met on a cruise. She called Dottie and me one day and said she was getting married the following Thursday. We asked, "To who?" He was a complete stranger to us. Alas, the union was brief, and after the divorce, she never married again.

When my marriage to Paul was crumbling, Adelaide counseled and consoled the kids and me. And there wasn't even a question when she invited us to live with her after my divorce. It's the way we were. And it was good for both of us.

At the time, my children (Alex was eleven and Ti was nine) and I were living in the Garden District, several blocks from Adelaide's home, and it made sense to jettison one of the properties and move in together. Adelaide wasn't joking when she said, "I think you'd better come here because your house is directly across from McGehee School and they ring that bell every morning at eight o'clock and that would wake me up and I couldn't live there."

(Adelaide had no children of her own, yet she was eminently capable of motherhood. One of our favorite family tales involves the time when Alex was sick as an infant and refused to take his baby aspirin. Adelaide was in charge that day, and she noticed that when Alex crawled around on the floor, he would pick up whatever he encountered and stick it in his mouth. So she simply placed the aspirin on the floor and waited for Alex to do his thing. Problem solved! On another occasion, I had been invited on a trip to Bordeaux when Ti was just four months old. I didn't really want to leave her, but Adelaide said, "Go! Go! Go! I'll take care of your baby!" So I did, and she did—and Ti was just fine.)

Once my divorce was finalized, we packed up and moved into her house on Prytania Street near Second Street, a magnificent late-1800s Greek Revival mansion. Adelaide had always been fascinated by that property. As a little girl, she went to school next door at the chapel and vowed that, one day, she would live there in that nice neighborhood. It was during the Great Depression, when no one had any money, but somehow that little girl formed that idea. As an adult she saved and saved, and in the early 1960s she made her dream come true. She couldn't afford many furnishings initially, but that was OK because she believed it was more important that the bones of the structure should show through. She adored every inch of it.

It truly was a dream house—8,000 square feet and three stories tall, with imposing columns framing the entrance and floor-to-ceiling windows on the upper floors. (Lally says that when she learned her cousins Alex and Ti were going to live there, her semi-joking first reaction was, "Well, that's not fair!") You'd open the front door and right there was a gorgeous circular staircase that didn't seem to have any visible means of support—just beautiful. The place was considered an architectural gem because it was built in squares—the living room and dining room were completely square, twenty-two by twenty-two feet, and the ballroom on the side was like two joined squares, topped with sixteen-foot ceilings. All the windows were floor to ceiling. The kitchen was all copper-topped counters and came equipped with two refrigerators, two stoves, two ovens and cabinets galore that held enough silverware, china and cocktail accouterments to serve upwards of 200 guests. No kitchen table, though—this place was built strictly for entertaining. It was enough to make a (Mardi Gras) queen envious.

In the foyer was a beautiful mural painted by Vera Reinike that depicted Louisiana bayou scenes, and it was illuminated by a giant chandelier. I'll never forget that mass of ornate crystal and tapered light bulbs. Once, when the kids were little, we'd sought safe haven at Adelaide's during hurricane Camille. We put mattresses down in the foyer for everyone to sleep on, but when we looked up, we saw that mighty chandelier slightly swaying above us and abandoned that idea.

By far the most interesting feature was that ballroom, twenty-two by forty-four feet, ringed by petite chairs, with an ornate ceiling inlaid with gold leaf. We'd always have to remind my kids and their cousins that the chairs were for decoration, not sitting, a concept that puzzled them. Yet it didn't stop them from kicking off their shoes and skidding from one end of the room to the other on the highly polished floors. Ti tells the story of showing the room to one of her schoolteachers, who asked whether the furniture had been sent out to be cleaned. "No, ma'am," she said apologetically. "This room is just for dancing."

And dance we did! To live music! Thank you, piano wiz Freddie Palmisano and all the other local musicians who entertained us. People still talk about the soirées that Adelaide hosted there: spontaneous parties with people we'd just met at Commander's; Lally's fabulous wedding and the cousins' birthdays; costumed slumber parties for the girls during Mardi Gras; sumptuous Christmas dinners; and formal events for 200. It was non-stop fun. One of my fondest memories is that whenever we'd have a party and "Mack the Knife" came on the stereo, wherever my brother John was and wherever Adelaide was, they'd just stop talking and find each other and dance.

Reporters from the society page followed us because our guests often included a cavalcade of entertainers, writers and film folks who came through town to promote their projects, as well as friends from all walks of life and from all over the city. At any given event, you might rub shoulders with the mayor, Rock Hudson, Joan Fontaine or an artist from the French Quarter—or all four. So many wonderful people cut a rug in that house—Jane Powell, Bob Hope, Phil Harris and Kaye Ballard, among them—and a few really stand out.

There was pioneering comedienne Phyllis Diller, an absolute love and a barrel of laughs, who once tried to teach Adelaide to sing. Those two were good about sending each other funny postcards from wherever they were. Adelaide would come into the house and find me in tears of laughter over something Phyllis had written. But my favorite memory of Phyllis is more poignant than funny. Phyllis came over to the house one night and I said, "Phyllis—my goodness you look fantastic. You look so healthy and beautiful. What have you gone and done? And please, no face lift jokes."

"Do you really want me to tell you?"

"Yes, yes, yes."

"Well, I got rid of all the negative people in my life. I still send some of them checks, but they are not in my life."

How about that? Pretty good advice, I'd say.

Truman Capote once came gift wrapped. The writer was staying at the Royal Orleans Hotel, and he'd come over every day for lunch at Brennan's. I didn't know him all that well, but I'd see him regularly. It was Adelaide's birthday and I hadn't had time to get her anything, and even if I had, what do you get someone who had the most fabulous taste in the world? So that day he came in for lunch, and in a sudden fit of inspiration I said, "Would you mind if I gave you to my sister for her birthday? We're having a dinner tonight, and I'd like you to come and surprise her." He said, "Sure!" He arrived just as she was having cocktails with friends. Ti answered the door and there he stood, wearing a blue velvet suit with jodhpurs and a red bow tied to his head. I said, "Adelaide, this is your present: Truman Capote is here to dine with you." She was absolutely stunned, and Truman couldn't have been more of a delight. Just a delight.

Tough-guy actor James Coburn was another delightful guest whom we got to know very well when he was in town doing publicity for a movie. We had him over to the house a couple of times. One night, Adelaide and I thought he must have been tired of traveling and eating in restaurants, so we served him a meal of red beans and rice and gumbo at home. I guess he really enjoyed it, because the day he left, he had six dozen roses sent to the house.

And then there was Carol Burnett, whose comedy variety show I adored. She dined at Commander's with our friend, the writer Peter Feibleman, and we asked them to come back to the house for a spontaneous get-together. (This was one of those nights where we "stole" the pianist Freddie Palmisano away from his regular gig at Mr. B's Bistro; one of the greatest joys in my life was hearing him play.) Carol was feeling pretty good as Freddie entertained us, and she insisted that we all line up in the ballroom and do a chorus line. With our arms around

A STYLISH MENTOR

Lally Brennan says that her Aunt Adelaide inspired her to play a similar role in the family today: keeping the younger generation of Brennans close, being a role model at work, throwing parties and counseling them on life's ups and downs. Here are a few of her memories of her beloved aunt:

"One of my first and best memories of Adelaide, from when I was about age four, was when Brennan's was being featured in a big photo shoot in one of the national magazines and they needed children in the picture, so my brother Ralph and myself were enlisted. Adelaide took me to Gus Mayer's department store to buy me a green velvet dress, with a little white collar, embroidered with flowers that looked as though they were coming up out of the garden. Ralph and I had to sit on the patio at Brennan's, and Adelaide gave me a flower and said I had to look at it when they took the picture.

"Then I remember going to her house on Eleonore Street and playing in her shoes. She had these blue ottomans that opened, and that's were the shoes were stored. She had tiny feet, so her shoes were the closest fit for me as a child, and flopping around in Aunt Adelaide's shoes, I felt all grown up.

"She would always have bowls of macadamia nuts around the house. They usually came from Jim Nabors, who had a macadamia farm in Hawaii. She probably captured his heart, and he'd just send cases of nuts to her house.

"After she moved to Prytania Street, Adelaide would stage black-tie Christmas night parties in the ballroom. I think you could start attending when you reached sixteen, so Ralph and I were the first ones eligible. On Christmas night, after everyone had already done all the traditional things with their little kids, we'd put on formal attire and go to another party. It was just magical. The ballroom, the lights, the music, the food, the gorgeous people—all just the way my Aunt Adelaide wanted it to be.

"After many of her other parties, everybody would leave and I would just kind of follow her around as she straightened up. That's the way I am too. I want to have everything straight before I go to bed. I'd tag along behind and help her clean up and ask her questions, and she'd just have these wonderful answers."

each other's backs and kicking our legs as high as they would go (not very far in my case), we reveled in the silliness and pure joy of the night.

It was truly a fairytale kind of life. We worked hard and liked to play hard, and we shared that with the most interesting people we could find.

All these people undoubtedly were attracted to Adelaide's personal style, which today would remind people of Cher and Madonna—just as original but more elegant, complete with a long cigarette holder. When someone would ask her, "What are we wearing tonight?" she'd reply, "Nothing fancy—just basic sequins."

She loved to make an entrance by descending that winding staircase in gowns accented with furs or feathers and exquisite but tasteful jewelry. One slight exception was a necklace that connected to what looked like a gold bar. At just the right moment in a party, Adelaide would lean forward in her slightly décolleté top and push a little latch, releasing three prongs that would serve as a swizzle stick. She'd then dip them into a flute of champagne to re-energize the bubbles—while flashing the naughtiest smirk you've ever seen.

Adelaide didn't drive, but she traveled in a Rolls-Royce Silver Cloud that once was part of the Queen of England's fleet. She and Dick schemed together to get that Rolls. It was gorgeous—with a teak wood interior, a bar equipped with a few "Sazeracs in waiting," and a TV—and it was prone to frequent breakdowns. For important occasions, Adelaide would hire a limousine to follow her and her driver in the Rolls in case of an emergency.

Her "aura" followed her into the business world as well. When we were opening Brennan's in Dallas, she moved into a hotel suite there for a few months—and persuaded the manager to decorate the rooms entirely in Fortuny fabrics. I'm sure they had no clue what they were getting into (until the bill came), but it was hard to say no to the lady.

Paul Prudhomme used to tell this wonderful story—oh, how I wish he were still here to tell it himself—that sort of sums up Adelaide's unique style sensibility. The way he told it, we were doing some improvements to the landscaping around the patio in back of Commander's—replanting and so forth. The woman in charge of the project had cordoned off the perimeter with white stakes and string. Well, one day, Paul sees Adelaide going in and out of the restaurant through the back entrance off the kitchen, and she's carrying a bucket of paint and a brush. Very, very odd, especially for her. So he wanders outside and there's Adelaide painting the string green! Even though nobody in a million years would have noticed, it bothered her. She knew that white string didn't fit in the garden. And she knew that she was the only one who could paint it correctly! No one else. So Paul gathered the kitchen staff to "watch Ms. Adelaide paint string," and they brought her a chair to make it easier! Paul always said that Ms. Adelaide was "probably the best character I've ever seen in any kind of a play or any kind of human situation."

What an environment in which to raise my children! But I wouldn't trade it for anything, and I know they wouldn't either. Even though I was working long hours and had a lot of child-rearing help from those around me, I was determined that motherhood would always come first in my life. I always told my kids that if they ever wanted me home or really needed me for some occasion, I would be there. They took me up on it a few times, just to see if I meant it, and I did. I didn't always make it to their sporting events, but they understood and it never became an issue.

We had an arrangement where the women in our family, including our British nanny, Grace, sisters-in-law Lynne and Claire Brennan and Lynne's sister-in-law Georgia Trist, would take turns looking after all of the kids—all told, there were eighteen cousins, with six of them being just a year or two apart in age. (To this day, they remain close and throw an annual "cousins party" just for themselves.) During any given outing, there always seemed to be just enough children around to fill a station wagon to capacity.

I was extraordinarily lucky with this help. I can see Ti now as a two-year-old, refusing to take off that crazy cowgirl outfit that her Auntie Adelaide had given her. I can see her walking out the door with Alex, and Alex running ahead of her and getting into Lynne Brennan's car. Lynne was Dottie's best friend all through high school and had married Dick. Her father was a doctor and the sheriff of St. Bernard's Parish, and the family owned a drug store and a bank. Well, because Dick and I worked at night and on weekends, Lynne became the chief organizer of the children, the camp counselor. Oh, they adored their Aunt Lynne. She would take those kids everywhere—swimming, up to the park to climb the hill, on bike hikes to the river, horseback riding, or on an outing across Lake Pontchartrain. It was just organized play, and my children and their cousins had a fabulous young life while I was at work. When I got to Commander's, I would frequently walk over to the playground and sit on the bench to watch the kids, and then I might take them back to my house and we'd have great meals together. But Lynne had properly detailed activities that involved a schedule and a car that held maybe eight kids. I can just see them all coming in. Alex had been rolling in the mud playing football and I would say, "OK, stand here in the yard, and I'm going to hose you off before you come in."

I'll never forget one day when I was able to play chauffeur. I was returning from the equestrian place with a carful of our hot, sweaty and smelly brood. I stopped to buy them their favorite snacks of Fritos and cherry-flavored slushes. As we headed home, the car in front of me stopped suddenly and I ran into it. A second later the car behind us rammed our big old Cadillac. When I whipped around to check on the kids in the back, all I could see was this red stuff with yellow chunks streaking down the rear window. Blood and guts! I've killed my family! Once I calmed down, I realized that it was just slushes and corn chips. The car was demolished but no one was hurt—and my brood have never let me forget that day.

During my daily talks with my kids, we frequently make reference to their somewhat unorthodox upbringing and how it shaped them into the independent, creative, loving—and fun-loving—people they are today. Here are their takes on life with Adelaide and me:

ALEX

"I was the only male in the house—even the two dogs were female—so I remember there were a lot of things in which I was not included. Of course, I was always loved, but even my room was sort of not a part of the main house. I lived in the room over the kitchen. In the old days, the kitchens were often separated from houses because of the danger of fires. I'm not sure why they put me back there—anyway, it was an uproarious way to grow up, and totally different from what my friends were experiencing. Not only were Mom and Aunt Adelaide at work at the restaurants, but they would come home and entertain people, from movie and TV stars to sports figures. There was always this amazing cast of characters coming through the house at all hours.

"It was crazy fun times with all of the families mixed together all of the time. We were constantly doing things with cousins and aunts and uncles. The way business and the family were all mishmashed together could have been a recipe for disaster. But for us, it was just a magnificent way to grow up. We really lived for life. We got the most out of growing up in New Orleans."

TI

"I had no clue that we were living an extraordinary life with Aunt Adelaide. You don't think about it as a kid. Uncle Dick and Aunt Lynne lived nearby with my cousins Lauren and Dickie. We spent as much time with them as at home sometimes. Theirs was a fun household with a pool and always lots of kids visiting—much more "normal" than ours. But I didn't know until later how unusual it was for me to be upstairs in my room and yell downstairs, 'Mom! I've got a calculus test! You and Bob Hope (or whoever) keep it down so I can study!'

"Years later when I read *Midnight in the Garden of Good and Evil,* John Berendt's marvelous book about a murder case among Savannah's bohemian elite, I remember thinking that our household would have fit right in—sans murder, of course.

"I just remember that Mom and Adelaide were so very close—my full name is Ti Adelaide, after all—and yet so very different in terms of style. Mom was more straightforward and keen on discipline and achievement, whereas my aunt, while wildly intelligent, was full of quirks and merriment. To cite just a few examples:

When we went to New York, Adelaide would usually treat me to a Broadway play or musical, and invariably, the seats in front of us would be empty. When I inquired, she said, "Well, I don't know why I would go to the theater and not be able to see. I am not as tall as I would like, and there always seemed to be a tall man in front of me. So Johnny, my ticket broker, just started offering me the two seats in front of me."

She would dab perfume on her body just before she tucked in for the night. When I asked her why, given that she was sleeping alone, she replied, "Well, who *do* you wear it for?"

Adelaide didn't cook—that was left to helpers named Sadie and Ethel. But on their days off, she would sauté liver in butter for Pud, the world's most spoiled Yorkie that she had gradually "stolen" from me (without any protest from Pud). One day I asked her, "Why do you feed Pud way up on the copper kitchen counters?" Adelaide replied, "I think it's the only time she gets to look me straight in the face. I want her to know what I look like." Her other dog, a Labrador mutt named Elvis Mae, must have been jealous, especially when she saw Pud sleeping in Adelaide's off-white four-poster bed with silk sheets and gorgeous lace.

Her closet held at least a half-dozen furs and accessories: stoles of mink and sable, a weird monkey coat and hat, pink and light-blue mink wraps, and a fox piece complete with the head (which Pud, at some point, chewed off). I remember this collection well because it was my job to take it to storage every summer.

For much of my teen years, Adelaide employed two male domestics, George Tibbs and Bobby Thomas, whom I adored and who were quirky in their own right. Tibbs could throw together a dinner party for 200 without requiring Mom or Aunt Adelaide to lift a finger (of course, it helped that our restaurant kitchen was a few blocks away). During one soirée I saw him take a big swig straight from a bottle at the back of the bar. He saw me looking, and he looked back plaintively, as if to say, "Oh, please, kid—I am working so hard here, give me a break." I did. I loved him, and never told anyone—until now. (That moment did shed light on the three times he managed to drive Mom's station wagon into the Palmetto overpass canal, though.)

That brings us to Bobby, the man most likely to have answered the door at those parties. He stood about 6-foot-4, was built like a linebacker for the Saints and talked like Prissy in *Gone with the Wind*. Swishy? I think he invented swish. Bobby was always—*always*—cold, so Adelaide had him wear a white cook's jacket over his multiple sweaters—even if it was July in subtropical New Orleans. Bobby would also pull a wool hat snug over his Afro, the perfect complement to his tight black polyester pants and platform shoes. He was in charge of the dogs' afternoon walk, so he'd sashay behind them, mumbling to himself or singing like Prissy. Those not used to this triumvirate would either stare in amazement or hurry along in fear. Needless to say, I loved both men and the flavor they brought to our household.

"Amid the eccentricities and occasional madness and social swirl, there was one constant—Mom and Adelaide were always there to talk to about anything and help me navigate life's thickets. My cousin Lally says the same thing. When you brought a problem to either of them, you wouldn't get the quick, pat answer. You'd get a reasoned, thoughtful solution or a list of options to consider (and yes, the occasional stern 'suggestion,' if warranted). To have those resources to draw upon as a teen and still today with Mom, has been the greatest gift of my life."

• • •

The final years of my dear sister's life were dotted with episodes of tragicomedy, as, I suppose, befits a true New Orleans character. I was working on the *Commander's Palace New Orleans Cookbook* in 1982, a follow-up to the *Brennan's New Orleans Cookbook* that I helped write in 1961 (I hate putting together cookbooks—so much time, so many meetings—but people want recipes! No good cook cooks with recipes. I'd rather be running the restaurant than working with someone writing about it. I can't believe I let Ti talk me into *this* book. Talk about complete role reversal. She keeps telling me to quit rolling my eyes.), when Adelaide's doctor called me. She had failed to return for a doctor's appointment and she needed care.

What in the world was he talking about?

I badgered him into telling me. She had ovarian cancer. She hadn't told anybody. She was in complete denial.

The world stopped.

It was awful. So, we did what we do: we circled the wagons. Dottie, who was well versed in these things by now, having fought her own battle with breast cancer a few years earlier, essentially moved in to care for Adelaide. We convinced her to at least try treatment, and she had surgery. After that, she did OK for a while—she looked good and was able to attend a family party or two.

Then the cancer returned, and she refused any more treatment. We set up a hospital room at home and had nurses around the clock. There were some laughs along the way, however. One day Dottie had Adelaide all bundled up in her wheelchair to go out on the upstairs porch for some fresh air. She didn't want anyone to see her (this frustrated a few of her friends who wanted to say goodbye, but we honored her wishes), so the upstairs porch was perfect. As Dottie and Ti went to move a chair or something, they heard little yelps from Adelaide and turned back to find her wheelchair rolling towards the railing. The giggling went on and on.

The last day of Adelaide's life was horrible, chaotic, and even (later, anyway) funny. Our close friend and doctor had equipped us with morphine for when the pain became overwhelming. That day arrived, and when the nurse went to get the morphine, she discovered that it had been replaced with water. Clearly, one of the other nurses had a drug problem. Imagine, stealing from a dying person.

There was no time to investigate the situation, though. Adelaide was in mortal pain. We needed morphine *now*. I called the doctor, who said to meet her at the hospital where she could procure the drug for us immediately. I ran to get Ti to drive me so that I could run into the hospital pharmacy to meet the doctor as fast as possible. Ti happened to be in the shower. She jumped out and, with wet hair and (later she told me) not even wearing any underclothes, off we went. We were two blocks from the hospital when we heard a siren—a policewoman wanted to pull us over. Ti continued to drive the two blocks with the police behind us so I could run in to get the morphine. Surely the police would understand. I remembered the officer who stopped us the day Owen died and ended up escorting us and helping us all day.

That wasn't to be this day.

The policewoman explained that our license plate tag was expired and that she needed to see Ti's driver's license. In the rush to get to the hospital, Ti didn't have her license on her. We explained the situation to the officer, who didn't care and said she would have to arrest Ti for driving without a license. Unbelievable! I was not in good shape. The doctor actually came out to confirm the story to the cop, but she said she had to proceed with her arrest. Ti told me to go get the morphine and take the car home—FAST—and that she would be fine. So I did.

Now Adelaide's dying and Ti's in jail. Ti did reveal that after she tried everything to change the officer's mind, she eventually gave her a piece of *her* mind. God help both of them.

The entire family—I mean all of us—were at the house. We called a judge friend, who was horrified and intervened, and Lynne and I went to get Ti out of jail. She was white as a ghost. That's when she told us about her lack of undergarments. Good god, how the laughter sliced through the tears.

That night our dear friend Father Tommy Bouterie came to the house and said a mass with the entire family in Adelaide's bedroom. (It was a big bedroom.) It was surreal. She died at one a.m. and we buried her at ten a.m. that same day, August 4, 1983.

I did not go to the funeral. I haven't been to a funeral since Owen's. Can't do it. I am supposed to be so strong, but I am a blubbering idiot making a fool of myself when I get in those situations. The people who love me understand, and I know Adelaide would have approved of my absence and my choosing to grieve in my own way.

Remember that Gail Sheehy book *Passages*? This was a big passage. The house was so empty without Adelaide and the kids. Alex was in Houston running our restaurant there, and Ti left soon after finishing graduate school to work for a real estate firm in Houston. Plus, there were three full-time employees to keep that house running, so something had to give. I loved the house, but not the way Adelaide had. It had been a great passion of hers, but now it contained too many memories.

Dottie was getting divorced after some more turbulent times, during which her husband of thirty years was indicted for some financial misdeeds. She called one day and said, "Let's fix up the house next to Commander's and move in together." (The house on Coliseum Street had been part of the original deal when we bought the restaurant.) So, we did. It was the beginning of a new era—different, but just as wonderful in so many ways. And of course, Adelaide was still with us every moment.

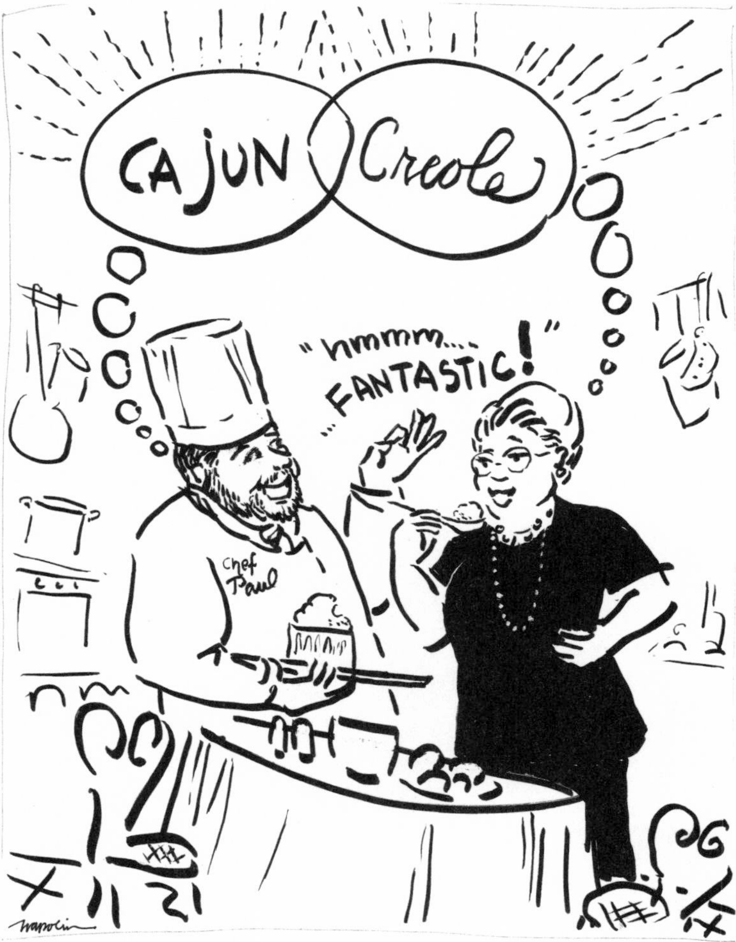
CAJUN
Creole
"hmmmm.... FANTASTIC!"
Chef Paul
napoli

8

Creole-ize It: Pioneering Modern American Cuisine (1974–1983)

"NO MATTER WHAT WAS ON THE MENU, WHETHER IT WAS A CREOLE INGREDIENT OR NOT, IT HAD TO TASTE LIKE SOMETHING THAT WAS COOKED IN NEW ORLEANS."
—GENE BOURG, FORMER *TIMES-PICAYUNE* RESTAURANT REVIEWER

Once we removed the roux from the gumbo and the venom from a food critic, I began to have the time of my life at our new home base in the Garden District. But getting to that point tested me as I've never been tested.

Sometimes I think people look back on the last forty years of Commander's Palace, with its joyous jazz brunches, string of awards and high-profile chefs creating now-iconic dishes, and assume that it was special from day one, the way that Brennan's had been an uninterrupted smash for my eighteen years there. But I promise you that was not the case. Not by a long shot.

Still smarting from our departure from Brennan's in November 1973, my siblings and I licked our wounds and tended to the five restaurants that we ended up with in the legal settlement. I was still confident that we had the ambition and know-how to create something that would surpass what had gone before, and I knew I had plenty of energy for the task. Invention—and reinvention—were now hallmarks of our heritage, so why not once more at

Commander's? For the short term, however, keeping everything afloat was our chief worry.

Now that Ti, Alex and I were living with Adelaide in her home a few blocks from Commander's, it was more convenient for me to juggle both business and family needs. Good thing, too, because Commander's was one needy project. (Raising my kids was a breeze by comparison . . . most of the time.)

Emile Commander had established a restaurant in the great, grand hulk of a mansion in 1893. (For years we thought the founding date was 1880, based on some internal documents we had, but recent research has proved the younger date to be correct.) Through the decades it enjoyed several reputations, including that of a luxurious private home. The second floor featured several small rooms where guests could dine discretely, and that gave rise to rumors among the tour guides that Commander's had been a brothel. That's just not true, but it was believable enough that my mom warned me as a child not to walk on the side of the street of "*that* Commander's." Most folks, however, knew it as a respectable dining destination for the neighborhood.

By the time we bought the place in 1969, Commander's was coasting with a boring, traditional Creole menu and had suffered under careless and some-times fuddy-duddy management. We had brought over a few people from Brennan's to oversee the staff that was already in place, but they couldn't seem to pull it together.

That was the situation we faced as we plotted how to turn the place into our family's new flagship. Shortly before we assumed day-to-day management on February 27, 1974 (I remember that well because it was the day after Mardi Gras), my siblings and I gathered in the garden and asked ourselves, "Well, what in the hell are we gonna do, gonna do, gonna do?" Eventually, we came to the conclusion that we'd dive in and run the restaurant the way we knew how, and our mantra became "Let's just go to work. Again." And that's what we did. It was an interesting experience that I don't wish to repeat.

Everybody did what they did well: Dottie grabbed the front-door duties at lunch (and stayed there for more than twenty years); Dick was in charge of get-ting the kitchen organized (it had a room with stoves but you couldn't really call it a restaurant kitchen); Adelaide represented us at public events and spent time in our restaurants in other cities; and Adelaide, Dottie and Charlie Gresham figured out how to give the décor a champagne makeover on a beer budget. Even John started coming in in the evenings after tending to his food brokerage business. My role was to figure out the menu, decide who was going to prepare it and keep us afloat financially.

We agreed to have one of us there every shift—a Brennan On Duty (BOD). We knew that a good number of our guests would follow us there from Brennan's, and we were going to make sure they knew that a familiar face would be waiting to take great care of them.

But mentally transitioning from running a thriving, shiny gem into reviving a dowdy, out-of-date operation was tougher than I expected. I admit that I moped around for a while, causing my siblings to label me "Pitiful Pearl." One day, I found myself sitting in a little coat-check room near the entrance, bawling my heart out. "I can't work in this place! I'm ashamed of it! How can I ask people to come here?" (I may have been Hurricane Ella, but I was fully capable of occasional self-pity; besides, Owen wasn't there to tell this smarty pants to go fix it.)

The others probably had similar feelings at some point, but they came up with a solution to their frustration: start tearing the place apart and make it fantastic. During the first few years, we moved the bar from the front of the house to behind the kitchen, where it is now; vastly upgraded the kitchen with new stoves and modern equipment; and spruced up the downstairs dining room décor.

At one point around 1976, John went upstairs and poked around the underused space next to the small dining rooms to see what might be done with it. A bunch of refrigerators were stored in the hallways, and there was a room where employees changed their clothes, which was pretty dark except for the light coming in from a little window above the commode. John stood on the seat so that he could see out, spied the patio and wonderful old trees below, and said, "Oh my God, this is all out of place!" He came running down, grabbed Charlie and said, "Go look at the view that's been hiding!"

Charlie made a quick assessment and came up with a design plan, and by the next day we were knocking out the back wall of the changing room. Within a month we had our Garden Room, seemingly nestled within a giant oak tree and full of light from floor-to-ceiling windows that overlooked the patio and courtyard. We borrowed the interior design from a room in Dottie's house that had latticework with a mirror behind it. While it was being constructed, we took some of our regular customers up there and they immediately said, "Oh! *That's* going to be my table from now on!" Still, we had to convince many folks that the second floor was not Siberia, as it is in so many restaurants, so we launched a "formal word-of-mouth" campaign. It took a short while for news to spread, but once it did, a seat in the Garden Room became one of the city's most coveted reservations, and it gave us much-needed traction.

Before any of this transpired, however, on the eve of our taking over full-time daily management, we were whacked by a couple more crises that tested us yet again. Dottie, a former model and my kid sister, who was just forty years old, developed breast cancer and had to have surgery. In the early 1970s, when you said "cancer," everybody heard "dying." It was very different then, and women did not talk about it, especially if they had breast cancer. First Lady Betty Ford had not yet gone public with her breast cancer diagnosis; she really broke new ground when she did that in 1974. Dottie did too, by being open about her

HUE AND CRY

One of Ti's favorite stories from her childhood reveals how Commander's Palace acquired its distinctive exterior color:

"Aunt Adelaide and Charlie Gresham were always full of grand ideas, and after one of their many tours of world-class eateries, they came back with a doozy. The exterior of Commander's desperately needed a paint job. The city's blistering, humid weather is hell on wood, and the paint had begun to flake like coconut frosting. It was beige in those days, to fit in with most of the Garden District mansions, which were painted in white or earth tones. Their idea? Why not paint Commander's aqua? Paint was paint, and aqua cost no more than beige.

"I was a scamp on a bike, living about four blocks away from Mom's all-consuming business. Pedaling past the restaurant one day, I hit the brakes. I was mesmerized. I was appalled. There was a huge bluish-green splotch of paint on Commander's pale wall.

"Now, Commander's is not small. It juts out here and there. It has balconies and a turret—a style of architecture that Aunt Adelaide dubbed 'Victorian Cuckoo.' It already was a thumb in the eye of some who were used to the Garden District's more sedate Greek revival gems.

"My instant thought: 'Aqua? They wouldn't . . . would they? Oh, God. They would—it would be just like them! They are!'

"I pedaled home as fast as a banana-seat bike would take a skinny, reeling, thirteen-year-old girl.

"'Mom! Mom! There's a big patch of some weird blue color on the wall at Commander's.'

"'Yes! Isn't it great?'

"'You're not going to paint Commander's that color are you? How could you? How will I go to school tomorrow after everyone has seen that? It's stupid! It's crazy!' It was, in fact, the perfect way for a restaurant with peanuts for an advertising budget to declare itself revolutionized.

"'It's brilliant,' Mom said, ending the discussion. 'And Charlie says it will fade beautifully.'"

POSTSCRIPT I: "Aunt Dottie later turned to Charlie for advice on painting her home. One afternoon he showed up, dressed impeccably in his customary three-piece suit with a cane and a pocket-watch chain across his belly. Offered a drink, he asked for a whole pitcher of Negronis and then, oddly, a folding table and a chair. Charlie hauled the setup across the street to the little park opposite Dottie's home. He sat there alone, staring and sipping for about an hour and a half. He then rang the doorbell and said one word: 'Pink.' He left, and Dottie's house was shortly painted pink."

POSTSCRIPT II: "Incidentally, today my house is painted a bright coral, which is the same color that the Parlour Room at Commander's was painted before the post-Katrina renovation."

experience and, afterward, counseling others who were going through the same ordeal. She was always there for whoever called, often going to see them in the hospital, and she'd bring them nice gowns to make them feel pretty. Since she was known in town as such a beautiful, feminine and elegant lady, she was the ideal person to provide inspiration. But first she had to get through her own crisis, which involved radical surgery and painful rehabilitation. In response, the baby of our family showed the strength of the South's famous live oaks, which bend in the hurricane but survive and thrive. Tears would trickle down her face and mine as I watched her do excruciating rehab to rebuild the strength of her upper arm, where muscles had been removed. No complaining. Just march on— and look elegant while you do it. I, on the other hand, was stunned that she had to go through this and that we might lose her. I was pretty much numb.

Then one afternoon as I arrived at the hospital to visit Dottie, a friend handed me that day's newspaper and said, "Go outside and read this."

I couldn't believe the article in front of me: a food critic at the *States-Item*, Richard H. Collin, decided to weigh in with a thoroughly negative review of Commander's while we were still finding our way as a restaurant and struggling to find the right chef. "Commander's Palace is a place to avoid like the plague: it is a blatant tourist trap with no vestige of grace or skill," he wrote. That was one of the nicer sentences. He gave us not a three-star rating, not a two- nor one-star, but a *zero* grade—a black X, signifying "unacceptable," that shot from the page like a bullet between the eyes. Hell, we didn't know they even gave out zero stars. People think of me as a pillar of strength, but that day I was blubbering at the cruelty of it all. Back then, newspapers could affect your livelihood and reputation. So Dottie was staring down cancer with three young children in tow (having added sons Daly and Brad), and now we were all facing financial jeopardy if we couldn't get things turned around. Quickly.

Being tarred with that critique was a gut-check moment where all of us had to dig really deep. I was damned if that was the way this was all going to play out. But before we did anything, I had to walk into Commander's and face my new team and my guests and address this review. Dick, Adelaide and I met on the patio and decided that day that we were going to make Commander's Palace into something extraordinary, like this city and country had never seen. We vowed to get up and go to work every day and just get after it. And the truth of the matter was that the critic had hit upon some basic flaws, however badly overstated.

I knew right away that I had to deal with Mr. Collin. A few weeks later, I called him and invited him to my home for a cocktail and to discuss food, and this being New Orleans, he couldn't resist. We chatted for a bit, with no confrontation, and then I delivered my message: "I read your review and we have really taken it to heart. And I want you to know that this is going to be a great restaurant. Keep an eye on us. We are about to begin day-to-day operation of Commander's Palace, and from now on, we are going to get up and go to work every day to make it the best damn restaurant in the country."

That was all that was said. I had to get it out of my gut. I had to do something.

He seemed amused as he finished his drink and departed, and I don't think I ever encountered him again, except for another negative review of Commander's that he wrote in 1980. (Eventually he would get his comeuppance at the hands of journalist/screenwriter Nora Ephron, who wrote a damning article in a national magazine that accused him of unethical reviewing practices.)

Now that we'd been slapped around a bit and had stood our ground, we actually had to get busy turning the place into something great. Finally, I felt re-energized and ready to get on with the mission.

As I continued to read everything I could find about where food and restaurants were headed, it became clear to me that a revolution was stirring as the baby-boom generation began making good livings and indulged in leisure pursuits. The dining scene in America had begun to awaken, and fascinating things were happening in certain pockets around the country. The Culinary Institute of America had just moved to a new campus in Hyde Park, New York, and was providing state-of-the-art training to students who would soon lead the profession. Among them was Larry Forgione, who in the 1980s would be referred to as the "Godfather of American cuisine."

On the West Coast, Alice Waters and her partners at the then-unknown Chez Panisse in Berkeley, California, hired Jeremiah Tower and began proclaiming the superiority of produce acquired from farmers they knew. Wolfgang Puck in Los Angeles and Michael McCarty and Jonathan Waxman of Michael's in Santa Monica touted fresh, seasonal California cuisine, including exotic pizzas and extravagant salads. Jeremiah wrote the first-ever "regional cuisine" menu at Chez Panisse in 1972 and went on to run one of my all-time favorite restaurants, Stars, in San Francisco.

James Beard, with his writing and cookbooks, was alerting everyone to what was happening across the country, particularly in New York, home to innovative restaurants such as the Quilted Giraffe, the Four Seasons and Lutèce. Julia Child and Graham Kerr were teaching national TV audiences about the glories of French cooking techniques, and Robert Mondavi was spearheading a domestic wine renaissance in the Napa Valley. I got to know Bob in the '70s and became a friend and disciple, shouting from the rooftops that American wine could hold its own with its European counterpart—so much so that when we opened Mr. B's Bistro in 1979, we decided to have one of the first American-only wine lists (and a foreign-only beer list as well). That shocked New Orleans, a city with strong ties to France.

All over the country, interest in Asian cuisines was deepening, and upscale Italian restaurant menus were starting to expand beyond red-sauce staples to embrace dishes from various regions.

In Europe (and soon New York), something called "nouvelle cuisine" was becoming influential. Chefs were throwing out the heavy sauces and Escoffier recipes and introducing clean, simple presentations made from pure ingredients. (I investigated this during my travels abroad and determined that some of the best aspects of the movement were already being practiced in New Orleans, and that the silliness and fussiness—tomato water, anyone?—would be laughed out of town.)

Nothing had fully coalesced on a national level, but my homework was telling me that something was afoot—and that we had better be a part of it.

Meanwhile, the restaurant culture in New Orleans had become frozen in time, despite our efforts at Brennan's to shake things up. Beef Wellington, crabmeat imperial and oysters Bienville still held sway at too many places. Cooks cooked what restaurant owners told them to cook, and the menus didn't change. The modern concepts of chef-driven restaurants and celebrity chefs were unknown. And this was in a city that probably was ahead of most in terms of dining.

My visits to France had taught me that the basic tenets of their cuisine, even in nouvelle form, weren't that different from what home cooks were doing in

Louisiana. They seasoned their food with food, not just salt and spices, and so did we. Onions, carrots and celery form the base of so many French dishes. Well, replace the carrot with bell pepper and that is our so-called Creole trinity. Of course, we usually add garlic. French soups and sauces were often based on intense stocks, which is something good New Orleans cooks had always done (our now-famous turtle soup depends upon the richness of veal stock, which takes hours to make). I argued that our Creole redfish courtbouillon was a close cousin to fish *à la nage* in top French restaurants. As for the idea of making friends with your regional farmers and fishermen to ensure quality sourcing, why, New Orleans cooks had been doing that for years.

On a similar front, I was convinced that Louisiana cuisine, in both its countrified Cajun and refined Creole forms, was a world-class indigenous cuisine—America's best—that was poised to break out of home kitchens and into restaurants. Interest in regional cooking was stirring across the country, and we already were at the forefront of that approach. But I knew it could be better. Much better.

So the potential was there to do something dynamic and revolutionary while still respecting tradition. We'd take the best aspects of modern French cooking and "Creole-ize" them. Transforming classic trout amandine into Southern pecan-crusted trout is a good example. My brother Dick said, "I don't see any almonds around here, but I trip over pecans walking to work. Why don't we make use of them?" Thereby we created something that we would call "Haute Creole." All we needed was the vehicle, and I was determined that Commander's Palace would be it. I didn't know exactly where I was going with these ideas, but standing still would not be in the plan. It would just take a little time.

• • •

During the first year and a half or so of our running Commander's full-time, we went through two head chefs. Both were old-school Europeans, but they lacked the foodie gene and had no clue about what we were trying to achieve. While I was searching for that creative force that might transform some of our ideas into reality, I happened to talk to my friend Terry Flettrich, a TV personality at our local WDSU station. She was moving to Maine, and we were having a little goodbye lunch.

"Well, how's it going?" she asked.

"It's hell. It's just not there. We are not there yet."

"Well, what is it?"

"I really need a chef. *Really* need a chef."

"Wait one minute—let me tell you about Paul Prudhomme. He and I have been doing cooking classes together. He's fantastic and I think you two should meet."

Terry arranged it, and as soon as I began talking with Paul, I sensed I had found a kindred spirit. It turned out that he had been a busboy at Brennan's long ago, but I hadn't recognized him. He had run a hamburger stand, traveled the country and cooked in New Orleans at Le Pavillon Hotel and Maison du Puy. Now he was teaching New Orleanians about Creole cooking, as well as the secrets of Cajun cooking that he had learned while growing up on a farm in Opelousas, Louisiana, where he was the youngest of thirteen children. At 300-plus pounds, Paul looked the part of a master of hearty country fare. Wildly talented and ambitious, he shared my obsession with food.

A few weeks after our initial meeting, he returned and said, "I'll do lunch for you and try to get the kitchen and the systems organized." And the next thing we knew, he was working at Commander's night and day.

Paul was one of the nicest guys you'd ever want to meet. You couldn't have an argument with him. If we had a disagreement over a dish, he'd say, "Well, let's taste it." And then we'd break down why a dish worked or didn't. His palate was the best I've ever seen.

Hiring a chef whose specialty was heavy Cajun dishes at a time when much of the world was going mad for spare, pretty nouvelle cuisine sounds counterintuitive now, but it was just the thing to ignite a spark at Commander's. It was also risky. At the time, there was just one Cajun restaurant in the city, the Bon Ton, and Cajun culture in general was looked down upon as backwoods and déclassé in many quarters. We had to tread lightly at first, but we knew, as Paul would eventually prove, that once American taste buds were awakened to a distinctive and authentic regional cuisine, their cravings would be unleashed.

Paul and I started talking—a lot, every day. We'd start on a bench by the elevator and then migrate to stools right in the kitchen. He'd tell me where he had eaten recently, what his mother cooked, what he thought about French soufflés, how we could "Creole-ize" various dishes, and on and on. I truly felt that we were discovering and creating things, given that there were no Southern Foodways Alliance or James Beard Foundation or CIA seminars to guide us as there are today. The cooks would come around and we'd all taste and taste and talk and talk. Through these conversations it became clear that Paul was trying to make us into Cajuns, while we were trying to make him into a Creole—and all of us loved every second of it. The end result was something that would shake up the city and, ultimately, America.

Paul had never been a chef—he was a cook—and didn't have the training and background to organize a kitchen or teach and develop people. But that would come. (Upon his passing in October 2015, he was quoted in the obits as saying that I taught him "about making a buck"; given how successful he became, I took that as a high compliment!) But he had extraordinary taste buds and cooking skills and passion, and he did hire some fine cooks at Commander's and Mr. B's Bistro, including George Rhodes, Greg Sonnier, Paul Miller and Frank Brigtsen, who became outstanding New Orleans chefs in their own right. He helped get our kitchen up and running and was just a terrific guy.

It was the seasoning that made the magic happen. My son, Alex, calls it the "pow and wow!" approach to describe what happened when his food hits your tongue. Anybody can make gumbo, but when you tasted Paul's gumbo it was *Paul's gumbo*. He had seasoning boxes in the kitchen, with about a dozen compartments, from which he'd create special mixes for fish and meat. The surprise and complexity of those flavors made all the difference in the world. (Later, Paul launched a collection of Magic Seasoning Blends for the commercial market that has been phenomenally successful.)

At Commander's he inherited a menu that was staid and filled with classic Creole dishes. In contrast, some of the cooking he wanted to introduce was heavy and rustic Cajun. I happen to like to eat that type of food, but at the time, I thought it would be just too much for our guests. He'd put a sauce on part of a dish and another sauce somewhere else, and I would find myself saying, "Stop it, Paul. Calm down. Let's do something simple." So we went through that learning period, and I was working on him as much as he was working on me. I'd say, "No, no, no Paul, you've got to do it this way," and he'd say, "But did you taste it?" And I would usually respond, "It tastes magnificent but *look* at it! Think

VOODOO MIX—OR SOMETHING

As head of private parties at Commander's Palace in the late 1970s, Marcelle Bienvenu worked closely with Paul. Both hailed from the bayou country of southwestern Louisiana and shared an affinity for the Cajun food of that region. She shares her impressions of watching him startle the food world:

"Paul was incredibly creative. He always had these pieces of paper in his pocket with some kind of seasoning mix on them, and I would say, 'It's voodoo mix or something!' I was kind of curious about what a fantastic mouth he had and how he wanted to get everybody's mouths all fired up. It used to scare me because I thought that he meant peppered. But it was all these other seasonings that he came up with. I will never forget when he came out with a mirliton [chayote squash] carved to resemble a pirogue [a little boat]. And he fried it and then he filled it with fried oysters and fried shrimp. Then made a béarnaise sauce with tasso [spicy ham] in it. And I said, 'I never had *that* when I was little.'

"So he really took a lot of the ingredients and kicked them up all kind of ways. And when he did blackened redfish, I thought, 'Oh, nobody is going to like that.' My mother would say, 'It's just burnt and I am not going to eat it.' But he was of the right time to start preaching the gospel of Cajun cooking. People were ready for a change—nationwide, not just here. People were looking for something else, and I think that the flavors he introduced people to were something that nobody had ever had. Paul was bigger than life, and he said, 'Y'all gonna like this.' And people did. It was something so unusual on their palates that everybody went, 'Yeah, that's pretty good.'"

about the calories! Look at the way it looks on the plate. No! No! No! You have to improve this. Lighten it up."

It got interesting because we began to find common ground, even on his signature gumbo. When he arrived, Commander's was serving a traditional seafood gumbo, based on a roux of oil and flour. I wanted something lighter, so I asked Paul to eliminate the roux and make it more like a bouillabaisse, yet keep the rich flavor. "You can't do that. Too fancy," he said. "This is New Orleans and they want real gumbo." Back and forth, back and forth. Finally, he came up with a delicious version without the roux and it was much lighter, reminiscent of bouillabaisse but without the saffron. And our guests loved it. So the question became, if we could do that with the gumbo, could we lighten other dishes we had in the house? Paul tried and usually succeeded.

He introduced a dish that eventually caused a mini-sensation across the country. The idea came out of one of our weekly "foodie meetings," which could be attended by any of the staff. You'd have the best cooks there, along with Dick and Dottie and Paul, and we'd all sit around a table on the patio. The first thing you'd say at the meeting was, "Does anybody have anything exciting to talk about? I read about this or I did this or I went to this restaurant." That day, someone asked, "What's the best way on Earth to cook and present fish?" One of our cooks spoke up and said that the best way was to take a just-caught fish, season it all over and sear it over an open fire in a very hot cast-iron skillet until the flesh is caramelized.

Paul said, "OK, I agree with you that that couldn't be better. I've eaten it that way a million times in my life. Let's go into the kitchen and see if we can re-create it in a restaurant." Paul took a whole fish (probably redfish, red snapper, flounder or pompano), worked with the cooks and came up with what came to be known as "blackened" fish. It was phenomenal. We put it on the menu at Commander's as "seared redfish," and as "charcoal-grilled fresh fish" at Mr. B's because I didn't care for the word "blackened." Later, when he served it as his K-Paul's restaurant using redfish, "blackened redfish" became so popular nationwide that fishing restrictions were implemented to preserve the species.

Another of the restaurant's signature dishes, bread pudding soufflé, came out of a foodie meeting held as Commander's prepared to host the American Cuisine Symposium in 1983. Having invited the country's top culinary pros to explore regional cuisine at a series of dinners and seminars, we needed a unique dessert that would have its roots in the region, so we turned our attention to bread pudding. Commander's served a perfectly good version, but so did a lot of restaurants. Everybody likes it, but they often don't want to eat it as a dessert after dinner because it's too heavy. "C'mon, Paul, help, dammit! We have to do something different!" is probably the way I phrased it. So he thought about it and wound up turning the ingredients into a soufflé, into which was stirred a whiskey sauce.

It was an immediate hit at the symposium, which was attended by the top people in the food and hospitality industry, including Larry Forgione, Jonathan Waxman, Michael McCarty, James Villas, the *New York Times*' Marion Burros, Julee Rosso of The Silver Palate, and representatives from top culinary schools and food companies. Our guests soon fell in love with it, and it has never left Commander's menu. (Many years later, chef Jeremiah Tower told me: "When I had that soufflé, all I could think of was the arithmetic—and I could see my new car! Anybody who hasn't stolen that idea for the soufflé is just crazy.") We had a guy named Mr. Lou, who had been in the Army, and his sole job was to take the kitchen's giant mixer and whip up that Creole soufflé. All. Day. Long. I'm glad we sold a ton of it, but I could never quite understand why it became a phenomenon. The same thing had happened at Brennan's with the Bananas Foster. It, too, had been *the* dessert in town. But can you tell me why? I guess that when you take very simple, comforting ingredients and elevate them in some attractive way, it strikes a chord within people (and, of course, the whiskey or rum sauces don't hurt!). My favorite dessert, though, is still Nellie's sautéed bananas, which Dottie now makes.

One challenge that Paul faced when he was with us (and would face for most of his life) was controlling his weight, which, according to his obituary, got as high as 500 pounds. His knees couldn't sustain that strain, and he suffered terribly. Dottie tried to get him to go to a psychiatrist to deal with his eating habits because she envisioned the restaurant being dumped in her lap if something were to happen to him. (Or us.) He wasn't alone in this, though: I was getting bigger and so were several of the people who worked for us. It was simply the restaurant lifestyle. Dottie laid down the law: "I know you are eating ice cream when I turn my back! I know this therapist and he's going to come talk to you and fix your head so that food won't be the first thing you think about in the morning."

We tried Dottie's program for a while, but it had a negligible effect (except for the fact that years later Paul would marry the therapist's wife!).

Aside from his tasting and cooking abilities, another thing that impressed me about Paul was his willingness to take some of the incoming generation of Brennans under his wing. Alex had just gotten his driver's license and spent a couple of summers driving Paul between our restaurants and running errands, soaking up Lord knows what kind of wisdom. And my nephew Dickie recalls that when he was a teen and learning the ropes in the kitchen, Paul would come up to him and say, "You know that everybody is looking at you, so you need to always do your best." That simple admonition has stayed with him for nearly forty years.

I learned an incredible amount from Paul, and I think he was as talented as any of the chefs who have gone through our kitchens, but when he came to work for us, very few people in the city knew who he was, so we set about raising his profile. We'd send him around town to cook for special events, and just as we would later do with Emeril Lagasse, we'd have Paul meet with every newspaper and magazine food editor who came to town. Though by nature he was somewhat shy, he could turn on that 1,000-watt smile when he needed to, and eventually he began cooking for events all over the country.

By the time he left us, Paul Prudhomme was becoming a household name, having appeared on NBC's *The Tonight Show with Johnny Carson* (the show's producers had asked me to appear, but I persuaded them that Paul would be a far more engaging guest) as well as morning shows all over the country. And within the culinary world, he emerged as one of the most influential chefs in the country and brought respectability to the profession. If Paul wasn't *the* first of what came to be called celebrity chefs, he certainly was among the first. He didn't know anything about that part of the business, so I taught him everything I knew about publicity, because my brother Owen had taught me the same things.

I think the first national attention he ever got was when our friend from *Bon Appetit* magazine, Jim Villas, let us know he was coming down to do a story. He called and said he wanted to write about gumbo (remember, this was still an exotic dish to most of the country), and I told him, "Boy, do I have the guy for you to talk to! Let me tell you about Paul Prudhomme." And that's the way it started.

On the day of Jim's arrival at Commander's, I had someone take every ingredient from the prep kitchen that goes into a gumbo and put them on the table. When Jim came in, I introduced him to Paul and said, "How about that? There's your gumbo and there's your cook. And here's your picture right here." They sat down and got to know each other, and a few months later we got a cover story in *Bon Appetit*.

Paul was so easy to present to people because he genuinely loved food. He had a magnetic personality, an engaging Cajun accent and extraordinary taste buds. There couldn't have been a better ambassador for the cooking of Louisiana, and we made the most of it. Given our rapport and sense of adventure, this was a very, very happy time for both of us.

• • •

My education continued on a number of fronts during those years, particularly when it came to wine. I was getting to know many of the top French producers—the folks from Barton & Gustier were among my favorites—who would stop by the restaurant to taste and talk as they toured the country promoting their latest vintage. I'd get out maps of France to see where their vineyards were located and try to understand why their wines tasted the way they did, what grapes they were using, etc. Wine people fascinate me, and soaking up their knowledge has been one of the great pleasures of my life. I'll never forget being invited to a tasting event staged at the Four Seasons in New York. It was one of the most spectacular parties I've been to. They had the top California winemakers pouring their best wines, and they sat me at the head table between James Beard and Alexis Lachine, a delightful Russian who was a noted wine writer and entrepreneur. There were something like seventeen glasses at each place setting.

"I'm no taster," I confided to Jim. "I know what I like, but I can't tell you what grape this wine is made from."

"Neither can I," he said.

"Well, you're no help! What about this guy on the other side of me?" I said, indicating Alexis.

"Oh! He knows everything about everything!"

Alexis was that kind of guy, and we became good friends that night. (Mr. Lachine somehow got the impression later on that I had named my son after him, but that wasn't the case.)

After we finished that round of tasting, there was an intermission and they reset the table with about seventeen more glasses. The re-setting was rather amazing for me to watch, and I filed that information away for later use. The other remarkable thing was how miraculous the food and wines were. It turned into one of the most divine evenings I've ever had, though it ended on a disconcerting note. Toward the end of the event, Jim leaned over to me and said, "I've got to get out of here. I've got phlebitis and it's acting up." I had arranged for a car, so we took him to the hospital. They took care of him and got him back to his house, but the whole incident was truly scary.

All of my experiences with Jim were, shall we say, vivid, but one of his visits to New Orleans was particularly memorable. We had been to lunch and had a little wine, and I had something important to do that evening. I said to him, "Look, I've got to go home and take a nap. What about you? What are you going to do?"

"I'm going to go home with you and take a nap."

So he came to the house. I put him in Daddy's bedroom and I went down the hall to my room. I was in the bathroom and a knock came on the door. Well, I opened the door and there he was, Jim Beard, all 300 or so pounds of him, with a towel wrapped around him (and there was no towel big enough to go around Jim Beard). He stood there and said, "I'm too big for the shower!" My daddy had a shower bathroom; he didn't have a tub. Well, I said, "Give me ten minutes, and I'll be out of the tub and you can come in here." Unbelievable. But that's how well we got to know each other.

He was always teaching me things. I gave him Creole cream cheese one morning, and I said, "To me, this is one of the great tastes. I love Creole cream cheese. I think this could be on our breakfast menu. But what can we do to make it look good?"

"What's wrong with it?"

"It's just blah white."

"Well, put a couple of prunes on it." He wasn't into food for looks—he was all about the taste.

Another time, we went to eat oysters during one of our first-ever restaurant outings in New York, at the Grand Central Oyster Bar. I started to make a cocktail sauce like I'd done all my life and Jim said, "Now wait a minute. We're going to have some of the best oysters in the world. Put that away and let's taste the oyster."

That was pretty interesting because they always had oysters from everywhere, from all over New England, this bay and that bay, and he was right. And I've learned to love to eat an oyster that way. I mean, he was very knowledgeable about food, but he wasn't pretentious in any way.

• • •

Given Paul's success and ambition, I knew that he would probably go on to other things at some point, so we engaged his talents in as many projects as we could. By 1978 he held the position of executive chef for our family's restaurants, and he and I created the menu for a place we were opening in the French Quarter called Mr. B's Bistro, on the corner of Royal and Iberville. We had been dying to get back to the Quarter, and John and Dick had found a space that used to house the beloved Solari's Grocery Store (a New Orleans version of Dean & Deluca, if you will) but was now occupied by a garage, a cheap Chinese takeout eatery and a pornography shop. They struck a deal and soon we were in business.

I really loved Mr. B's—it was modeled after the kind of place you'd find in France, where a cook at one of the elite restaurants would branch off and do personalized cooking at the more relaxed bistro level. Many watchers of the city's dining scene proclaimed that Mr. B's was the beginning of a new genre of New Orleans restaurant, a genre that flourishes now, especially post-Katrina. At a time when formal dining meant stuffy dining rooms and tuxedo-clad waiters, Mr. B's roared onto the scene like a convertible with the top down, loud music blaring. It's fun to think of the amalgam of influences on us at the time: the great bistros of France; my mother's home cooking; Paul's rapidly evolving, ramped-up Cajun cooking; a bit of a backlash to nouvelle cuisine; our growing confidence in our regional cuisine; and on and on. We loved what we were doing and so much of it came through in our racy new outpost. We let our hair down with a menu that included barbecued shrimp, the hickory-grilled Gulf fish, pasta jambalaya, cream of eggplant soup, Gumbo Ya Ya (chicken-Andouille sausage gumbo with a dark roux), and "Bananas Faster" (a whimsical milkshake-like version of Bananas Foster), some of which are still on the menu. Mr. B's turned out to be a big success and remains so to this day under the steady hand of my niece Cindy (John's daughter). Meet her and you will not soon forget her restaurant or her infectious laugh. From the start, nearly every member of the next generation of Brennans spent time there, learning their craft in the front and back of the house.

Once we had Mr. B's up and running, Paul turned his attention to operating his own French Quarter restaurant with his wife, K Hinrichs, called K-Paul's Louisiana Kitchen. It quickly became a sensation, with lines out the door and down Chartres Street. For a time he juggled working there and in the Commander's kitchen, but the demands became too great. I was upset at first when he finally announced that he was leaving us—K-Paul's was a small place and not put together very well, whereas we paid him handsomely to work in a great kitchen—but I eventually got over it, and we remained friends for the rest of his life.

While it is true that Paul's presence boosted Commander's reputation immeasurably, particularly toward the end of his five-year stay, we still struggled a bit until we found our footing in the late 1970s. For the first time, we were advised to do a little advertising and, in particular, to tout our lunch prices and our 25-cent martini promotion. The reasoning was that, while we were attracting guests who knew us from Brennan's and the folks from the surrounding Garden District, the general public wasn't as aware of us yet. Taking out a few newspaper ads worked, and we only had to do it for a short while.

Marketing was the bigger thing, and we had to do it every day. Adelaide became a pro at this by staging and representing us at public events. We got a major boost in that area courtesy of Dick, who came up with the idea of combining two of New Orleans' finest institutions: food and jazz music. We were trying to rev up our lunch business, and one day when I was in Houston, I got a call from Dick, who excitedly explained the light bulb that had gone off in his head. He loved Dixieland jazz, with its impertinent, buoyant rhythms and celebratory spirit, and he reasoned that tourists, and a fair number of our regular guests, would love it too—especially if they were drinking expertly made champagne cocktails and Ramos gin fizzes and eating those famous Brennan egg dishes and flaming desserts. So Dick hired a band to perform at the weekend brunches and then sent his children and some of their cousins downtown on the streetcar the day before with flyers that said something simple like "Take the streetcar to the historic Garden District for Jazz Brunch at Commander's Palace."

Dickie, who was also working as a busboy, recalls that his dad kept nervously asking how many customers he thought would show up for the kickoff event. Dickie said all the people he had talked to on the streetcar line had seemed really interested, so he guessed 100 folks might participate. Of course, way more than 100 showed up just in the first hour, and we soon had to turn folks away.

Those early brunches also got a big boost from a friend of ours, the glamorous dancer Chris Owens, who owned and performed at a popular club on Bourbon Street. Chris showed up at one of the first brunches, and Dick said to me, "Put her in the middle of the dining room." We knew that all the old ladies from uptown would get so excited when Chris walked into the room—and they did. I later found out that Dick always sent out a bottle of Dom Perignon for her, and she would smile and sip it as everyone came by to "ooh" and "ahh" at her. Chris was wonderful. She was there to support us and let us know that she cared and would help us in any way she could.

Since then, we've thrown a New Orleans–worthy party nearly every Saturday and Sunday, almost always to a full house and always swinging to the sounds of just two band leaders, Alvin Alcorn and Joe Simon.

Another reason that I look back on that era with great fondness and pride is because it marked the arrival into the business of some of the younger Brennans. John's son Ralph had learned the ropes at Brennan's on Royal Street and then became a CPA. We sent Ralph to New York to work at '21,' and he eventually returned to New Orleans to work at Mr. B's before launching his own collection of restaurants. Alex and Dickie had both grown up working at Brennan's and Commander's, but as they went off to college, their paths in life weren't yet clear.

Alex had had a fabulous childhood but didn't like studying. He attended Louisiana State University in Baton Rouge but had no direction in his life. He came home that first summer and spent a lot of time waterskiing, hunting and fishing. I asked him what his plans were and he said, "Well, you know, we're going to hang out and have a good time."

Oy. This kid's not doing well in school, and he keeps asking me for a job in the restaurant because he says it's the only thing he knows how to do. Finally, I got fed up and said, "I can't give you a job. What do you know?"

"Well, I can do what everybody else over there does."

"Oh, you really can, eh? You want to start as a housekeeper? You don't know anything about the kitchen. You don't know anything."

We kept this conversation going, and I was up to here with his not doing anything with his life. Finally, I said, "OK, I'm giving you a ticket to Europe. And I'm going to give you a weekly allowance. And I'm going to send you over there to get a job and learn French. I want you to learn everything you can learn, and I want you to call me every Sunday at 3 p.m." Phone calls were expensive back then.

Alex says it scared the hell out of him to be sent an ocean away from the family, but that's what it took for him to become the restaurateur—and man—that he is today. He attended a couple of culinary schools and worked nights at various restaurants and really threw himself into it. Of course, I was bombarding him with packages of books and magazine articles that I thought he should read. One feature had a bunch of photos of French chefs who were talking about their favorite perfumes. One of the photos was of a debonair guy with white hair and a mustache and a big smile on his face, whose wide-open arms beckoned the reader in. I wrote in the margin, "He looks nice. Try to get in with him," and shipped it off. The photo was of Roger Vergé, from the famous Moulin de Mougins restaurant in the South of France. Alex, being the dutiful son, took up my challenge. I had refused to get a job for him, and it was time for him to prove himself. He showed up at Moulin de Mougins' back door, introduced himself to chef Vergé and talked his way into a fantastic job at a Michelin-starred restaurant in one of the most beautiful parts of France. Talk about a finishing school! That's when we both knew that he had found his calling.

Alex returned to the States and worked at the Four Seasons and Maxwell's Plum in New York before deciding it was time to return home. We had an opening at our Houston restaurant, so we sent him there, and a few years later his cousin Dickie joined him. (Alex is still in Houston today and has maintained the restaurant's position as one of the city's very best.)

Dickie, who was about two years younger than Alex, followed a somewhat similar path. Dick and I saw to it that he learned the ropes at Mr. B's and Commander's, in between studying at LSU and Loyola. After he graduated with a degree in finance, I sent him to apprentice with Larry Forgione at his new restaurant, An American Place, in New York. Dickie then moved to France to study the language and cook in some of Paris's top restaurants. By the mid-'80s he was ready to return to the States, so he decided to move to Houston to help out Alex, who was having a tough, tough time because of the city's economic depression. I helped them the best I could with what I thought were some wise marketing suggestions, but not everything turned out the way we anticipated. I'll let them tell the story:

MORE THAN FIFTEEN MINUTES OF FAME

When Ella's son, Alex, and Dick's son, Dickie, finished their stints in Europe and New York in the 1980s, they wound up at the Brennan's in Houston during a period when the city was suffering from a collapse in the energy business. Here, they recall Ella's very sensible—though occasionally off-the-wall—advice on how to stay afloat:

ALEX: "By the time I got to Houston, our restaurant was already about twenty-five years old. It had been a grand success early on, but it had grown tired. And then, about five minutes after I moved there, the price of oil dropped by two-thirds, literally within a week, and it was the great oil depression that lasted a number of years. It was overwhelming. Some of Brennan's best customers jumped out of office towers to their death. Mom used to say of me, 'He thinks he caused the depression!' because I really took it to heart. So the family took a long, hard look at the restaurant and said, 'Look, we have got to remake it, but we need to remake it *not* in the mold of New Orleans. Let Brennan's in Houston become more of a locals' restaurant by adding some regional flavor to the menu.' That helped, but still there was this deep depression in the city.

"At the same time, we had a general manager who'd been there for a number of years, and when I stumbled upon a few things that he shouldn't have been doing, we parted ways. After I'd been there a while, my cousin Dickie decided to come to Houston, and I remember us having this conversation: 'Did your dad (Uncle Dick) tell you that we are running this place?' Dickie said, 'No. Did your mom tell you we were running this place?' They never told us! I mean, we just went to work every day. Very typical of our family."

DICKIE: "I was living in Paris, and I started getting calls from Alex—we grew up really close. He said, 'I think that if you come to Houston and help me at Brennan's, then your dad and Ella won't send a general manager over here and you and I can probably run the restaurant.' He was mostly interested in not having to work under somebody, so he and I kind of came up with a strategy for running the place. I was twenty-five at the time."

ALEX: "You know, there was a lot of pressure from the family to make Houston successful. There was a night that stands out for me when we had maybe fifteen or twenty people in the dining room. I mean, it was empty. And a fellow I knew from around the corner who ran another restaurant came in and sat down at the bar. He ordered a drink, sort of threw it back. I asked him how he was, and he said, 'Nobody came tonight. Goose egg. Threw a party and nobody came.' So it was really tough times.

"Mom and I talked about all of this and she told me about her 'four walls' philosophy. We can control everything that happens within these four walls, but nothing that happens outside, right? So don't waste your energy on worrying about things that you can't control. You got fifteen people in the dining room? You need to make fifteen customers into fifteen friends, and make sure they walk out talking about their experience. She was a cheerleader all the way."

DICKIE: "When Aunt Ella came to visit, she never made us feel bad that we were having a real rough time. Instead, she said, 'We've got to do something. We are going to make this thing work.' She was always communicating with her friends, so the next thing you know, Raymond Burr was coming to spend a week with us. He was a dear family friend and he loved Houston. They had just opened up the Menil Collection art museum, so he wanted to come to town anyway to see that, but he mostly wanted to hang out with us and they were going to do some stuff with

TV. We got all kinds of media that Raymond Burr was hanging out with Dickie and Alex! And then it wasn't long after that that Andy Warhol did a commercial for Brennan's."

ALEX: "You know, we really tried all sorts of wacky marketing ideas, including one where we'd do a TV commercial that would get people's attention. We needed something that really grabbed them, startled them or would make them think differently about Brennan's. So Mom and this marketing advisor hired Andy Warhol! If I am lying, I am dying! Andy Warhol was to be a front man for this commercial. We went up to New York and filmed a short commercial, and there was Andy Warhol talking about Brennan's of Houston."

DICKIE: "Just picture Andy standing there, saying, 'When I am in Houston, I go to Brennan's. When you go to Brennan's, tell Alex and Dickie that Andy sent you.' And it was just a twenty-second commercial that we put on local TV in Houston. Brennan's hadn't had a Brennan (in charge) for a good fifteen years, and we were trying to let people in Houston know that these two young Brennans from New Orleans were here and running the restaurant. How did we convince Andy Warhol to do it? Aunt Ella, are you kidding? I mean, that's just the kind of world that we grew up in."

ALEX: "We put it on the air and it was a disaster. Houstonians did not exactly take to Andy Warhol, of all people, telling them where they should eat in Houston. The phone calls that I got were . . . well, let's just say a lot of them were interesting. But I mean, Mom has always wanted to be outside of the box. She has always been a voracious reader, a student of business and marketing in particular. And I remember her saying, 'This is sweaty palms marketing. If your palms aren't sweaty when you are doing it, you are doing it wrong.' Mom was always willing to try different things. And it was sort of back to the 'four walls' marketing: first you make a friend, marketing from within the restaurant, and then tell the story to the world. That has been the greatest lesson that I have learned from her."

That first decade or so at Commander's had proved to be so enriching, even given its rocky start, and by the time of Paul's departure, I felt that my career had reached another peak. On the home front, we had settled into a wonderful life with Adelaide in her home, and I watched as my son and nephew embraced the family business. Ti was growing into a studious, independent young woman whose career path lay before her, with seemingly unlimited options. My siblings and I had successfully reinvented Commander's Palace with a new look, new traditions and a highly influential menu; we were being recognized as among the leaders of the hospitality industry, thanks in part to the dynamic interchange between me and Paul; and we regained a foothold in the French Quarter with a stylish and very different restaurant that was an instant success. Life couldn't have been sweeter.

Little did I know that we were just getting started at Commander's.

Frank Brigtsen became a protégé of Paul Prudhomme when the chef hired him at Commander's Palace in the 1970s. He now runs his own self-named restaurant in New Orleans, where on busy nights, he frequently cites his favorite Ella Brennan quote: "The best restaurant décor is a fanny on every seat." Here, he recalls another lasting image from his stint at Commander's:

"I was in the kitchen between lunch and dinner prepping. And, of course, Commander's has an open kitchen, so Miss Ella came walking through with Caesar Romero, the famous Hollywood actor. And she's talking and pointing at this and that. A busboy behind them dropped an entire tray of china, and there was a loud crash. And Mr. Romero went 'Oh my God!' and Miss Ella didn't even flinch. Total professional. Although I'm quite sure that afterwards she sent a little message back to the chief steward to make sure to admonish that young man for being so impolite."

9

Are You Sure You Want to Run a Restaurant?

"IT WAS THE MOST EXTRAORDINARY
SERVICE I'VE EVER HAD IN AN AMERICAN
RESTAURANT. YOU WENT TO COMMANDER'S
PALACE AND YOU UNDERSTOOD WHAT YOU
HAD BEEN MISSING ALL ALONG."
—RUTH REICHL, FORMER EDITOR OF
GOURMET MAGAZINE, TO THE *LA TIMES*

I don't like to talk about the idea of legacy. In fact, I hate it and have never thought in those terms. Makes me seem old and pompous. Besides, it's for other people to decide whether I've left a noteworthy legacy, not me.

But I do like to think that our family's restaurants and all who have worked in them have helped to improve the quality of hospitality and service in New Orleans, and perhaps the rest of the country. We have come so far since taking over that run-of-the-mill Vieux Carré on Bourbon Street. The best ideas originated with my siblings, my teachers in New York and, especially, my coworkers, who have refined these concepts in the crucible of day-to-day service.

So, instead of dwelling on what I might be remembered for, I'd like to share a few of the things I've learned over more than sixty years in the business—principles and practices that Brennan restaurants are still executing and improving upon with every meal served.

STICK WITH IT.

At Commander's, Dick and I shared the role of restaurateur, not just owner. A restaurant owner hires a chef. But a restaurateur has to make sure the chef does what he or she is supposed to, and keep the place running smoothly. The roles are very different. If you're a restaurateur, you have it in your blood. You love it. What you're trying to do is create something that's good, not average, because it's gonna be what you do with your life. It's a lifestyle, not a job.

When you're a restaurateur, the first thing you do when you wake up is call whomever is running the kitchen that day. Everything OK? Yes? No? What do you need? You check all of that. Then you head over there and see for yourself that everything is in order before the doors open. Make sure the restaurant is absolutely clean, especially the restrooms. Position the tables in their proper place—the staff have probably moved them in the course of the day, and if you don't put them back where they're supposed to be, servers will bump into guests. That's needless and avoidable. Makes me very angry. You can't let things like that happen.

When you're done with that, you take out the reservation book and talk to the kitchen about how it looks for that day. Will it be extra busy? Any parties? Are we prepared for this couple's anniversary or that person's birthday? Communication between the front of the house and the kitchen is essential.

Take a moment to walk outside, front and back, and check the sidewalks to see if everything is welcoming and clean. After that, try to grab an hour to sit down and communicate with the team, and make it very personal. The dishwashers, waiters, captains and front-door people need to know that you care about them and are doing everything you can to back them up and make their jobs as efficient as possible.

The next thing you know, the door opens! From then on, you're going back and forth between the kitchen and dining room until the last meals are served. You're tasting everything all day—Dick used to keep a bunch of plastic spoons in his pocket for that purpose—to make sure the kitchen is doing its best work, every shift. Then it's back out front: Ms. Smith just came in with a client she wants to impress and would like you or the chef to say hello.

THE LIFE OF A RESTAURATEUR

To remind us of our responsibilities—and our lot in life—we have hanging in the office a poster with a cheeky essay titled, "The Life of a Restaurateur" (sometimes attributed to Canadian restaurateur Dominique Chapeau):

"A restaurateur must be a diplomat, a democrat, an autocrat, an acrobat and a doormat. He must have the facility to entertain prime ministers, princes of industry, pickpockets, gamblers, bookmakers, pirates, philanthropists, popsies and prudes. He must be on both sides of the political fence and be able to jump the fence.

"He should be, or have been, a footballer, golfer, bowler, tennis player, cricketer, dart player, sailor, pigeon fancier, motor racer and a linguist, as well as have a good knowledge of any other sport involving dice, cards, horse racing and billiards. It is also most useful, as he has sometimes to settle arguments and squabbles, that he be a qualified boxer, wrestler, weightlifter, sprinter and peacemaker.

"He must always look immaculate when drinking with the ladies and gentlemen mentioned in the first paragraph, as well as bankers, swankers, theatricals, commercial travelers and company representatives, even though he has just made peace between any of the two, four, six or more of the aforementioned patrons.

"To be successful he must keep the bar full, the house full, the storeroom full, the wine cellar full, the customers full and not get full himself. He must have staff who are clean, honest, quick workers, quick thinkers, non-drinkers, mathematicians, technicians and at all times on the boss's side, the customers' side and stay on the outside of the bar.

"To sum up: He must be outside, inside, offside, glorified, sanctified, crucified, stupefied, cross-eyed, and if he's not the strong silent type, there's always suicide!!!"

To ensure consistency, we instituted a policy called BOD: Brennan On Duty. That means that someone from the family is on premises and taking an active role whenever the restaurant is open. We don't have, and never have had, formal titles for the family members, but in a practical sense, everyone is empowered and equally responsible for the success of the operation. Such a system requires tremendous dedication and commitment on everyone's part, but the results are satisfying and the rewards are tremendous.

A restaurateur plays an essential role, but today I think many restaurants operate without one. My view is: if the chef is trying to be the restaurateur, he or she is not minding the kitchen. As a restaurant grows and becomes more important, you need to have the chef, the restaurateur and the operations/purchasing people working as a team. And that's how we run Commander's today.

NO PRAYING AT THE ALTAR OF THE RESTAURANT—HAVE FUN!

We have been reading so much recently about how people are buying "experiences" and not "things." We feel like we have been attuned to that for a long, long time. Years ago, Alex put it into words that we are in the business of "creating dining memories." I think many restaurateurs and chefs believe they are in the business of selling dinner. Selling food. They are missing the biggest part of the equation from the guests' perspective and a major part of the enjoyment and fulfillment of the life of a restaurateur.

As you can tell, I was born with a competitive streak, which I channeled into a desire to succeed in business. It was a natural and healthy part of my growth, but Owen taught me that I needed to balance it by helping others succeed as well. "You have to meet everybody in the restaurant business," he said. "You have to make friends with them because they are in the same business as you. We're all in this together, and New Orleans is a great city, so let's get going."

At first, some of them maybe didn't want to be friends with a little sawed-off kid from a tacky restaurant in the French Quarter. But eventually we got to know everybody, mainly because Owen insisted. And as we grew and improved, so did many of the restaurants around us.

Owen thought about hospitality, which was in its infancy as a business in America. At some restaurants, customers would venture in and if they didn't know the people who ran the place, God help them. So Owen taught us to always greet *everyone* at the door, be warm and friendly, learn their name and give them yours. (Owen was terrible with names his entire life. After he died, I opened his chest of drawers, and it was full of these little pieces of paper with somebody's name on it that he had written down ten times. He was trying. He wasn't good at it, but he was trying.) "Treat people as you want to be treated," Owen preached. Remember that the customer is always right. And when he's not right, you have to make him think he's right.

"One must come across as sincere," he said. So if you don't like people, don't work in the restaurant business. I didn't have to bite my tongue very much because I generally like people. Generally . . .

Drawing from my experiences at Café Lafitte and the Old Absinthe House, I developed the mindset that a restaurant is not a church, where you have to be quiet and kneel and you can't talk or laugh. No! There should be no praying at the altar of the restaurant or chef! The whole point is to come in and have a ball. That may be especially true in New Orleans, but I think it should be true pretty much everywhere. The most exciting thing for me is to go into a restaurant and see a bunch of people around a table having a spirited but friendly conversation. That's what this business is all about. When people are served a great meal and enjoy the company they're with, most of the time they never want to leave. They stay and stay.

It's all about making people feel special. We found out years ago at Brennan's Vieux Carré, where we had a bar back by the kitchen, that regulars would come in through the back door rather than the front door. It made them feel like they had an "in." That was also true at Arnaud's across the street and at Antoine's. People always went in through the back door.

When we moved to Royal Street, the building's layout didn't allow for that. And when we came to Commander's, the bar was in the front of the house. So we soon moved it into the kitchen, where it's been ever since. Having it there pleases the cooks, who get a kick out of seeing people come through their domain. Sometimes guests will stop and chat, and sometimes the cooks see

BOTTOM LINE: IT'S ALL ABOUT VALUE PERCEPTION

Joe Henican is a member of the board of directors of the Commander's Family of Restaurants and has advised the family on financial matters for more than thirty years (his ultimate reward was to have a dish named after him on the Commander's Palace menu—Shrimp and Tasso Henican). Here, he explains Ella's refreshing approach to managing the bottom line:

"The thing that makes the biggest impression on me about Ella is that she's not a Harvard Business School business person. Although she's very comfortable in reading a balance sheet or an income statement, she understands that that's not how you run a business. It's a tool to use and it gives you some sort of objective measure, but what she understands and what she practices is that there's a lot more to a successful restaurant business.

"There are several key factors: labor, food cost and pricing on the menu. The approach that Commander's and Ella have always taken is that they don't want to be the most expensive restaurant in town. They want to provide value for their customers. They perhaps leave money on the table, as it's said. That really guarantees a loyal customer, a customer who enjoys the experience and enjoys the feeling of hospitality that's created.

"Ella steps into the restaurant and she senses whether there's excitement, whether there's interest, how the people are enjoying their meals. I've seen her get up from the table and lead a second-line parade around the restaurant—up the stairs into another dining room. She didn't feel like there was enough going on and that movement and excitement needed to take place, and so she made it happen. You can see the response of the customers when that happens and how it really enhances their restaurant experience."

people waiting a little too long at the bar so they'll bring them something to nibble on. It's a very interrelated thing now.

The whole idea of welcoming people behind the scenes has been with us a long time. Putting the chef's table in the kitchen went right along with that. *The Wall Street Journal* did a story saying we had the third chef's table ever to be done. We didn't even know that. But we'll take a good idea wherever it comes from. In this case, Alex had seen Charlie Trotter's chef's table in Chicago and immediately instituted one at Brennan's of Houston. Well, we were quick to copy him at Commander's. It's a magical place where you are truly in the center of the action. That table is very special to all of us. It's like a magnetic force. We meet there during the day for one-on-ones with a cook or a manager or a salesman. Then at night the chef's table guests are designated the "Kings and Queens of the Palace." The culinary team creates a special meal and serves and interacts with these guests all night. Wines are paired with the courses, special cocktails come out of the adjacent bar, and all the other guests want to know who is so special that they get to sit there. Usually those tables are reserved six months to a year in advance, but we like to think it's worth the wait.

MAKE IT RIGHT. IMMEDIATELY. EVERY TIME.

On occasion, there are nights when everything seems to go wrong in the kitchen. It doesn't happen often, but for whatever reason there is a meltdown. It's a terrible thing to have happen, and the only thing I knew to do was say to the team: "Stop. Collect yourselves and listen to the person in charge. Give me the checks, and I'll talk to the guests." Then I would go out in the dining room and say to those whose orders were delayed, "I'm terribly sorry, there's a problem in the kitchen and it's going to take a little while to resolve. Would you care to wait? Give us a half hour. If you can't wait, we'll pick up the check for whatever you've had. I know this is your special night and we're ruining it. We take responsibility for that. We want you to come back on another night and be our guest."

To follow up, I would take their name and address, write them a note and tell them to call anytime and book a return date so that we could make up for what we'd done. And most people are as nice as can be, though you'll always have a

UNBROKEN SUCCESS

Tim and Nina Zagat are the founders and co-publishers of the famous Zagat Survey, *which has ranked Commander's Palace as New Orleans' top restaurant for eighteen years and counting—that's every year except for the year the restaurant was closed to repair the damage from Katrina. And the Zagats tell us that streak is longer than any other restaurant anywhere. Ever. Here, they assess some of Ella's contributions to that streak:*

NINA: "Somebody can be a fabulous chef and not see how to shape what they're doing into a comprehensive menu for a restaurant so that consumers get the kinds of choices that they want and dishes that just hit the spot. Ella's got that talent to be able to pick great chefs, and then help those chefs put together a menu that will be great for her restaurants."

TIM: "Nobody I know has brought on more important chefs than she has. But she also has the other elements of a restaurant: One is a great understanding of hospitality—where you walk in the door and you feel welcome. That's very important, and many restaurants don't get it. And the other is she creates an environment that other people enjoy being part of. Her restaurants are something of a party. At least, when she's around, you *feel* like you're having a party."

NINA: "Yeah, and she's got a real passion. Part of being really good at this is having a passion for food. It's not that you necessarily can create it yourself, but she definitely has that passion and shares it with the chefs that she's selected to work with her."

TIM: "Décor, ambiance, service and cost are all major influences in terms of your feelings about a restaurant, and she's got it all as far as I'm concerned. Her restaurants give you very, very good food, very pleasant ambiance and wonderful service. I mean, when you get it all, you're pretty happy."

jackass. If there is a letter of complaint, our rule is that it must be handled by sundown that day. There is even a sign hanging in our office: "The Sun Shall Not Set on a Guest Complaint."

So never let a situation linger and get any bigger. Apologize. Kill them with kindness. If you do that, they will come back forever. They want you to take the blame, so do it. More often than not, we did something wrong. Don't equivocate. Apologize profusely. Multiple times. I tell young people to remember this in life and in the restaurant business: apologies cost you nothing.

WE'RE CREATING DINING MEMORIES.

What passes for good service now in America, even a couple of decades into the "foodie" revolution, is an embarrassment. Maybe people don't care. "Food drop-off," as opposed to truly gracious service, is good enough for too many restaurants. I realize there are many welcome exceptions to that assessment, but on the whole I believe this country's restaurants should be much further along.

I believe that exceptional service became the number one thing that set us apart from other restaurants (and enabled us to win awards from the James Beard Foundation and other organizations). We worked very hard at it from the beginning and studied what others were doing, and now we learn from people who work for us.

Our service philosophy is simple: we are in the business of creating dining memories. Some restaurants want to be known for food, some for the volume of their business, some for their appeal to celebrities. Our goal is to balance sumptuous food with perfect, warm and professional service in a way that results in a memorable experience. Period. It's the mission that drives every decision we make.

When I saw the formality in Paris and London during my first visits, I knew immediately that that was not going to work here. People in New Orleans don't want you to join the party, but they don't want this formality either. They want to be comfortable. They want something in-between. So over the years we developed and embraced some practices to help us achieve that goal. Here's how we hope diners will view the Commander's experience, from the first phone call to the last warm good-bye at the door:

It's about enveloping the guest in warmth and professionalism at every point, beginning to end. Everything centers upon the guest being extremely well taken care of, from the bar, to the kitchen and dining room, to the front door, to maintenance. The guest gets what he or she wants, when and how he or she wants it.

It starts with the reservationist. Do the potential guests feel a smile through the phone, or do they sense an attitude that the person is doing them a favor by taking their request? We're happy you want to come, so when you hang up, you have to feel that sensation or we've blown it before you arrive. To hear how it should be done, just call and listen to our Jimmy Boudreaux say, "Well, Mr. Shapiro, you know we'll have your table for you. You're the big chief. The team will be ready."

The guest's next encounter is likely to be with the valet. Does he guide you to the door with a warm but respectful greeting? (At Commander's we still have a problem with the way the valet parkers dress; they get hot working outside, so their uniform is more casual than we would like. You can ask them to not hang on the fence and to stand up, but even that can be a challenge. It's the nature of the job, given the heat.)

Once the guests are inside, they should feel that they can relax and have fun, knowing that we are aware of what they need before they are. To achieve that goal, we train our staff to fill out "short forms," which communicate information about our guests to the entire team, so that they're prepared for the next visit. They're easy to fill out, with boxes to check off—celebration, birthday, anniversary, flowers, send extra appetizers, etc.—and a big spot to write a note: "Judith recently moved here and is a dear friend; her husband is Nat." Little notes in the computer system are not enough. We want a piece of paper that can be passed from hand to hand, so they're done in triplicate—one for the maître d', one for the kitchen and one for the Brennan On Duty. They're a tremendous tool: when a guest needs to impress someone, our greeting them with a big "Hello, Mr. Smith, we've got your table ready with your favorite wine" is much more effective than saying, "Hi, table for two?"

Once the guests are settled in, the servers do things very quietly. They remain in the dining room but stay out of the way so that they don't interrupt conversations. So much of good service happens in the moments when the guests don't

FOUR MORE ELEMENTS OF SUCCESS

Beginning in 1985 with the opening of Union Square Café in New York City, Danny Meyer emerged as one of the most successful and admired members of the hospitality profession, today overseeing restaurant ventures on three continents. He recalls the inspiration he received from studying Ella's career:

"Everybody says that this is a pretty tough business, but I'm not sure if they actually know what they mean. I think it is relentless, and I think that the stamina that it takes is remarkable . . . so to have done that as long as Ella has done it is an amazing thing.

"This business also demands a huge amount of humility, because hospitality is a humble act. It's the belief that in the service of you, I am actually going to be taking care of myself. But I have to be the guy that gives the hug first. And if I give the hug first, I trust that I am going to get it back. It takes that. So now you have got stamina and humility, and the kicker is that you have got to have really, really high standards as well. There is absolutely no way in the world that Commander's Palace would be where it is today, or where it was yesterday, or where it was ten or twenty years ago without a combination of those three essential ingredients from Ella.

"I would add a fourth one, though: a person who has made it to where Ella is today also has had . . . a little chip on their shoulder where they had to prove something to somebody. And happily, they are using these acts of hospitality as a proving ground for something even bigger than the restaurant. You make the naysayers go away by making people feel great and taking care of a community of cooks and servers, and the community of people who live nearby, and the community of people who come to break bread in your restaurant, and the community of people who live in your city. What an awesome way to deal with that."

know they're getting it. They look up, and the waiter or captain catches their eye as if to say, "I'm here if you need anything, but I don't want to disturb you needlessly." Service should appear and disappear magically at all the right times.

We still sometimes have a problem with young waiters who want to take over and recite the whole menu. One night we had a young man wait on us, and I had to remind him that we already knew the menu. But he kept right on and told us things three times. Finally, I stood up and said, "Are we in Commander's Palace?" But I do know they work really hard at it.

Another thing we started was "gang service." Guests love it. Here's how it works: A runner brings the food into the dining room. The waiters stay in the dining room, where they belong, and everybody who's available comes over and makes sure that everyone is served at the same time. (That way you avoid having just one person saying, "OK, who got the salmon?") The person who leads the service at that table directs those who have come over to assist. The other waiters help get the food on the table and then they go away. We get a tremendous number of parties of six or eight because people in New Orleans go out to dinner for conversation and family celebrations, and the gang service approach helps to avoid interruptions in the dialogue.

Of course, the food has to be prepared to come to the table at the right time. If it comes too early, it should be sent back and redone without the guest's knowledge. And shame on that captain and manager for not being aware if a dish needs to be put on hold. This requires good communication, trust and respect between the kitchen and the dining room.

When it comes to wine, guests should feel confident that they can get as much or as little help as they need. If they say, "Bring me a lovely bottle of pinot noir," they should trust that we'll do that and not break the bank.

Ti likes to say that when service is done well, it transports our guests to "an oasis in a turbulent world." I like that, but there should be a bit of showmanship too: rushing to the table to pull out a woman's chair when she returns from the ladies room and then handing her a neatly folded napkin, or making eye contact with the host to see if it's a good time to clear the plates or if another bottle of wine is needed. Body language is so important; it can convey deference and professionalism—or a tired and disinterested attitude.

One of the best practitioners of this was George Rico, who became our maître d' at Commander's after starting as busboy. I never saw anyone so graceful. He could move between tables with an appropriate urgency, but his movements were ballet-like, not athletic or jerky. I used to like just watching him move, with his eyes darting around to make sure every detail was just right.

Soon, he became the best maître d' in New Orleans—ever. He was focused on one thing: making our guests feel like "Big Shots." Where else do you get that in life? I think there is an entire generation that has missed out on that experience. But I never met anyone who didn't like it. It's a gesture of respect, but done with flair and style. I always joke that George spoke Honduran with a Chinese accent—half the time you had no idea what he was saying. But he did it with grand gestures—big, big smiles of recognition, a firm handshake with an arm on the shoulder—saying, "Hey! The Big Chief is here!" or "Mr. So-and-So's in the house!" If he knew you well, he'd give you a quick, manly hug, but with eye contact.

With female guests it was always, "Hello, pretty lady." I never met a woman who didn't like that. I asked George once why he often used the man's name but seldom the woman's. He told me that one time he'd said the name of the man's girlfriend, not his wife, who was accompanying him that evening—so that didn't go well. And when a lady would arrive at the door apologizing for being late for her reservation, he'd invariably say, "A pretty lady's never late at the Palace." Or sometimes, "Oh, please, take your time. We've got nowhere to go and all night to get there." Everyone within earshot would smile and relax.

George was a key part of the Commander's experience for more than forty years. He took great joy in making you feel important and very, very welcome. It's a rare gift. Often we see young people who attempt to work in the front of the house fail because they have so many hang-ups and aren't expressive. They're too worried about embarrassing themselves—too reserved, no eye contact, stiff body language. That won't do. We don't need a shy little girl at the door who waits for you to speak or who says, "Can I help you?" Ugh! No. No. No. We want an over-the-top welcome: "Welcome to Commander's. How are you all tonight?"

"We're great. We have a reservation, Shriver at eight, but we are a little late."

"You're never late at the Palace, Mr. Shriver. It's good to see you again. Your guests are already here; we'll show you and the pretty lady right in."

Why not? Who wouldn't like that welcome? It's fun, and it lets our guests know we're on their side and that we're not going to make them feel bad if they're late. What's the point of that?

And all of this is done with big gestures, lots of eye contact. Nothing meek.

Toward the end of the meal, we know that a huge percentage of our guests will order dessert, and we like to make it a bit of a show. Many of them order the bread pudding soufflé in advance, when we take the meal order, and when it is paraded to the table, heads turn throughout the restaurant. Other guests will go for one of the flaming dishes, which we execute with flair and precision: Café Brulot, Café Pierre or Bananas Foster.

The end of the meal is equally important. For our style of service, the check should never be presented until the guest has given some indication that he or she is ready. Like the rest of the service, the timing should be about what is convenient for the guest, not the service team. That means the server has to stay nearby so the guest can catch his eye. We also have food runners to bring dishes from the kitchen and a front waiter and a back waiter to assist the captain, along with a manager in every room.

The overall idea is that our guests should feel when they are leaving that they have been graciously received and that their service was personalized in some fashion. Did the BOD come by? Did the manager send them a trouble tree (cocktail samples served in tiny glasses perched in a metal tree)? Did the band sing a special song at brunch? Did they get a tour of the wine cellar and garden? Did we paint "Congratulations on your new job, Helen" in chocolate on a dessert plate? And on and on.

As the guests get up to leave and head for the door, we give them a big goodbye and ask how the meal was. They should feel thanked by multiple people as they leave. And they should never *ever* feel rushed. In any way.

We *are* glad they came, and we try hard to convey that.

Finally, we never, ever, ever put out the garbage until after the restaurant is empty. The garbage room is refrigerated so no neighbor has to walk by a smelly dumpster or garbage room. The garbage is picked up by appointment, so it is never sitting out on the street. Community relations are just as important as guest relations.

EARN EACH OTHER'S TRUST AND RESPECT.

When I worked at the Vieux Carré after WWII, we used to say that we had to tell a few of our employees to wear shoes when they came to work, but even before that we had to say, "No, wash your feet before you put on your shoes." Perhaps that sounds demeaning today, but it truly reflected the caliber of some of the people who would show up at our door to ask for a job. We asked one guy how long it took him to drive home after his shift and he replied, "Three beers." When I would complain about this, Owen would say to me, "Teach, teach, teach, don't train, train, train, because they're not animals."

I had no professional training myself, but I was well schooled in the common-sense lessons my family taught me growing up, so I set out to apply them when I got to hire people. Eventually I learned that you deal with one person at a time, and you relate to that person as a human being. I would tell every new employee: "I am trying to earn your trust and respect. I want this to be a great restaurant, and I want you to be a very important part of it for a long time." I would say that to the cooks, to the dishwashers, to all the employees.

That's the attitude we try to instill in our people. That sense of professional satisfaction from someone on our team, in whatever position, makes me as happy as a compliment paid directly by a super-pleased guest.

Later, when others assumed the hiring duties, I still made it a point of knowing the dish and pot washers, and I would visit with them. They were part of the business, part of the team. Washing dishes didn't mean they were down at the bottom; it was a very important part of the whole operation. And we have taken many folks from washing pots and made them cooks—only because we got to know and like them. We'd start giving them every chore in the kitchen that they were capable of doing and watch them grow from there.

Today, the quality of the people we can hire in the restaurant business is extraordinary, top to bottom, compared to what it was. It used to be that nobody wanted their sons, and certainly not their daughters, to be cooks or waiters.

WHAT IS YOUR BUSINESS'S SIMPLE TRUTH?

Spurred on by his mother's fascination with business principles, Alex explored the psychology of his customers at Brennan's of Houston to try and understand why they did—or did not—return:

"There was a period in the 1980s, when I was in Houston, that some of the first truly rock star business books began to be published. *Thriving on Chaos* was one in particular that dealt with the culture of business. Mom read every one of those books she could get her hands on and would buy multiple copies and hand them out to everyone. I just got absorbed in it and was really trying to understand the culture of our business.

"But I'll never forget being asked one day, 'Well, there are a lot of other great places in Houston, so why do people choose to come to your restaurant?' And I had one of those moments where I just started spewing out stock phrases, like 'best in class' and 'personal service'—I didn't have my elevator speech that would answer why customers chose to come to our restaurant. It seemed to be a pretty important thing, and I spent a lot of time talking it over with Mom and Ti and other members of our family. We also did some customer surveys and elicited the help of a business consultant friend of mine.

"It really turns out that people don't come to our restaurants to feed themselves. They don't necessarily come just to be well served. They don't come necessarily just for unique and wonderful ambiance. True, you'd better be world class in all three, but there is something beyond that. And it turns out that people will talk a lot about memories—'I remember we got engaged here,' or 'I remember we closed the biggest business deal of my life here,' and so on. So it dawned on me that the reason why people were coming back was that we were creating great memories for them. And that became a concept that I called 'Our Simple Truth.' I wrote a book about it, *The Simple Truth About Your Business,* and it was very well accepted, with three printings. The thought had never occurred to me that people would say, 'I liked your book, would you come talk to us about our business? But they did, and I did, and it's worked out very well."

But now, we have young men and women who are maybe putting themselves through school or who have tried school and want to do something they're passionate about.

The first thing we look for when hiring for the front of the house and for managers is people who take care with their personal appearance. Then, they must have a personality. You can't have folks who don't speak up, who are retiring. They have to be alive! They have to display at least some knowledge of the field, be it food, wine or views on dining. During the first interview, I'd find out where they'd worked before, what they expected of Commander's, and why they wanted to work with us. Then I'd say, "Well, I hope we'll have a long relationship. We're going to try to get you to learn while you're here so that you can grow. So that if you leave here, you can leave with more than you came with. We're going to give you back as much as you're going to give us."

When it finally came time for someone to leave, they would come and tell us that they were moving on. That comes out of developing trust and respect for each other from the moment they're hired. In the old days, they'd just not show up and that was the end of it.

As Commander's began to get recognized, we started to get people who wanted to come to work with us. Culinary schools would sometimes steer their students our way—that's how we got Jamie Shannon and our current chef, Tory McPhail—and others would seek us out because of the training we provided. The result is that our talent pool today is as strong as it's ever been.

BLEND RIGHT IN.

Sometimes, if you're lucky, people come to you fully polished, with skills that are immediately recognizable. They quickly grasp what we are trying to achieve and soon blossom as leaders. That was the case with Steve Woodruff, who's been with us more than twenty-five years. I think his title is Operations Manager. I just tell people he runs the place—and a couple others too. We're not much on titles in our organization. Looking back, I think that may have been a mistake, because a title can be a source of pride and identity for some people. I never had or wanted a title, so I didn't understand why anybody else wanted one. My role was pretty clear regardless of what my title was. We always liked "proprietor" if someone insisted on a title, instead of owner or president or what have you. It evoked the role of the restaurateur and the fact that you were there and not an absentee owner.

Anyway, when I hired Steve to replace our purchaser, I could see how bright he was after working with him just a short time. So I told him, "I want you to take my job." I knew he thought I was nuts or full of bull, or both. He'll tell you now that I meant it. But Steve had done his training with the Steak and Ale chain during the era of its founder, the great Norman Brinker. Norman's ranks were filled with smart, ambitious young executives who went on to launch restaurant concepts, from Chili's to Macaroni Grill and on and on. Steve liked mentoring young managers, but he also liked numbers. Steve says once you get used to the financials (which, Lord knows, are not complicated), the "numbers start talking to you." He means it's easy to see where your problems are and your opportunities. Then it's fun to lay that out and set those goals. Get the team focused on a goal and let them watch the results. Show them the numbers. You cannot teach them if they don't know the numbers.

Our company is focused on one number more than any other: the guest count. How many people came into each restaurant each shift? Do not talk to me about weekly sales. That matters, of course, but you can diagnose the patient best by that guest count. You can inflate sales by increasing your check average and get a false sense of security. Guest count never changes. I can compare Commander's in 2015 with Brennan's in 1958. And I do. Ti has a handwritten chart I wrote on the back of a file folder with the monthly and annual counts going back many years. If I ask a manager the guest count for yesterday or last month or last year and they don't know it, then I know they aren't taking their job seriously yet. Let's just say they will be aware of my displeasure, even if no words are spoken on the subject.

I have seen too many restaurants (and other types of businesses) where the people at the door or on the phone and even in management don't seem to care how many guests come in. They'd just as soon tell you "No, we're booked" than try to find a way to get you in. Here's the culture we want: "Wow! Great day! We did more than we projected and operations were smooth, guests were leaving happy . . ." Our projected numbers are posted for all to see (internally, that is; I've never talked to guests about our numbers). But having that team goal—"Hey, what are we going to do tonight?"—then going into the kitchen and saluting the team with "Way to go, ladies and gentlemen. Great night"—that's our touchdown. High fives, fist bumps (my granddaughter Lexie just taught me that) and smiles all around. That breeds a group of people striving to accomplish goals. But everyone knows numbers will never be more important than the food and the service. Those underlie everything we do.

So, these are things Steve came to understand. He brought some systems and smarts that we incorporated. And he keeps developing them. He has our reservations down to a science. Steve saw how our family worked as a team alongside the chef and the financial officer, and he now works on that key team with Ti, Lally, Tory and front of the house manager Don Strunk. They have been a solid team at the top of our New Orleans restaurants since 1997. We like to paraphrase the definition of leadership from Jack Welch, the former longtime head of General Electric: "'a constant interactive process aimed at consensus'; failing consensus, leaders must lead." That's it. That's how we do it. This team is so in sync and has such respect for each other that there just isn't tension. Differing points of view where they occasionally agree to disagree respectfully, perhaps, but that's OK. Their talents are complementary. Tory handles the kitchen with lots of input from Ti, me and everyone else. Don handles the front of the house with similar input. And what a job he does. We love that Don often says, "There are no obstacles to excellence at Commander's." Lally makes everything look beautiful and is magical with the guests and the team, Ti handles numbers with our magnificent CFO (and good-time gal) Arlene Nesser, and Steve handles "operations."

Ti likes to say, "There is no air between them." By that she means team members can't play them against each other, because the respect—even love—between the members of this team is so strong. They always have each other's backs. This has led to an amazing culture at Commander's that is at the core of our success. Strong united leadership. Nothing can replace that.

If you assemble the right team and invest the effort to teach them, it makes for a rewarding place to work. You lay down the ground rules, and if they don't want to follow them, they leave. It's absolutely amazing. When you treat people decently, they act decently. I like to walk into the kitchen in the morning and say, "Good morning, ladies and gentlemen." You can literally see them stand up a little taller.

The most important thing is to have the team—kitchen and dining room—understand that they have to work together. The job of a restaurateur is to make sure they *want* to work together.

RINGING BELLS AND WHISTLES— CELEBRATE WINS AND KEEP IT CONSISTENT.

My role—and I've passed this along to Ti and Lally at Commander's—was to encourage and celebrate the culture of hospitality we'd instilled, to boost the restaurant's esprit de corps. If I showed enthusiasm, an emotion I value above most others, the team and the restaurant were enriched. I rewarded team members verbally for their winning moments, and I did so in front of whomever happened to be around. To yield to distractions and miss out on these opportunities was like throwing out a sack of oysters before they'd been opened and eaten. Praise—sincere and prompted by genuine delight—is how we built toward truly gracious hospitality. It's a circular process: compliments inspire the staff to ever more thoughtful service, which in turn inspires more compliments. Without investing the energy in praise, entropy takes over and the hospitality wheel slowly grinds to a halt.

Celebrating every "win" is a part of our system. It's a must. Call it "ringing bells and whistles." Bells and whistles can go off for a good thing or a bad thing. The point is to create a memory and not miss the opportunity to celebrate one of life's grand little moments or to make an impression on someone you need to hold accountable. And that holds true even—and especially!—when the restaurant is hectic with business and you're so caught up in preparing for a shift (or recovering from one) that you're tempted to let the moment pass unnoted.

We still give out awards at our "summit suppers" and company picnics. We share great service stories and guest letters in our training sessions and post them on our bulletin boards. Nothing magical—you just have to do it. And never stop. Again inspired by Jack Welch, we refer to this as making "a fanatical commitment to the consistent execution of the fundamentals." Love that saying. So we developed an award for employees with that standard in mind: the Fanatical Commitment to the Consistent Execution of the Fundamentals Award. We love to say it real fast.

Today, Commander's Palace has about 200 employees, approximately the same number as when I stepped away from daily management in 2004. Getting a steady, strong performance out of large groups is always an epic challenge, so we have developed systems to make it easier to execute consistently. But they must be rigorously upheld. Otherwise, performance will begin to decline at the system level, just as it can at the personal level. And before you know it, managers aren't attending pre-meal meetings, thus missing their chance to communicate and motivate.

At Commander's, we are willing to change anything, but team members have to justify that their new way is better. One time we discovered that someone changed our coffee recipe, basically on a whim and without a clear justification. So we reverted back to the original formula. Changing something because it's easier/faster/cheaper isn't good enough. The new way has to represent a marked improvement and be agreed upon by the team.

RUN AHEAD OF ME OR BESIDE ME— I WILL NOT PULL YOU UP THE HILL!

Hurricane Ella.

Oh, yes, I'm well aware of what the folks I've worked with have called me over the decades, usually behind my back and with their eyes rolling. I've earned the title, damn it, and wear it proudly!

It probably started when I was thrust into my career at the Vieux Carré. I'd get up in the morning and start getting dressed, and my mom would immediately start telling me about everything that was going on in the restaurant. (She had great sources.) So by the time I burst through the door of the restaurant, my

A LEADER MUST BE HEAD CHEERLEADER
AS WELL AS HEAD SHERIFF

Ti illustrates how the system works with a few stories about her mother and some other folks:

One day while working with my adored cousin Dickie Brennan at Commander's, I asked him how his weekend had been. He looked at me with a big grin and said, "Well, I decided to pop the question."

"Oh my God, did she say yes? How'd you ask her? When? (Hugs, kisses.) I've got to call Mom."

"No, no, no—don't do that!"

"Why not?"

"'Cause we won't get anything else done today. You know how she is. She'll break out the champagne and on and on, and we have so much we need to do."

At the time, Dickie and our cousin Brad and I were working to open Palace Café, on Canal Street, a major new downtown restaurant. Well, we called Mom anyway and she did exactly what Dickie predicted, which, of course, was as it should be. She celebrates accomplishments at work, but when a big moment in our family's life occurs, she goes through the roof with love and congratulations.

Then it's right back to work!

Mind you, work doesn't have to mean drudgery, least of all when it comes to building staff morale. A touch of outrageousness never hurts. Our current chef, Tory McPhail, may be a star, but he doesn't miss a chance to knock himself down a few pegs. He showed up at our company picnic one time in the ugliest yellow shorts (they drooped to mid-calf) plus a silly T-shirt and hat and carrying a toy car shaped like a hot dog. Apparently a certain meat company had offered him a chunk of change to represent them. Tory turned down that offer, but meanwhile they had sent him every logoed item on the shelf. He was a sight. And even though he had a cold and a hoarse voice (whether from too much work, a hunting trip, or a most eligible bachelor's nighttime carousing, I'm never sure), he was prepared with an arsenal of corny hot dog jokes. ("Let's be frank . . .")

The very same week, our CFO, Arlene Nesser, had coaxed our front of house manager, Don Strunk, and maintenance chief, Ted Oggs, into wearing drag outfits to support the skit her team developed to boost 401(k) participation. Their performances are now legend. I personally will never be able to look at the ordinarily imperious Strunk without remembering him in old-lady drag, lamenting his need to eat cat food since he forgot to set up a 401(k) account before retiring.

"If only I'd known!" he keened in a falsetto that threatened to shatter stemware. It brought down the house.

The sign-up was a big win. I had no clue any of this was happening until I walked into the room. It demonstrated to me that our culture of creativity and camaraderie had spread throughout the business without my taking charge. Bingo! The culture takes on a life of its own.

Not that we don't do our part! Not so long ago, Lally and I were dressed up as cheerleaders to kick off a series of staff seminars called Aqua Blue U, so named in honor of the restaurant's exterior hue. We sported outfits with "CP" emblazoned on the chest, pom-poms, wigs and go-go boots— all colored aqua blue. I guess the takeaway is that staff members get a kick out of seeing "authority figures" drop the sternness and intensity of their daily workplace persona and make fun of themselves.

mind had already arrived and was on fast-forward. One day somebody said, "You know, Ella, you never say 'good morning' to anyone." Well, it's not that I meant to ignore people; it's just that I had already said "good morning" two hours earlier to somebody else, so I was done with that and was on to the next thing. But I did need to be reminded to be more pleasant and to give that sincere greeting and ask people how they were doing, even if my mind was racing with all that lay ahead that day.

As a restaurateur, I always seemed to be dealing with a dozen details and a few big plans all at once, so if you combine that with a constant desire to push everyone to do their best—and a certain natural impatience, I suppose—I can see where a nickname might develop.

Eman Loubier, who was a fine but sometimes wild-child sous chef for us at Commander's under Emeril, says that he was "intimidated as hell" by the sight of me and Dottie sitting on those stools in the kitchen. He felt like we were constantly checking up on him. Heck, I was just having fun watching all of the action. It was like a ballet, the best part of my day. And if I made a few suggestions, they weren't out of anger. I got over being angry with people a long time ago—it's a big waste of time and energy. If I were to go into the kitchen now, I might just say, "Goddammit, the floor is wet!" and leave it to someone to take care of. (The floor *always* seems to be wet, by the way. I think Tory took the mop with him on his trip to Australia and forgot to return it.)

Alex, who worked at our restaurants from a very young age, says one of the most important lessons he learned from watching me was how I dealt with people who weren't giving their best. He recalls countless times when I would confront a slacker and deliver my mini-sermon: "If I am working this hard, why won't you? We are all running up the hill in this business, and we are all running up a hill together. You know I will run alongside of you, but I will be damned if I have to pull you up the hill." Eventually, if you say it enough times, you'll find that your team is accomplishing more than they ever thought they could.

Having said that, I'm also keenly aware that the restaurateur and the chef must set a professional tone for the operation. We don't allow excessive screaming and yelling in the kitchen or anywhere else. That's no fun for anyone. During lunch service one day at Commander's, Emeril just blew up. He was causing a commotion that wasn't good for the restaurant, it wasn't good for anybody. So I took a manila file folder and proceeded to make a sign in print large enough for him to see from where he was working on the line: "You're too goddam smart to be so goddam stupid!" He read it and pulled himself together. It was amazing. I guess he had just had it up to here and things weren't going the way they needed to go, so he was upset. But our approach has always been "ladies and gentlemen serving ladies and gentlemen." Emeril understood that, and we never saw that kind of outburst again. (Or if we did, it's forgotten now!)

When things do get out of hand, a restaurateur has to practice conflict resolution. I picked this up from Owen. He told me that if you have two employees who are at odds, you say, "OK, let's all go out to the patio." And we'd sit there, and I would say, "May I get you something to drink? Would you like a Coke? Coffee?" I'd bring it out to them and say, "OK, let's talk." If they started going after each other, then I'd say to one of them, "Stop! Do you hate him? 'Cause you sure sound like it. Why do you hate him?"

"Well, I don't hate him, but he did this and he did that . . ."

I'd let them talk it out, one at a time, and then remind them that it's just all in a day's work. "Tempers get short, but you have to keep all of the guests and your coworkers happy, so let's calm down and enjoy it and make sure we understand that each of us can have a bad day. Now, do either of you want to leave, or go home and relax, or sit under a tree in the park for a bit—or do you want to go back to work?"

And ninety-nine percent of the time they'd say, "Let's go back to work."

STAND UP AND BE COUNTED. OR JUST MAKE SOMETHING HAPPEN.

There are times when you just have to stand up and do something.

How do you know when to stop what you're doing, stand up, and take a stand on something? In your business, in your city, in your industry? You know in your gut. Just listen to it. You're supposed to be *everything* you're capable of. You can't be lazy or selfish. Get in there. Stand up and be counted. Go over, under or around. Just make something happen. For the betterment of all. We used to call it the common good. I still believe in it . . . deeply.

Perhaps my first lesson in this came when I was a young woman working in the French Quarter. It seemed as though every summer one of those horses that pulled tourist-filled carriages would drop dead from the heat. It was awful. Some summers several horses would die. You just assumed that someone who cared for the horses, or the city, would do something. But they didn't. So finally my dear friend Marilyn Barnett and I set out to rectify the situation. I like a beautiful horse pulling a carriage through the French Quarter as much as the next gal, but not if it's cruel to the animal. And believe me, the heat and humidity of a typical New Orleans summer can be cruel to both animals and humans.

Well, it turns out mules can handle the heat much better than horses, and one of their biggest needs is access to water. So we persuaded the powers that be to have the carriage trade shift from horses to mules, and we pushed to have troughs of water positioned here and there throughout the Quarter. We got with the city and we got the rules changed. So if you prefer horses to mules, blame Marilyn and me. But there are no more dead horses.

Years later I got involved in another sticky issue that I felt threatened the city's well-being. I was against gambling/gaming coming to New Orleans. Do you know that gambling is still against the constitution in Louisiana? So the politicians legalized "gaming" instead. That is just the type of shenanigan I knew would ensue.

I had been through this before. Back in the 1950s, gambling was outlawed except in certain parts of the city, mostly on the outskirts of town. Trust me, this was not good. I knew that if we tried this again, there would be trouble just like before. I knew there would be corruption and that that corruption would hold our city back. We needed to operate in a more businesslike way and push forward in developing our port, our medical industry and adding value to the natural resources we have, etc. What we didn't need to do was take the easy money and become a one-industry town. Our hospitality industry is strong, but it and the whole city and region are better off when the economy is more diverse. What we didn't need to do was trust our governor that this process would be fair and pristine. What we didn't need to do was believe a bunch of pied pipers saying that one casino across from the French Quarter would generate 60,000 jobs. That's what they said.

But as if all that wasn't enough, there was something else that worried me to my core. I love the people of New Orleans. I do! But I thought this sent all the wrong messages. I believe that you can and should enjoy life fully, but you can't let it get out of balance. The parties are more fun if you've been fully engaged and working hard. Possessions, which I don't personally put much stock in, mean something if you've worked hard for them. But because I know our people,

I thought encouraging gambling was sending entirely the wrong message. It's trying to get something for nothing. Trying to "luck out." I am of the school that the harder you work, the luckier you get. Gambling doesn't jibe with that. I had visions of our people taking their paycheck straight to the casino and blowing it. Call me matriarchal, call me Big Brother, I don't care. I just hoped for better.

I got involved in the campaign to keep gambling, and specifically the proposed casino, out of New Orleans, but we lost. Well, the governor pushing the initiative went to jail, there were corruption scandals left and right, and the casino in New Orleans employs around 2,500 people. Though the issue still irks me on some level, I can sleep at night knowing that my colleagues and I stood up for what we believed was best for our city.

KEEP IT UP, KEEP IT UP, KEEP IT UP— IT'S ALL ABOUT KEEPING YOUR STANDARDS UP.

With all of these things, it's the day-in, day-out execution that matters. That's how you separate the men from the boys. Anybody can do these things for a few months, or even a few years. But try forty, fifty, sixty years. If you're going to be in the restaurant business, you have to ask yourself: Can you keep your staff motivated with one more speech about a great service experience? Can you write one more heartfelt letter to a guest disappointed that he didn't get a window table? Can you quietly ask one more waiter why he served from the wrong side? Can you tell one more manager why it matters that his shoes aren't shined? Can you explain to one more cook why veal stock, not beef stock, is critical in a certain sauce? Can you tell one more reservationist that he or she needs to find a way to get our locals in when they want to come?

Can you?

Can you do it again? And again? And again? Can you muster the stick-to-itiveness, effort and energy? And enjoy yourself all the while?

If so, you might have what it takes to run a restaurant.

We have a saying posted in the restaurant that speaks to this: "Nothing in the world can take the place of persistence. Talent will not; nothing is more common than unsuccessful men with talent. Genius will not; unrewarded genius is almost a proverb. Education alone will not; the world is full of educated dere-licts. Persistence and determination alone are omnipotent."

A FINAL THOUGHT ON "LEGACY"

If you want to see what I'm most proud of in my career, just come to Commander's and watch Ti, my niece Lally or my nephew Brad in action as one of the BODs. Or go to Houston and check out what Alex is doing at Brennan's. Come see how my nephew Ralph and his children, Katherine and Patrick, have given new life to Brennan's in the French Quarter. Visit one of the fine places run by my nephew Dickie, his sister Lauren and my niece Cindy. They're their own people, each with their own style and way of doing things, but they're family, and I hope only the good things rubbed off on them. I am very, very proud of them all.

ABOVE, LEFT: *Lynne Brennan, Dottie Brennan, Alex Brennan-Martin, Ella Brennan, and John Brennan.* ABOVE, RIGHT: *Adelaide Brennan.* BELOW, LEFT: *Julia Child, Eugenie Vasser, JoAnn Clevenger, and Ella Brennan in a second line.* BELOW, UPPER RIGHT: *Ella, Adelaide, and Dottie.* BELOW, LOWER RIGHT: *Ella and Adelaide talking with a friend.*

ABOVE, LEFT: *Lindy Boggs and Ella Brennan in the Garden Room at Commander's Palace.*
ABOVE, RIGHT: *Emeril Lagasse and Ella with the Celebration Dessert.* BELOW: *Brennan family in Vail, Colorado, mid-1980s.*

ABOVE, LEFT: *Adelaide and Ella on the porch of the house on Prytania Street (photo courtesy of Roddy McDowall).* TOP, RIGHT: *Dottie Brennan, Ti Adelaide Martin, Ella Brennan, Tory McPhail and Emeril Lagasse at the Chef's Table in Commander's Palace.* ABOVE, RIGHT: *Adelaide, Ella, and Alex Brennan-Martin.* BELOW: *Front of Commander's Palace after Hurricane Katrina.*

10

Lighting a Fire: Emeril Lagasse, Jamie Shannon and the Commander's Palace Classroom (1983-2001)

"SHE IS EXTREMELY DEMANDING, BUT NOT HARD TO WORK FOR. YOU HAVE TO BE ELLA BRENNAN TO BE BOTH."

—EMERIL LAGASSE TO THE *TIMES-PICAYUNE*

We knew Paul was going to leave Commander's sometime in 1982 to join his wife, K, at their K-Paul's Louisiana Kitchen restaurant and further develop his career. Though we often had spirited discussions about the Commander's menu, we had a warm relationship and parted on very good terms, with Paul offering to help out until we found a replacement.

But where would we find the next Paul Prudhomme, someone who could take charge of the kitchen and execute the ideas we had for the restaurant? There wasn't anyone on the team we felt we could promote, so we hired one or two chefs from the outside who proved to be OK but still didn't have all of the qualities we were looking for. Eventually we called in a recruiter, and he sent us a couple of people whom we interviewed, but nothing clicked.

Then he sent me the résumé of someone named Emeril Lagasse, a kid from Massachusetts who had gone to Johnson & Wales culinary school in Providence,

Rhode Island, which wasn't that well known at the time. I scanned it and said, "I don't want to hire this boy—he's twenty-three years old!" He was cooking at some place on Cape Cod, Massachusetts, and he had cooked at a businessman's hotel in New York, so I decided to reject him right then because I didn't want to bring him down to New Orleans and then reject him.

But this recruiter stayed on my back, and a recommendation came from Larry Forgione of An American Place, whom I respect very much. (Years later I would send Dickie to work for Larry in New York.) So I finally gave in and said, "OK, I'll bring him in, but I'm telling you right now I don't think it's going to work."

In the two months leading up to his visit, Emeril and I began calling each other about once a week, just to chat about his views on cooking and his outlook on life. In high school he had been a musician with a scholarship to the prestigious New England Conservatory of Music, but he had switched to a culinary path, which I found intriguing.

Emeril recalls that I picked his brain relentlessly during those talks: "OK, so tell me what you have been cooking the past week. And why. And what ingredients you've been using. And why." Or, "Tell me your philosophy about getting people excited about food." Then we'd talk about service and wine: "Do you like wine? What wine do you like? How do you study for wine?"

I really, really wanted to know what this young man might bring to the table before we met him.

Finally, Emeril arrived in New Orleans around dusk on a Sunday. The airline had lost his luggage, so he looked a bit discombobulated when he emerged from the cab in front of Commander's. I had just walked some guests outside to say goodbye, and when I spotted him I said, "You must be Emeril Lagasse." He replied, "I *know* you're Ella Brennan."

"Well, come on in."

We sent our maître d', George Rico, to get him some toiletries, and then I invited Emeril into the kitchen and asked him what he thought of all the great aromas wafting about.

"Well, it kind of smells like my mom's kitchen."

What a perfect answer! And completely sincere. That's when I began to suspect we might have someone special.

On Monday Dick and I sat down and visited with Emeril and his wife, Elizabeth. We got somebody to drive them around the city so they could see what it looked like. He came back and we talked some more, and then we asked him to make something in the kitchen. I don't remember what he made, probably an omelet with something else, but it was very good. Dick got up from the table and called me over: "I think he looks pretty good." I replied, "I'm shocked, but I agree."

Here was the key: I could tell more from our conversations with Emeril than from what he cooked. You look in a man's face and you can tell an awful lot. There are a few questions you have to ask anyone you want to hire: What made you want to be a chef? Can you cook in this environment? How do you feel about restaurants and what's going on in the business? How do you feel about cooking in a Creole restaurant all the way down in New Orleans? Emeril's answers were honest. He interacted with us very well, and there was a strong attraction on his part to becoming a chef.

Emeril went back to Massachusetts. We called him a few days later and made him an offer, which he accepted right away. But it took us an eternity to get him to Commander's. If I remember correctly, he and his wife were expecting a baby, they had to sell a house in Massachusetts and buy a house in New Orleans, and it would be a month before he could start.

While we waited, I got a phone call from a guy I knew of but didn't know well, and he said, "I understand you hired that Lagasse guy."

"Yeah, what about it?"

"Well, you know he can't cook."

"What the hell are you talking about he can't cook?"

"No, he's full of personality but he can't cook."

That shook me up, so I got rid of that guy on the phone and went to Dick and told him what I'd heard, and he just said, "Oh, God. What are we going to do? Stop it?"

We decided, OK, you worry today and I'll worry tomorrow, because we've got a business to run in the meantime.

Soon after, Emeril came down and he quickly put our fears to rest. (Many years later I had a rather straightforward chat with the gentleman who had called and made us so nervous. Clearly he was just trying to hang onto an employee, but when he had the nerve to walk into Commander's one day . . . well, let's just say he had a greater understanding of what I thought of him after our chat.)

Emeril was a fast and eager learner, and it became clear that the kitchen staff would respond to his budding leadership skills. And yet he was very unworldly. He knew what he had learned in school and a little of what he had learned on the job, but he didn't know anything about Creole cooking or New Orleans. We had to get that into his head. We sent him to every restaurant in town, and I sat with him by the hour. I fed him books and newspapers: "Start reading! Start reading! Start reading! Make friends in the industry!" And he was like a sponge.

After he got going, Dick and I were in a position to introduce him to some of the nation's food writers. Food was becoming a big story in newspapers and magazines in a way it hadn't ever been. We wanted the rest of the country to know more about New Orleans, Emeril, the restaurant and what was going on down here. Writers would periodically check in on the telephone or come visit, keeping alive connections that had started with my brother Owen and were carried on by Paul. We suggested to Emeril that he maintain those relationships, so he'd talk to colleagues and writers every Saturday morning to find out what was going on in the food world and then suggest that New Orleans would like to be a part of whatever was happening on the American dining scene. He didn't have to say much. They got the message. And that's how Emeril became well known in this emerging foodie world.

Ti recalls a story from this era that involved Commander's being named to *Playboy* magazine's annual Best Restaurants in America list. Once I got word that we'd been included, I got excited because, as we all know, *Playboy* really did have good writers and good stories amongst the girly photo features. Well, I wanted that list, but I was not about to go into our local K&B drugstore and ask for a bunch of *Playboys*. Wasn't going to do it. I went looking for Alex, but he was nowhere to be found. There were no cell phones in those days, and I am not known for my patience. I finally tracked down Ti (who would have been in her late teens or very early twenties), gave her cash, and explained why she had to go right away and buy me as many *Playboys* as she could. They were still kept behind the counter at that time.

"Mom, *really?*" was her reaction to my directive. She was none too thrilled, but honestly, I figured it would be another one of those crazy things in life that would teach her to get past her fear of what other people think—what I call hang-ups.

She complied, and there we were on the list, with K-Paul's and Lutèce and a bunch of other great places. And Ti apparently recovered from her trauma.

Dick kept the restaurant going while I did what I had to do with Emeril or Paul or, later, Jamie Shannon, be it arranging for them to cook at a charity event or give a cooking demonstration on a TV show. It used to be that chefs weren't really out in front of the public, but we pushed them out there and put them in a position to learn. I had Emeril reading every major newspaper food page in the country, and the business pages, along with *Forbes* and *Fortune*. I felt he had to understand where his customers were coming from and be able to talk about whatever was happening today.

As we know, it worked very well. And could he cook! Emeril furthered the evolution of Haute Creole cuisine and expanded on what Paul had been doing with Cajun, but he also brought his French-Canadian/Portuguese heritage—and his own insatiable curiosity—to bear on the menu.

Emeril was eager to try new things, and so were we. One of my favorite sayings is, "If it ain't broke, fix it anyway." We want to continue to evolve, but we had to be careful because we didn't want our guests to be guinea pigs. Proposed dishes had to be thought out and thought out and thought out, and then tested on my siblings and me, long before they ever came out of the kitchen.

We were happy to have him tweak some of the signature dishes, but we made him prove himself before we were comfortable introducing something as "an Emeril Lagasse dish." But when those dishes worked—wow! That's how we got Veal Chop Tchoupitoulas, stuffed quail, rack of lamb with Creole mustard crust, and on and on. Eventually, he wanted to try adding elements of other cuisines to our Haute Creole base. Many different cultures were represented in New Orleans, he reasoned, so why not reflect some of their flavors on our menu?

I was fine with that and encouraged him, but again, he had to make a convincing argument. I told him that to understand the food, you have to understand the culture. And if you understand the culture, then you will understand the people. And by understanding them, you will understand the food. We encouraged him to travel and develop contacts, not just with people at the world's top restaurants, but also with the farmers and fishermen and food producers in our backyard of Louisiana. That way, if he came to us with an idea to do something Asian inspired, we could make sure that it was justified and that he had done his homework. "What do you know about Asian ingredients or Greek ingredients (or whatever)?" I'd ask. "Where does this fit in with our history and culture, and where did the dish come from? Why does this dish make sense?" With each series of discussions we'd both learn something, and the menu would slowly evolve in a thoughtful but exciting direction. That's how we became a team.

Of course, one of the most important things about changing a menu is to give the cooks a challenge to do something exciting and different instead of repeating, repeating, repeating. To do that, you have to get a general feeling of what the public wants, what they are looking for, what's becoming popular, what's appropriate for the season. But every now and then you've got to say "Strawberry time!" And you do the strawberry shortcake, which this town is nuts for. And a few weeks later you have a new olive oil, so you take it out in the dining room and show it around. You tell people this is a new one—you can try it on the salad today and see if you like it. Or, you have some fun with the soft-shell crabs. We had a couple that would catch them for us. They'd load them on a Greyhound bus to the New Orleans station, where they would be put in a taxicab and driven to the restaurant. The most fun thing to do was to have a cook get the crabs out of the cab and then go into the dining room and say, "Look! They just came in by taxi!" before giving them to the kitchen. Little things like that immediately made the customer feel really good.

Emeril fit in beautifully. He was one of those guys who understood that running a kitchen or a restaurant was about far more than food. And did he work! He had a good personality and wasn't one of those yelling and screaming chefs. He got along with people, and he immediately let them know he was going to be a good leader and help them. He did have his moments though. On those rare occasions when he would act out, I'd sometimes slip a piece of paper into the pocket of his chef's jacket and tell him to read it at the end of the night. He'd fish it out as he was leaving and would find that I had written something like "Leave

UNLEASHING EMERIL'S POTENTIAL

Emeril's evolution into a full-fledged chef-owner was hastened under Ella's tutelage during his nearly eight years at Commander's Palace. Here, he traces his learning path:

"We were great communicators. Serious communicators. The restaurant was evolving, the customer base was growing and the staff was growing. We truly believed that we had some magic going on. I was very involved in the front of the house as a chef. I was very involved with the customer, but Ella really didn't know that it could also be done from the kitchen. So we learned that together and made that evolve together.

"I would have some of our local customers come into the kitchen and just say, 'We don't really want to see a menu tonight. What are you doing?' So Ella and Dick allowed me to have what we called 'weapons' or 'toys.' I would have soft-shell crabs, but they weren't necessarily on the menu. And I would have a veal roast that wasn't on the menu. It was a very interesting way for me to sort of cook and create and begin to think outside the box with our customers. And then one day she said, 'I just don't understand why you don't take over the whole restaurant.' And I said, 'What do you mean?' And she said, 'Well, now you know as much about service as most people do, and you know more about the customer than most people do, so why don't you just be the general manager?' I said, 'I really want to do that. Can I do that from the kitchen?' So I became her general manager, her right hand with chef's whites on. It was a blast, and we really added some layers of magic again."

your ego at home," and that seemed to solve the problem. Probably ticked him off at the time, but it solved the problem.

I'd also occasionally remind him of our "7 Ps" motto: "Prior proper planning prevents piss-poor performance." I had actually forgotten about that until he brought it up recently, but I'm glad he's carried it with him.

That reminds me of the time he royally screwed up and ran afoul of the authorities. I was at home one night and got a call from him: "I'm in jail!" Seems the police had heard about his buying fish from a sportsman instead of a legitimate fish dealer, so they arrested him. I said, "Stay there. I'm either going to get you out or I'm going to join you. Just stay there."

It worked. I called one of my customers who was a judge; Emeril was released and nothing was put on his record. It seemed as though every day something crazy or wonderful was happening. You just had to take it and run with it.

Now don't get me wrong, it wasn't all work. Ti and Lally say no one was more fun at a party than Emeril. They all were close in age and were running around and working hard, but they were enjoying all that New Orleans had to offer. Lots of late nights dancing, I seem to recall. And he became a mentor in his own right, particularly with Jamie Shannon, whom Emeril would pick as his successor following his decision to leave Commander's in 1990 after nearly eight years. Emeril and I had occasionally talked about how it might be time for him to start his own restaurant, ideally in partnership with us, but he was insistent upon opening a place in the still-to-be-redeveloped Warehouse District across Canal Street, while I wanted something in the French Quarter. We were both stubborn—and both absolutely right—so he somewhat reluctantly departed the Commander's "classroom" and struck out on his own with Emeril's on Tchoupitoulas Street. I was one of his first customers and have continued to encourage him every step of the way in his fabulous career.

We had made our mark in the culinary world. Jeremiah Tower would tell me years later that Commander's, with its dedication to cooking with local ingredients and its professional but comforting service, inspired his influential Stars restaurant in San Francisco. Johnny Apple of the *New York Times* had picked up on it, too, calling Commander's and Stars "the two most democratic restaurants in America." I was proud that our approach and efforts were being recognized.

Looking back on any accomplishments or awards, mentoring is the thing I remember most fondly. I love seeing it continue today at Commander's, but like everything else, I had to learn how to do it. When I started out, I knew nothing about people skills. Had never heard the term. I was just trying to do my best by working with people one-on-one. But Owen began to talk to me a good bit

EMERIL, HONESTLY

New York restaurateur Drew Nieporent (Nobu, Tribeca Grill, Batard) had admired Ella's career for years before finally getting to know her at various culinary events. Here, he recalls a particularly telling encounter:

"I sat on a panel in New Orleans with Ella once, close to the time when Emeril left. And it was very much in the moment of Emeril's celebrity. He had just become huge. And somebody from the audience asked Ella what she thought about Emeril. I am somewhat of a provocative person, so I thought, 'Oh, this is going to be interesting.' She thought for a while and she didn't say it right away, but then she goes, 'I don't think he's ever hurt anybody that I know.' And I thought, 'Wow, that is an extraordinary answer.' It's like, if she was bitter or angry, it might have come out. Instead, she really thought about it: 'He's great. He hasn't hurt anybody.' That, I thought, was a pretty honest answer."

about this. The first book Owen gave me was Dale Carnegie's *How to Win Friends and Influence People*. (It was an excellent book, and still is.) I began reading all kinds of books about relationships, more books than anybody can ever imagine.

Later on, if I liked a book, I'd buy a copy for everybody. It took me a long time to realize that people didn't read them. I find that to be very strange. I mean, if somebody gives you a book and it's interesting, not a dull, stupid book, why wouldn't you want to read it? But they didn't, so day by day I had to talk them through what I'd learned.

I have had the great good fortune to have had several people mentor me, before I even knew what that term really meant. I think one of the smartest things I ever did was to realize how much you can learn (and how many mistakes you can avoid) by being willing to seek out thoughtful advisors and mentors. People who think they know it all are foolish or egotistical or both. I was a John F. Kennedy fan, and he was famous for wanting to surround himself with people that were smarter than him and then truly listening to them. It doesn't mean you always accept their counsel, but you truly hear them. At the end of the day, you always have to keep your own counsel. But if you do that in a vacuum, your odds of success are minimal.

I, of course, had Owen and Adelaide. But I also had Ralph Alexis in the 1950s. He had knowledge and experience I didn't have, particularly in finance and business. (He also had wisdom. You can have a lifetime of experience and still have no wisdom.) People who do the mentoring see something in the person they're working with. They see a reason to give their time to this person. No need to waste your time on someone who is not receptive. I'm not sure what Ralph saw in me in my twenties, but he gave me so much. He understood business in a way that I did not, yet. He spotted problems and kept me up to date. Just as important, perhaps, he bought me the first bottle of great wine that I ever tasted. It was at a restaurant, and he ordered Chateâu Pontet-Canet, a Bordeaux that probably was from one of the fine vintages of the late 1940s. So he started me on drinking good wines, and pretty soon I was able to speak up and say what we should have. He was just an extraordinary man, generous with his time and intelligence. People who are smart, worldly and kind, and who also like good wine, make wonderful mentors.

Later came another man, younger in years than me but ahead of me in certain ways. We first got to know Joe Henican when Ti was looking for a new lawyer for our company because our beloved longtime lawyer, Edward Weggman, was nearing retirement. Joe instantly became a favorite of ours for his willingness to disagree without being disagreeable. He would point out alternative ways of looking at a situation, and he seemed to always have a story to make his point. He gave and gave of his time at first as our attorney and later as a member of our board.

Along the way Joe became the CEO of a company with 13,000 employees, so he was a businessman facing issues of all sorts. He always said we had the same problems, just with a few less zeros. To have the advice and friendship of this man has meant the world to me; it has given me comfort when facing hard decisions. And this character is a barrel of laughs. The culture of our company is work hard, play hard, and enjoy yourself and the people around you as much as humanly possible. We have belly laughed through more board meetings than I can count, thanks to Joe Henican. I will never be able to thank him enough. His adorable wife, Marge, says that if I were any younger, she would have thought we were having an affair. All just fun and love.

One day Ti got the idea that since we couldn't come up with a way to properly thank Joe, we should break our longstanding rule about not naming dishes after people. We were all in. But what dish? We change the menu so often that there were few dishes that would be on it forever. But there was one. We called it Shrimp and Tasso—a magnificent dish from the Jamie era with shrimp in Crystal Hot Sauce beurre blanc, five-pepper jelly and pickled okra. Very *us,* bursting with flavor. We can't take it off the menu or there would be a revolt. So, it is now Shrimp and Tasso Henican. That dish graced the cover of *Saveur* magazine in April 2013. We never told Joe of our intention, we just did it. I think he loved it. However, in typical Joe style, he had to have a comment. Being a handsome six-foot-four-ish and not scrawny fella, he said, "If you have to name a shrimp dish after me, could it at least say 'jumbo shrimp?'"

I would be remiss if I didn't mention my dear friend Leah Chase, the chef and proprietor of Dooky Chase's restaurant, who is a role model for me rather than a hands-on mentor. Whether she is teaching the neighborhood children in Tremé about respecting a business establishment that is trying to make a living and supporting lots of people, or feeding and advising the leaders of the civil rights movement, or organizing citizens to support the arts—this lady is a leader. She is the embodiment of walking the talk. She lives what she preaches and she preaches about her belief in the "common good." And that is something I wish people talked about more. This "me, me, me" take on life is the pits. Leah never bought into that. She gives and gives and gives, even when she is in the midst of tough times.

I remember Leah showing up everywhere to support everyone after Katrina, when she had lost everything. *Everything.* She just put her head down and started working on their comeback. She used to joke, "I can't die now, I owe everybody money." She is the epitome of a class act. Leah helped, as much as anyone in this city, bring everybody together after the storm. She did it with love, with compassion, with an occasional stern "talking to" and, of course, with food. I admire her so.

When I combined the wisdom I had received from Owen, Ralph, Joe and Leah, along with the values my parents had instilled in me and the things I had learned the hard way on my own, I eventually developed a management style that seemed to work for me and our employees. I began to understand that if you make one-on-one contact with somebody, you can reach him and earn his respect. You sit down with him and say, "How are you today? How are the children?" You open the door and get to know that person as a person and not as just someone you work with. You get him going and talking and telling you what he's thinking. And then you tell him what you're thinking. I would meet every new employee who came through our door and say, "I am going to come to work every day, and I am going to try to earn your trust and respect. And you should come every day and try to earn mine. I don't expect you to give it to me—I expect to have to earn it. You understand? I mean it. Watch me. I'm going to watch you. Let's see how this turns out."

Once you've planted that idea of trust and respect, you can begin to say to that person, "Well, why don't you do this? Why don't you do that? Ever know anything about this? Did you learn anything different on your last job? How did they do things?" That's the way we learned. Everything we did in the restaurant we basically learned from the people who worked for us. It's a two-way street and it has worked very well. But the culture of earned trust and respect is at the core of our philosophy and, I believe, of our success.

One thing I learned is that sometimes you may have to do a little mentoring of someone you have just met. If you can find a way to go about it that grabs their attention—even if it makes them angry for an hour—they may never forget it.

Years and years ago we did some renovations at Commander's. We closed a couple of days before a slow summer holiday to do something really exciting like replace a hood, fix a bathroom, and install some new kitchen equipment. As restaurateurs, we try like hell to never close. Not just because you are losing money hand over fist while you pay everyone and have no income, but because you will frequently run into some bureaucracy preventing you from opening again.

I was pressuring our contractor to get us open by the next day—let's go! But for two days he kept telling me he couldn't get the permit to open. I asked him for the name of whoever was in charge of granting that approval, and off I went to City Hall. I politely shared my story with the gentleman, and then he shared that he would get to it after he dealt with the other permits on his desk. So I waited and I waited. When the gentleman went off to lunch, I prepared a surprise for him when he returned. I had cleaned and organized his desk—it was a mess! Let's just say that when I walked back into Commander's with the permit that day, our contractor was stunned.

Now, I have never, and would never, bribe anyone—not even a few hundred dollars to get a permit processed. But I have cleaned a desk that needed cleaning. The lesson is that we got what we needed not by throwing our hands in the air or getting in someone's face, but by being persistent and creative. Everyone was treated respectfully and not a single voice was raised, but a point was made!

Sometimes, if I'm fortunate, I can cultivate a rapport with our managers over business philosophy, which I think is the most exciting thing in the world. I do. I want to know why: Why did a business go in a certain direction? Was it happenstance or was there a clear strategy? Did it succeed? Did it fail because it was a poor strategy, bad timing, poor execution, or poor leadership? I want to know because I just want to know, but also because I may be able to apply the lessons to our business. Every book or article that I read, I scratch out the words "oil business" or "hotel" or whatever, and I write in "restaurant." Then I write a half dozen or two dozen names on the top of the publications and distribute them. I try to get them thinking. Poor Ti gets a shopping bag full of articles every week—sometimes twice a week.

I try to share the things that motivate me, that excite me. Business—creating something out of nothing—is exciting. Terrifying at times, but exciting. We call it "entrepreneurial terror." It will motivate you and keep you up at night. But when it works, when your new restaurant (or store/company/division/hotel . . .) succeeds, wowee! That is exciting!

But you must be fueled by intellectual curiosity in order to create your business, improve your products, change your strategy or become an expert in your field. You have to go and experience things whenever you can, but you also have to read and get that knowledge in your head—constantly. You cannot stagnate or you'll just be a dummy. Really. And I don't have time for that. You have to be

IMPRESSIVE IMPRESSIONS

Juan Carlos Gonzalez, chef at Ti's SoBou saloon in the French Quarter, began his career at Commander's Palace in January 2000 as an extern from the Culinary Institute of America. He recalls his first encounter with Ella:

"During one of my first days, Ella was sitting at the chef's table in the kitchen and called me over. She told me that she knew every one of her employees but did not know me, so I must be new. She introduced herself, asked me some questions, and we talked for about thirty minutes. When I look back on that conversation, it amazes me that with 200 employees, she could spot the new one within minutes of sitting down. And she not only wanted to know my name, but also to know about me. I have never forgotten that."

Eman Loubier, chef-owner of New Orleans restaurants Dante's Kitchen and Noodle & Pie, worked at Commander's Palace from 1990 to 2000 under Jamie Shannon, rising to chef de cuisine. He recalls his early interactions with the woman who ruled the roost:

"I tell people that you haven't had your ass kicked until it's been kicked by a seventy-five-year-old woman, and I'm referring to Ella Brennan. When I started at Commander's, I was definitely intimidated by her because of her reputation. She would spend a lot of time in the kitchen sitting high up on one of those stools—there was one labeled 'Ella' and one labeled 'Dottie'—and she noticed everything. One day, I said to her, 'You intimidate me. You stare at me a lot.' She said, 'I am not staring—this is what I like to do. I like to watch people do what they like to do.'

"Eventually, I got used to it. Chef Jamie had talked to Ella about me before I arrived, so she gave me an extra eye and watched what I did in the kitchen. For one reason or another, she decided I was worth talking to and helping along.

"I was about twenty-five, and I was very bullheaded. Ella would say that about me too. I didn't see the bigger picture; I was looking through a tube. And I was living the chef life. You keep late hours, and when you get out of work, you don't go home and go to bed. You still have that adrenaline rush from working. And New Orleans is a twenty-four-hour town with plenty of cocktails to be had. You'd work hard, play hard and come in the next day and do it again.

"So sometimes Ella would have to get on my case. She wouldn't do it in the heat of the battle. But if something happened, she would hold court at the chef's table in the kitchen on Saturday afternoons, and I would usually be one of the people she'd talk to. Sometimes, she'd want to punch you in the head. But half the time you'd talk about the restaurant business or things outside the business. She'd flood my mailbox with magazines and articles—her copies were always highlighted—and then she'd quiz me. A chef can cook anything he wants, but if he doesn't understand how the business works, he won't be in business for long.

"When I started, my approach was 'This is a competition to see who's the best.' By the time I left, it was 'I am going to know these people for only a little while, so why not treat them the best I can? They're more likely to enjoy their time there and get more out of it.' I got that from Ella.

"She was like the hard teacher in school who was always busting you, and then you realize you learned so much because you weren't getting away with stuff. She never washed her hands of me, never said, 'I can't do this anymore.' I'm amazed she took so much time out of her life to spend with me. I never thought I'd have been worth it. I'd have fired me, but she never did. It's hard to overstate how much that meant."

---

willing to put in the effort. Teach me/us something. We will not drag you up the hill. Run beside me or, better yet, ahead of me.

Learning to love to read should become a part of life. And that learning can't be too specialized. Too many people have no clue what is going on in the world. It is terrifying. You must be aware. Once you get the thirst for knowledge, it's not work at all. It's thrilling. It's a necessity, like food. You have to feed your mind.

COMMUNICATING THROUGH READING

Ti feels anything but poor upon receiving "messages in a bottle" from her mother.

"I can't imagine life without them . . . the bags. They are everywhere. I hide them behind pieces of furniture. I can't keep up with her, but I can't throw them away. I will read every article she sends me. And I *love* it. They are so stimulating. I am spoiled. It's like I am the most well-read person in America. Only I'm not—*she* is. I get the CliffsNotes versions. They are all marked up with little notes—*The Wall Street Journal, The New York Times, Architectural Digest, Harvard Business Review, Nation's Restaurant News, Food & Wine,* novels, autobiographies, and on and on. If she tore it out, underlined it and wrote me a message, then she was trying to tell me something or wants me to think about something. I can't imagine missing a single one. I consider it one of life's great luxuries.

"Consider what I just grabbed from the top of the closest stack: a story about salt in cocktails; a story about the Arab states and American foreign policy; a story about the new female CEO at GM with a note from Mom pondering the timing of her appointment; and a story about the price of 'creature comforts' in New York City with a note that says, 'It makes you feel so poor.'

"I find every one of these to be like a message in a bottle. It has been a bigger part of my education than my MBA. And as Mom would say, cheaper."

Many of the best ideas that we implemented at Commander's came out of the weekly "foodie meetings" that we began under Paul. Keeping those meetings focused—food was the only topic allowed—and on schedule was tough, but they were productive and everyone wanted to attend. But if you were going to attend, you had better bring a tough skin. Every dish was on the chopping block. If a new idea was deemed better than a current offering, out with the old! Change was constant, but it required the stamp of approval from the group, and they were a tough audience. Spaghetti flowing out of an artichoke, just because the chef had never seen it presented that way? We would shoot down silly ideas like that in a heartbeat. But so many other ideas stuck and became part of the restaurant's fabric.

During Paul's time at Commander's, we hired a very bright advertising lady named Betty Hoffman. She would often sit in on those foodie meetings to learn where things were headed. The restaurant's motto under the previous owners had been "Commander's Palace—Dining in the Grand Manner." It certainly was that, but we decided the tone of that slogan could be intimidating. We wanted diners to come for grand occasions, but we wanted them to visit in between to see what was new as well. We were looking for a phrase that would capture the spirit of an evolving menu. Eventually, Betty and the group hit on "Haute Creole." It fit. It felt right. It was succinct yet said so much. We still use it today.

I believe Betty or one of us came up with the word "foodie" in the 1970s. We just needed a word to describe those meetings, and I had never heard that term before. Maybe somebody smarter than me could research the origins on the Internet. But we loved the word because it was much more egalitarian than "gourmet" or "gourmand."

While providing a forum for the healthy exchange of interesting new culinary ideas, the meetings also gave Dottie, Dick and me, and later Ti and Lally, a chance to see who was emerging as leaders in the kitchen. Future stars such as Tory McPhail (now Commander's chef) and Danny Trace (now chef at Brennan's of Houston) emerged in those meetings. Dottie always said that when she was in first grade they gave her a little seed and told her to put it in the dirt and water it and give it sun. When a flower bloomed, she never got over how amazing that was. She gardened the rest of her life. She loves planting seeds and growing flowers. Well, I love growing people and seeing how they turn out.

But some cases were harder than others. Let me introduce you to Jamie Shannon.

He was a young boy from the Jersey Shore who finished at the prestigious Culinary Institute of America in Hyde Park, New York. During his final year he went to the head of the school, Tim Ryan, and said, "I want to go around the country and learn all about American food, because American food is coming

A POWERFUL PRESENCE

Meg Bickford started her career at Commander's Palace directly out of college, a move that threw her into a major panic on her first day while working as a cook under chef Tory McPhail. But he and Ella spotted her talent and nurtured it, leading her to become the chef at Café Adelaide. Here, Bickford recalls her early impressions:

"When I first met Ella, I was a very young cook at Commander's, and it was very interesting when she came into the kitchen to have dinner. You'd hear whispers all around the kitchen: 'Ella's coming in! Ella's coming in!' Everybody would start wiping down and cleaning up and fixing their jackets, and there was just this feeling of a powerful presence. You'd feel her influence before she even arrived, and then she'd walk through and wave to everybody—'Hi . . . hi'—and she'd point somebody out and tell them they needed a haircut, you know?

"Since then, we've built this unbelievable relationship that means the world to me. Thinking of Ella as my 'boss' is maybe the fifteenth thing I might say about her. I consider her my friend and my mentor and my family. Listening to her talk, it's amazing the things that come out of her mouth, the ideas she has. It's how she lives her life—not letting someone walk by without saying hello and always making eye contact with people. She expects the same. And the attention to detail that she has—she'll watch you work and correct you on the spot, and it's not to be rude or bossy, it's because she wants you to be so much better. She has this belief that everybody around her can be great, they just have to put in the effort.

"One of the ways that she has inspired me is that in all the conversations we've had, there's never been anything about male versus female. Every once in a while she'll crack a joke, something to the effect of 'Well, somebody's got to keep the boys in line!'—but it is a joke. What is so inspiring is that I'm not a girl in the kitchen. I'm a person in the kitchen. Ella knew what she wanted, and she was going to work hard to get it, and nobody was going to hold her back, male or female, and it's not about your gender or your race or anything. It's about what you want and going after it. And if you want it and you go after it, then there's nobody saying you can't have it.

"Perhaps the best advice that Ella ever gave me was not to get fat and not to get old, because they were exhausting."

on strong." Ryan suggested that he start by coming down to New Orleans and working at Commander's. Jamie came in 1984 and never left. He went to work for Emeril, who was very good about setting up a career ladder for aspiring chefs and teaching them, teaching them, teaching them. (Emeril swears that after he introduced Jamie to me, the first thing I said was, "Please make sure he gets his hair cut." Apparently, I frowned at his ponytail. In any case, my request was ignored.)

Jamie was a bad boy. He would go out at night and sit around barrooms drinking, and he was the leader of the gang, if you know what I mean. I had to get into his head that we trusted him and really needed him to do his job. Emeril was there, but he was also all over the region doing charity benefits and cooking demonstrations. Jamie was a little young to be ready to accept the responsibility of a top sous chef. We had to get him to understand that learning and growing were more rewarding and exciting than playing around.

So we worked on him and worked on him, and eventually he became family. Jamie took Emeril's job after he left in 1991. We had five guys in the kitchen that had been working with Emeril—talented like you wouldn't believe—and everyone wondered whom he would choose. I had gone out and gotten Emeril, but we wanted his successor to be one of the guys he had worked with for so long. Emeril had mentored Jamie and told me to pick him, and it worked out wonderfully.

One of the most talented and beloved chefs we've ever had, Jamie was with us for seventeen years. Having learned from Emeril, he championed the use of local ingredients long before that came into vogue. People just naturally responded to his cooking. He was executive chef when the James Beard Foundation bestowed on Commander's the Outstanding Restaurant Award in 1996. Three years later, he won the Foundation's award for best chef in the Southeast.

MISCHIEF-MAKERS

Ti, who managed Commander's Palace with her cousin Lally during Jamie's run as executive chef, recalls her great friend and colleague—and the mischief he could create:

Horrific as Jamie's passing was, it is not how I choose to remember him. I think of him talking to me about a dish and having to go make it right then. I think of him on his porch swing with his son, Tustin, on his lap. I think of him cooking in the kitchen with women staring at him through the window. They had come not to eat but to see the six-foot-three, striking Irish man with the perfectly combed long, reddish ponytail, the droopy eyes with the naughty glint and the slow grin. He took a long, long time to mature. Very long. He was just bad, but in the most lovable way.

For instance . . .

We were supposed to be at the James Beard Awards in New York. I was there but he was late—very late. This was the pre–cell phone era, but somehow I had gotten word that Jamie had missed his flight from New Orleans. I sat nervously in my seat. Finally, he slid in next to me halfway through the ceremony. I gave him the cold shoulder for a while. Before long he explained that he had been at Jazz Fest with his friends from out of town and had hurried home to dress for his flight. But he told his pals, as they walked to their car along Bayou St. John, that it was a tradition after attending your first Jazz Fest to swim across Bayou St. John. Let's just say that was a bunch of malarkey that they unfortunately swallowed. As a result, flight missed.

So yes, he was bad, bad, bad—but in a fun-loving way. You just couldn't stay mad at him. We never told Mom about these adventures because they seldom affected his work, which truly did come first. The man loved to cook, to pour over old Creole cookbooks and to mentor. He mentored so many young cooks who still visit the restaurant and remind us about how he explained Creole cooking to them, how he worked beside them to show them how to butcher, sauté, age a duck, plate dishes, and on and on. He loved it. He wanted them to do well, and he wanted to be better every shift.

A sparkle in his eye, fire in his belly, and magic in his hands—that is how we remember our Jamie.

Just as important, he was a man who truly embraced the spirit of the region—Jazz Fest, the clubs, Mardi Gras, hunting, fishing—and the city embraced him. He loved the people he worked with and they loved him back. Which is why it seemed especially cruel when Jamie developed bone cancer in his leg. Ti and Jamie had just finished the *Commander's Kitchen* cookbook when he was diagnosed. They were on a tour promoting the book when Ti asked, "Hey friend, what's with the limp?" Jamie explained the pain in his leg, and she immediately set up an appointment with our doctor in New Orleans. That was the beginning of a long, hard battle. Jamie fought the disease the best he could.

Jamie's illness cast a pall over the restaurant. It was as though we had all been punched in the stomach. Everyone tried to rally, but we were just barely functioning. One day, we planned a surprise for him. All of us. We arranged with his wife, Jeannette, to get him out on the front porch of their beautiful old home while we gathered secretly around the corner. We put the word out to friends and family, cooks, waiters, and, of course, to Joe Simon's band, who has led our weekend jazz brunches for years. With about seventy-five of us gathered, we struck up the band and marched in a second line around the corner and past the front of his house. He loved it. We loved it. There was hope and fun and love thick in the air.

Jamie had to spend weeks off and on at MD Anderson Cancer Center in Houston, so his wife, mom and sisters, as well as Ti and Lally, took turns staying with him. He would pop into Commander's when he could, but those instances became fewer and fewer. One day some of Jamie's closest friends just couldn't take not seeing him anymore. I'll never forget when Jared Tees, Ethan Powell, Greg Collier and Eman Loubier loaded up in the middle of the night and drove to Houston. They were all so glad just to see Jamie. It was unspoken that this would be the last time. We were trying to figure out how to medically transport Jamie home at that point. But it was not to be. The guys saw Jamie for less than an hour before loading back up for the six-hour drive back to New Orleans for their brunch shifts. No one missed work. Jamie used to say, "If you hang with the big dogs, you got to get up and go to work with the big dogs." In his honor they wouldn't dare miss a shift.

Jamie would return to Commander's as often as possible, but he passed away in November 2001. He was just forty.

Jamie's family asked Ti to deliver part of the eulogy at his funeral. Here is a portion of her speech:

"Don't you know the food in heaven just got a whole lot better.

"I'm Ti and I worked with Jamie with my cousins Lally and Brad, my Aunt Dottie, and my mom, Ella Brennan. I think Jamie just thought of us all as one person in a way, so I think I speak for all of us today. Jeannette asked me to read a letter my Mom had written to Jamie in October of this year and to say a few words.

"This letter was written in October 2001 by Ella Brennan to Jamie Shannon:

Why do I love working with you?

You are a team builder.

You are a teacher.

You are a mentor.

You are creative.

You love food and wine.

You love people.

You are a great cook.

You have magic in your hands.

You have great energy.

You have a great sense of humor.

You have a desire for the better good of all.

You are loyal.

You are a builder.

You understand the restaurant business.

You are a great cook.

You are the best chef I have known.

You do it all.

—Ella

"So I wrote my own letter: 'Why I loved being your friend':

"Because you said you'd do anything the business ever needed except nudity or funny hats, and when the blender company that wanted you to pose nude with a blender like other famous chefs called, Lally and I had more fun watching you turn beet red on the phone with them.

"Because you ran that kitchen like the gentle giant that you were.

"Because in social situations you always turned the conversation away from yourself.

"Because when we traveled, just the two of us, for a month straight, you always held the doors, looked out for me like a big brother, and, unlikely pair that we were, I liked you even more when we got home than when we left.

"Because I always knew that your wife and son came first.

"Because you got so *incredibly* good at being a leader, a chef, and a TV host. Not because it all came naturally to you but because you worked so very hard at it.

"Because you didn't feel *entitled* to things.

"Because you cursed less than I do.

"Because you desperately wanted to get home from the hospital to see Tustin in his Halloween fireman's costume last month, but when that didn't work out, you just set a new goal.

"Because describing your wife to me and how she amazed you with all she did—working, being Supermom, renovating a house, taking care of you, and still being the fun-loving girl you met in an oyster bar—it brought tears to your eyes.

"Because when I was so mad at you for being late to the Beard Awards in New York, you had me crying with laughter as you explained that you had missed your flight because you had friends in town for Jazz Fest, and you had convinced them that it was a tradition that on their first Jazz Fest visit they had to swim across Bayou St. John as you walked across the bridge. And well, things just got a little carried away.

"Because you loved sincerely to see other people succeed.

"Because you helped more young cooks than any chef I've ever known.

"Because you'd stay awake all night wondering if the oyster dressing was right.

"Because you loved to call Tustin 'my son.'

"Because you loved your mom.

"Because you loved my mom.

"Because the phrase 'he broke into a smile' was meant to describe your face slowly forming into the widest full grin with those smiling Irish eyes, and you gave me and all of us here lots of those smiles—even at the end.

"Because you became, with as much hard work as I've ever seen, *simply the best*.

"Jeannette said I could tell this one last private story:

"Tustin, who was four, had come to see Jamie in Houston, just last week or so. He was coming to visit one last time before he headed back to New Orleans. When Mrs. Rayer and Tustin left, Jeannette sat down, and she shared with Linda, Anne and me that Tustin had never told either her or Jamie the words 'I love you.' That if they said, 'Mommy loves you,' he'd just smile, or if they said, 'Do you love Mommy or Daddy?' he'd maybe say yes or just smile. But as she had Tustin in her arms and they were leaving the ICU room for Tustin to go home, Jamie said, 'I love you, Tustin,' and he turned and said, '*I love you, Daddy.*'

"I know that if Jamie were perfectly healthy when that happened, he would have cried like a baby, and all I could think about was my friend being alone at that moment when Jeannette and Tustin walked out. I just thank the Lord that Tustin chose that particular moment to say, '*I love you, Daddy.*'

• • •

When his obituary ran in *Nation's Restaurant News*, Jamie was quoted about his affection for the city: "It is my home. I love the summer. The food is incredible. The people are outstanding. And then you have the music. It has so much culture and depth. I wake up every morning and say, 'I love New Orleans, and I love my wife and I love my job.'"

We all cherish his memory.

11

Two Passions, Many Loves

"IF THEY KEEP EXPOSING YOU TO
EDUCATION, YOU MIGHT EVEN REALIZE
SOME DAY THAT MAN BECOMES IMMORTAL
ONLY IN WHAT HE WRITES ON PAPER, OR
HACKS INTO ROCK, OR SLABBERS ONTO A
CANVAS, OR PULLS OUT OF A PIANO."
—NOVELIST ROBERT RUARK

Exploring the written word and engaging in lively conversations with smart, captivating people are my two greatest pleasures in life, even greater than a bottle of Chateau Pontet-Canet from a good vintage or Judy Garland singing "Get Happy." Maybe you play tennis or golf, or maybe you garden. I love to read and talk about the world with bright, funny folks. Working in the hospitality industry and living in New Orleans have allowed me to indulge in both pursuits to a degree I never could have imagined.

I've long had a fascination with good writers, and I marvel at how they can communicate an idea or an issue and distill it to its essence. The best ones engage in original thinking and present it in a beautiful, almost poetic way. That stops me in my tracks. It's the way they think that turns me on.

Maybe my infatuation began with Robert Ruark, a true man's man and big-game hunter who was known for novels such as *The Old Man and the Boy, The Honey Badger* and *Something of Value*. He even made the cover of *Time* magazine.

He blew my mind with his beautiful writing. Adelaide always thought I had a crush on him. Maybe I did. But it was about his mind. He seemed to know everything. Robert took me under his wing in the 1950s. He showed me around New York, took me to see Ella Fitzgerald for the first time, shared his deep knowledge of wine and suggested things to read. I loved him dearly, though I didn't know what "in love" meant at that time in my life.

The journalists I met over the years, however, may have fascinated me the most. They always had well-thought-out opinions that they could express to perfection. I first encountered them when Owen sent me to different cities to learn about food and wine. He knew Johnny Popham, the Southern correspondent for the *New York Times* and a gem of a guy. Johnny connected me to the stringers in London, San Francisco, Los Angeles, Chicago, and Paris and had them show me around when I was in those cities. Claude Sitton replaced him, and we enjoyed a similar relationship. What an education I received from them.

In later years, Turner Catledge, executive editor of the *New York Times,* ended up living next door to me when he retired. He got his paper very early every day, and after he read it, he would toss it over the fence for me. I had long gotten the Sunday edition but wasn't getting the daily at the time. I loved going out to get that paper in the morning, knowing Turner had already read it.

So many of the great writers had started out on newspapers, including Ernest Hemingway (wish I'd met him). They had to write fast, but they had to think and they had to know what was going on in the world. Put that together with a Sazerac or an Old Fashioned and you are in for a great evening. When some of these guys and gals also knew about food, well, we were off to the races. That would be R. W. "Johnny" Apple Jr., the great bon vivant and political and cultural correspondent for the *New York Times*. We would have dinner or brunch whenever we could, often with his delightful wife, Betsey. He was always just back from Russia or China or Paris and knew about their food and the politics, and he wanted to know about ours in New Orleans. Our meals together were vastly enriching and entertaining.

Now that I think of it, I wish I had put Johnny together with two other writers who had a strong interest in all things culinary and became close friends, Peter Feibleman and Marcelle Bienvenu. Peter was an award-winning novelist

AN ADMIRER TO THE END

New Orleans–based writer Julia Reed is a neighbor of Ella's and was a friend of the late Johnny Apple Jr. Julia recounts Ella and Johnny's final communication in 2006:

"Every single person that's ever written a piece about food knew about Ella. I remember going to see Johnny on his deathbed when I was in Washington, DC. We talked about how the following night I would be going to New Orleans to dine at Commander's. It was the first week that they had opened after Katrina. I came in to the restaurant and saw Ella and gave her Johnny's best, and then they talked on the phone, and then he died that night. But it was like Johnny wanted me to make sure that I went to Commander's to let Ella know that he was thinking about her in his last hours on earth, literally. I mean, she is *that* beloved."

and playwright who was raised in New Orleans and wrote the first (and best) cookbook defining the difference between Creole and Cajun cuisines. It was for the Time Life series and was called *Creole and Acadian.* He wrote it along with Louisiana native Marcelle, another character who, at one point, worked for us at Commander's Palace as a catering director. What a hoot she is. Marcelle later wrote *Who's Your Mama, Are You Catholic, and Can You Make a Roux?,* a darn good book with almost as much personality as Marcelle herself.

Probably the most memorable gathering of journalists I've ever been a part of occurred in 1988 when everybody in the political media world descended upon the Louisiana Superdome for the Republican National Convention. (No, I wasn't invited.) Naturally, many of those folks found their way to Commander's Palace.

The festivities all started a few days before the convention when my friend David Brinkley hit town and stopped by the house to chat. We decided to throw a party a night or two later for his ABC colleagues and some other folks. Well, the bash in our side yard was the most elegant crawfish boil you've ever seen. Dottie had the required newspaper on the table, but with beautiful silver candelabra centerpieces, silverware and silver-colored paper plates, and Baccarat glasses for champagne and cocktails. Freddie Palmisano came over from Mr. B's to play the piano, and Dottie's young son, Brad, who was living with us, greeted everybody at the door in shorts and a T-shirt (a signal that everyone could let their hair down). It was just dripping with media and political folks, including Peter Jennings and longtime *Washington Post* columnist Art Buchwald (talk about a great thinker—and salty storyteller). Everyone loved the informality of it, and I loved getting to hear the inside stories from some very smart people. There was champagne available all over the house, and they came and they stayed and they stayed and they stayed. Sander Vanocur of ABC News was the last one to leave. He seemed ancient even then, but he sure was fun.

A night or two later, I dined with Art, his *Washington Post* colleague Katherine Graham, Walter Cronkite and the piano-playing political satirist Mark Russell. (I would later read Katherine's memoir and it became my all-time favorite. How that lady made the daring decisions that she did in the midst of complete turmoil that was clearly going to change America forever, well, wow! And she did it all with grace and style and integrity. I was beyond thrilled. Just mesmerized. I thought she was the woman of the century, and I *still* think she was the woman of the century.)

Anyway, we wound up back at our house, where we danced and drank to records by Louis Armstrong and Ella Fitzgerald and munched on some treats that Emeril had sent over. Talk about a heady experience! I was thrilled beyond belief.

Over the years, a fair number of TV reporters and commentators also found their way into my circle. New Orleans native Bill Monroe became a dear friend when he worked as the first news director for WDSU. After he moved on to become a reporter for NBC's *Today* show and a moderator on *Meet the Press,* he always kept in touch and loved coming home. He was the prototype of the first-rate, high-ideal journalist guy and had a big heart. I met him originally through my husband, Paul, and Bill tried to help Paul with his alcoholism.

Oh, and I wish I had a nickel for every night I spent at Commander's with dear friend Lindy Boggs and her smashing daughter Cokie Roberts, the syndicated columnist and political analyst for TV and radio. Now, those are two of my favorites. After Lindy's husband, Hale, tragically died (he was in an airplane that disappeared in the Alaskan wilderness and was never found), right as he was about to ascend to Speaker of the House, we all encouraged Lindy to run for his seat. She did and she won. Later, Lindy was appointed by President Bill Clinton to be the United States Ambassador to the Holy See—and she lived on Bourbon Street!

Lindy was the epitome of a steel magnolia. Scores of politicians would tell me how she'd get them to change a bill in Congress with a smile and a wink and a few ever-gracious "daaawlins." Oh, the stories she told about Hale or herself fussing all day in Congress with their counterparts in the other parties and then going over to each other's houses at night. They actually passed bills, got things done and had the maturity to hold opposing thoughts in their mind at once. A better time.

And Cokie—what a smashing success and grand gal. She tackles the issues of the day by day and is a hoot to be with at night. What a great mind and every bit a Southern lady at her core. If the walls of Commander's could talk, you would know a few US or Vatican political secrets.

Of course, interacting with journalists can be a double-edged sword. I have always been a great fan of CBS's investigative news show *60 Minutes*. You always knew they pushed the envelope trying to get at the truth, the story. But you never expected them to show up on the doorstep of your restaurant, cameras in tow.

One day a waiter came running to my office to say that the show's notoriously cranky commentator, Andy Rooney, was at the front door. I got there quickly and found him perusing our reservations book and inquiring about the notations next to some names. He started asking in a not very friendly way what this little note meant and what that note meant. For one entry, I replied that it identified the guest as a local, to which he said, "So I see, locals get different treatment in your restaurant than tourists?"

I responded, "No, Mr. Rooney, we just don't think anyone should be a stranger in their own hometown." I am not sure what "scandal" he was attempting to unearth, but he and the cameraman trudged off and no story ever aired.

Fortunately, my encounter with Mr. Rooney was an exception. Much more often my relationships were friendly and enriching. I can't recall how I met David Brinkley, but we became close at some point, probably in the 1970s, and kept in touch regularly. David was smart as hell and delightful. He was in Washington, DC, and I think I was his New Orleans touchstone. He always wanted to know how things were going in our neck of the woods.

One particular night, I had been carping nonstop about how maddening New Orleans was. I had witnessed Houston, Dallas, and Atlanta speed by us in the 1970s and 1980s with shiny new airports, better schools and buzzing economies. I was mad—still am—that we blew our lead. That we let the schools go to hell and that the business community was hampered by an insular system of social strata. These other cities had meritocracies. I liked that. I guess I was really carrying on that night, because the next morning on his way to the airport, David called me: "Ella, I've been thinking so much about what you were saying last night, and I think you've got it all wrong. New Orleans has things no one else has. New Orleans understands how to live life. New Orleans is like Italy. Who cares if the trains run on time? It's Italy."

Sometimes it takes an outsider to remind you of some things. I know what he meant, and I do believe New Orleans has some things we can teach to the world. I do. We believe that life is meant to be lived, not endured. I think post-Katrina we have kept the best of our ways and traditions and have shed some of the worst. We have a work hard, play hard approach and a mentality of inclusiveness now.

But dammit, I was right about the schools at that time. We let down several generations. Now, post-Katrina, we're seeing a renaissance in our school system that educators are coming from all over the world to observe. Never thought it would happen in my lifetime. That hurricane had some silver linings.

I love to chew over issues such as these with two of my buddies who have a talent for writing and observation. Gene Bourg wrote dispatches for the US Army while stationed in France and then worked for various publications there as a civilian. Naturally, he fell in love with Paris and learned all about the country's food and wine. Gene later parlayed that knowledge into becoming the food critic for the *Times-Picayune,* so we didn't get to be really good friends until he retired from the paper in 1995. Sometimes you'll find Gene and me in the company of Ron Thompson, an advertising man in the *Mad Men* mold. I met Ron when his firm did some work for Brennan's at the very beginning. Adelaide and

I were crazy for him and his wife, Mary Ellen. Oh, the fun I've had with those two guys! And Ron can sing! At the drop of a hat. He knows the words to all the show tunes and the American songbooks that I love.

So for the last thirty years (and hopefully at least a few more) on any given Saturday night, you would find me with my two fellas, Gene and Ron, along with Dottie and our dear, funny friend Betty Fusselier; Lally and her fella, Stephen Parker; and Ti and her friends. Somewhere along the way I get Ron to sing.

"I REMEMBER YOU" IN SONG

Ron Thompson is one of Ella's closest friends and shares her love of food and wine and classic American popular music. Here, he reminisces about the times those passions have intersected:

"Ella's mantra was 'If you are coming to my party, I want you to have fun.' And she is fun herself—when you hear her laugh, it's contagious. So everyone responds to her.

"I think the reason that she and I are such close friends is that we love so many of the same things: books, talking about politics and theater, American musicals—I know virtually every song Fred Astaire sang, so Ella would say, "Ron, sing a song for me." Or we would be talking about a film or talking about a song and she would say, "Do you know that song? Sing that song for me." I would always joke that I would have to sing for my supper, because it would be after dinner and after having a lot of Scotch and a lot of wine, I was totally uninhibited. So I sang. I didn't care who was at the dinner table.

"There is a song that Johnny Mercer wrote that makes me think about Ella, and it has a closing stanza that says: 'When my life is through / and the angels ask me to recall the thrill of it all / then I will tell them I remember you.'

"And I do believe that."

It's grand. The whole dining room stops—then applauds. That's just how New Orleans is. My New Orleans.

It's certainly been fun to watch some of the younger folks make their mark as well. Walter Isaacson is another favorite from New Orleans who has done a little of everything. He worked at the *Times-Picayune*; served as editor of *Time* magazine and CEO of CNN; and has written biographies of Steve Jobs, Albert Einstein and Benjamin Franklin. No wonder I adore him. On my eighty-ninth birthday, Ti didn't know what to give me, so she came up with the idea of staging a dinner with fascinating people. She said her first thought was Hillary Clinton, but with her presidential campaign about to get underway, that would have been a *very* expensive dinner. The next thought was inviting Walter and his wife, Cathy Wright. Walter suggested rounding out the table with another fine New Orleans writer, Julia Reed, and her darling husband, John Pearce. She's a foodie, fun and as opinionated as me. That combo made for a delightful evening and a memorable present. Well, six months later Walter called and asked if we could do it again. When Julia and John couldn't make it, we invited our mayor, Mitch Landrieu, and his lovely wife, Cheryl. Now, these are fun dinner parties in Commander's main dining room, where the conversation takes raucous twists and turns and the wine is very good. Yes, there are some excellent perks to being in the restaurant business.

• • •

My fascination with writers is not only personally enriching; it also had some practical use early in my career when it came to promoting the city to the rest of the world. In the 1940s and 1950s, no one was promoting tourism in New Orleans. There was no convention center. There wasn't even anything similar because the city wasn't marketing itself. Those of us in the hospitality business were on our own, and if it hadn't been for Owen and a few others spreading the word to the outside world through their personal grapevines, we might still be in the dark ages. So in the absence of funds from the government or the business community, we did guerrilla marketing many decades before we ever heard that term.

One thing we knew: writers write. And when they came to New Orleans, the city always seemed to work its way into their novels or stories or magazine pieces.

And it was free. It took time and effort to cultivate those folks, but it was usually fun. We always thought that if we could get the spotlight on New Orleans—not just our family businesses but the city—we would get our fair share of rewards if we did a good job in our restaurants. All we had to do was sell New Orleans. The city is many, many things, but on some level it is a state of mind. And that is hard to duplicate. You arrive here and it doesn't look like the rest of the United States. People here don't act like they do in the rest of the country. The food is different, the music is different. We have history—we'll celebrate our tercentennial in 2018—and you can't invent history.

And that's where Pete and Al and Chris come in. That's Pete Fountain, Al Hirt and Chris Owens. Pete makes his clarinet sing—it's thrilling the way he and his band could mesmerize a crowd at his French Quarter club. He is a New Orleans boy through and through, and was one of the most frequent guests on *The Tonight Show Starring Johnny Carson*. And Al, a big guy with a big personality who could blow the roof off of his Bourbon Street joint with his trumpet. "Jumbo" was his nickname. And Chris Owens, my gorgeous longtime friend who still is wowing the crowd at her Bourbon Street disco with her endless energy and showstopping dance moves. I mean, Chris is a dancer—not a striptease artist or anything like that. She's just this flamboyant woman with unbelievable hair and makeup and costumes.

We were a self-appointed troop of ambassadors. When I had a writer from a newspaper or magazine show up at the Vieux Carré or Brennan's, I'd call down the street to those three and say, "OK, here I come. I've got a writer from *Look* magazine. Let's show 'em our town."

"OK, Ella, we'll hold some seats in front. Bring 'em on down."

Off I'd go down the street. That's just how we did it. We all knew each other, and even the bouncers and bartenders would get in on the act. And it worked. Those writers went home and wrote and wrote about New Orleans, and it really put us on the map.

Sometime in the 1980s, I got the idea to formalize that concept and expand it beyond journalists. I thought, why don't we just have a writers' conference? We'll invite writers of every sort to New Orleans, where they can commiserate with each other and meet agents and publishers and the like. We had a good tourism commission by then, and a bright go-getter named Beverly Gianna was in charge of its public relations. She made that happen. Our gathering later merged with another writers' conference that had started around the same time. The idea worked, though it wasn't quite as much fun as my traipsing down Bourbon Street late at night, drinking a Sazerac and going to see Chris and Pete and Al.

ABOVE: *Dottie Brennan, Cindy Brennan, Ella Brennan, Lally Brennan, and Alice Regan.*
BELOW: *Art Buchwald, Ella Brennan, and a friend.*

TOP, LEFT: *Ella Brennan in Pebble Beach, California.* ABOVE, RIGHT: *Dick and Ella Brennan in the courtyard of Commander's Palace.* ABOVE, LEFT: *Ella Brennan with a second line umbrella.* BELOW: *Daniel Boulud, Ella Brennan, Drew Nieporent, and David Chang at the James Beard Awards (photo courtesy of James Beard Foundation).*

ABOVE: *Ella Brennan and Paul Prudhomme.* BELOW: *Tory McPhail and Ella Brennan at the Chef's Table in the Commander's kitchen (photo courtesy of Sam Fritz Cusimano).*

12

Passages (1985–2005 ... and beyond)

**"ELLA SAID THAT WHEN SHE FELT LIKE
SHE WAS GOING TO START STICKING HER
TONGUE OUT AT THE CUSTOMERS, IT WOULD
BE TIME FOR HER TO RETIRE."**

—DOTTIE BRENNAN

Jamie Shannon's passing in November 2001 revealed several key truths about Commander's Palace: a talented kitchen team, assembled and trained by Jamie, was in place; the restaurant's high standing within the American culinary community had been maintained by Jamie and the rest of the team; and the operation itself was on firm footing under the management of Ti, Lally, Dottie and me.

By most appearances, we had become adept at managing change and planning for the future. The proof was in the continuous success and growth from Paul to Emeril to Jamie, and the confidence we had in the abilities of new head chef Tory McPhail. All of that, it seemed, came about more or less by design.

But if you were to go back and trace exactly how Commander's arrived at this stage in its evolution over the two decades leading up to 2002, you might shudder at the substantial role played by happenstance and unforeseen circumstances: health problems, relationship problems, weather problems, engineering failures. Yes, you can make plans, but then you discover that life seldom gives a damn. And that's when your ability to turn on a dime, dig deep and improvise really kicks in. One moment you're in a very good place, opening a zingy new restaurant, watching your hotshot chefs take you to the top of the heap, kicking the youngsters out of the nest (and later welcoming them back), and the next . . .

One morning in 1985, at the house Dottie and I share next to Commander's, I went to lift up my hairbrush and felt a sharp pain in my arm. Dottie's ex-husband had just had a heart attack, so she knew what was likely happening to me. My mom, my dad and Owen also had suffered heart attacks, but I didn't think my situation was as serious as theirs. Hell, I was just sixty-one. But Dottie knew, so she took me to Baptist Hospital, where the doctors looked at me and said they were going to do a bypass operation as soon as they could find a room. I tried to talk them out of it but they said no, no, no. So I had no choice but to let them do their thing.

Good thing I did. The double bypass operation was successful (lots of Creole cream cheese residue in there, no doubt), and I spent a month recuperating at a place we rented in Pebble Beach, California, sitting on the rocks by Carmel Bay and sipping that California wine I'd grown to love. (I felt so comfortable there that we would return for a month nearly every summer in the coming years.) You might say Hurricane Ella had been temporarily downgraded to a tropical storm, but soon I went right back to work—for almost another twenty years. The true significance of my medical adventure, however, is that it triggered Ti's entrance into the fold at Commander's.

Though she'd been an exceptional student and athlete in high school, Ti wasn't certain what she wanted to do with her life. She attended college at Southern Methodist University in Dallas and then Tulane for her MBA. At one point she got a wild hair and insisted that she wanted to go through boot camp with the US Marines, but a panicky Dottie and I steered her toward an Outward Bound program instead. That seemed to satisfy her craving for extreme adventure for a while. Bullet dodged, so to speak.

After graduation, Ti worked in real estate in Houston, then Dottie asked her to manage and try to sell a radio station in Beaumont, Texas, that she had been awarded in her divorce settlement. Though Ti felt totally unqualified being thrust into uncharted waters, she plunged in—sound familiar?—and within nine months had successfully sold the station. But just as she was wrapping things up and considering moving to San Diego, perhaps to pursue a writing career, I had my heart attack.

Ti says that during the drive from Beaumont back to New Orleans to be with me, she really examined what she wanted to do with her life and decided that her destiny was to come back home and be with the family, though not necessarily to join our business. At least not right away. I tried not to show it, but inside I was ecstatic. I had raised her to be independent and to take care of herself, and I hadn't pressured her to go into hospitality—she says I actively discouraged it—but my health problem brought her back to us anyway.

While I was recuperating in California, Ti started helping out at Commander's and launched Creole Cravings, a food products company. She has always been close to her cousins, especially Lally, Dickie and Brad, and her return home meant she could spend more time with them while she put her business skills to good use.

My setback also precipitated Lally's deeper involvement with Commander's. My niece had gotten married after attending SMU and moved to Memphis for nearly a decade. When her marriage faltered in the early 1980s, she came back to New Orleans, then spent a month in France with Ralph while he attended cooking school, and then returned home to heal. Fortunately for us, her father, John, coaxed her into working as a hostess at Mr. B's. It wasn't a job she particularly wanted, but she adored her father and gave it a shot. Anything to get out of her funk.

After a year or so, Ralph, who was running Mr. B's, and I worked out a plan for Lally to come to Commander's to do private-party sales and, eventually, fill in as a BOD. That's when I began sharing with her everything I knew about marketing, for which she seemed to have a natural affinity, and our always-close relationship deepened immeasurably. She is one of the warmest, most giving and loving people you are ever going to meet. And besides that, she's quite an eyeful and has a real touch of class. So, even though she never planned to be in the restaurant business, fate took over again and steered her back to us.

Lally recalls that I was always armed with a yellow legal pad. When she or anyone would come to me grappling with a decision, I'd draw a line down the middle of that pad and list the pros on one side and the cons on the other. That helps to clarify your thinking. And if the problem involved money, I'd do what I call a "declining budget." At the top you list the amount of money you have, and then you list the cost of the things you want and subtract those amounts. At some point you'll reach zero, but there may still be things that you desire. Well, you can't have that stuff. You have to prioritize. If you look at it on paper, it becomes obvious.

In the dozen or so years after my heart attack, Commander's was at the top of its game with Emeril and then Jamie heading the kitchen and Ti, Lally,

DR. ELLA PRESCRIBES RETAIL THERAPY

Besides learning hospitality, marketing and management skills from Ella, Lally also benefitted from her aunt's surefire method to mend a broken heart.

"I always felt like I could talk with my aunts about anything. *Anything.* Things I couldn't talk to my mother about. And I wouldn't be judged and I wouldn't get a quick answer or a quick fix. It would be, 'OK, let's think about this,' whatever the subject. You just always knew that there was going to be an answer full of caring and love and the attitude that 'we can get through this.'

"After I came to Commander's, I was going up to New York with Aunt Ella for an event, and we were in the car being driven into the city. I'd been going out with somebody and Ella asked, 'How's so-and-so?' And I just started sobbing and carrying on because we'd just broken up. Right away, Ella said, 'Let's go to Bergdorf's! Driver, *take us to Bergdorf's!*' And off we went. So a few months later, Ti was going to New York with Aunt Ella, and they were driving into the city when Ella asked, 'How's so-and-so that you've been seeing?' And Ti starts sobbing and carrying on, and Ella says, 'Oh God, here we go again! *Bergdorf's!*' So that's Aunt Ella's idea of fixing your heart when it's broken. Go shopping at Bergdorf's."

Dickie, Lauren, and Brad becoming more involved in running our restaurants (echoing what Alex was doing at the Brennan's in Houston). Once again we felt the need to expand to keep everyone happy. That led us in 1991 to buy the old Werlein's Music Store building on Canal Street and open the Palace Café, which gave us a prominent spot on the edge of the French Quarter. Ti had sold Creole Cravings, and she joined forces with Dickie and Brad and Lauren to launch this beautiful new restaurant. The venture—a grand Creole cafe geared toward a younger audience—was another hit (and remains so to this day under Lauren and Dickie's guidance).

Dickie and Ti established a working relationship reminiscent of the one I had with Dick, which pleased me to no end. Dickie mainly focused on the food and Ti the management, with enough overlap to make things work and keep them engaged. Putting a machine together is one of the most difficult things you can do. You have to get people who want to work together, who are willing to admit what they know and don't know, and play to everybody's strengths. It's not easy, and achieving it is one of the most important lessons a restaurateur will learn in his or her career.

Nearly a decade later, in 1999, we finally decided to try our luck in Las Vegas, which had become a booming (and probably oversaturated) culinary mecca. Every big-name chef and restaurant franchise seemed to have taken up residency there, and we fielded numerous offers before striking a deal to open a Commander's in the new Aladdin Resort and Casino. To run the operation we chose Dottie's son Brad, who had worked at our New Orleans restaurants and for esteemed restaurateurs Rich Melman in Chicago and Pat Kuleto in San Francisco. The restaurant did well, but the resort management company was plagued with constant financial problems, and the hotel was sold to Planet Hollywood. That was not what we had bargained for. We were there until 2008 and then took a lucrative buyout offer. Brad still lives there, to be with his kids, and flies to New Orleans often to help Ti and Lally at Commander's.

While all of this was going on, Jamie hired Tory McPhail, a talented culinary school grad from tiny Ferndale, Washington, and once he sensed the young man's potential, Jamie began teaching Tory everything about the Commander's kitchen. This was in 1993, and Tory caught on quickly enough to become sous chef at

HERE'S A TIP: BE DISCREET

Brad Brennan literally grew up in restaurants, under the watchful eyes of his mother, Dottie, his Aunt Ella, and his older cousins. Here, he recalls his earliest lesson in hospitality:

"My education in the restaurant business started when I was not yet ten years old. Mom would work the front door at Commander's at lunchtime, and sometimes I'd help her out. She'd greet the guests and I'd walk them to their table. People thought it was so cute. In fact, one day a person gave me $5, at a time when my allowance was 50 cents a week, and a few others followed suit. A little while later Mom got suspicious, and when she found out I was accepting tips, she got mad at me and made me go to every table and give the money back. The greatest lesson I learned from that experience was to keep my mouth shut.

"That incident aside, my mom did something very, very brilliant: she refused to be my boss *and* mother, which would have taken away her ability to jump in and nurture me through a hard situation at home. Instead, she let Aunt Ella be the boss and mentor. I've always known her to be a mentor in any situation. Any topic you put in front of her, she has the opinion and the solution and the direction to go in, and usually it's right.

"Aunt Ella taught me you're only as good as your customer's last bite. That last bite can destroy you. If it's unsatisfactory, then it becomes a race to get the situation back to being good again. So you never, ever, ever rest. I don't care what award you win—put it on the wall, look at it, then get back to work. You're never done. Ella is never done. This is her life, this is her culture, this is what we do. Our lives revolve around the restaurant."

Palace Café two years later. Tory loved New Orleans, but he also had wanderlust and spent a few years cooking in Florida, London and the Caribbean before returning to the Brennan fold in 2000 to help us open the Las Vegas restaurant.

When Jamie was battling his cancer, we knew that he would need a successor. A horrible situation, but it had to be dealt with. Ti told us all to keep our eye on Tory. It's probably the only secret the Brennan family ever kept, but we did. After Jamie passed in 2001, we named Tory executive chef in the spring of 2002, and the following year he was nominated for the James Beard Foundation's Rising Star Chef of the Year (in 2013 he would win Best Chef: South). Tory has just been phenomenal during his stints with us over these past twenty-plus years. He is part of our family. He's an extraordinarily accomplished chef and has a personality that is very controlled. There are no high points and low points and all of that stuff. A Rock of Gibraltar. He just makes me feel totally relaxed and comfortable. He teaches, hires people, writes the menu—everything—and of course Ti is looking over his shoulder and watching what he is doing. They work as closely as two peas in a pod.

Prior to Tory's second stint with our company (which has now surpassed fifteen years), we reorganized the businesses so that Ti, Lally, Dottie and I would manage Commander's (allowing Dick to work downtown with his children, Dickie and Lauren, and eventually retire), and Dickie would run Palace Café and other downtown restaurants he was planning. Ti really got into it, learning every inch of the business. She had worked with Emeril and Jamie on the food! the food! the food!, and implemented some new systems in the dining room that have without a doubt made our service the best in the city. I could see more and more that she was doing extremely well running the whole show, and she loved it. She was running it the way I did: You get up in the morning and you go to work. You go home when you're tired. And she learned the financial end of the business to make sure that everything worked out. I can't tell you how proud I am when I see what she and Lally and now Tory have accomplished.

(Ti's not through learning and I'm not through teaching, by the way. Not long ago, she was showing me some new plates that she wanted to introduce at Commander's. They were stylish and practical enough, but I think I blew her mind when I grabbed one of the plates off the stack and threw it on the floor.

"See? It broke into a few big pieces instead of a million small ones. These are perfect." She just looked at me . . .)

By late 2004, Ti, Lally, Alex, Brad and the team were really hitting their stride. They decided to open Café Adelaide and the Swizzle Stick Bar in the new Loews Hotel downtown near the French Quarter. Café Adelaide was to be a sassy downtown cousin to Commander's, evoking Adelaide's over-the-top style and naughty, though always ladylike, joie de vivre. The idea was to do playful modern Creole and to push New Orleans to really get serious again about cocktails. Ti and Lally had gotten a publishing contract to write *In the Land of Cocktails: Recipes and Adventures from the Cocktail Chicks,* a smashing little book heralding the importance of a well-made drink through irreverent stories and escapades. It fit right in with the artisanal spirits and cocktail movement that would soon sweep the country and made me long for a proper stinger, which the doctors had told me was a no-no. Sigh.

Seeing things so well in hand made it fairly easy for me to say "I'm out of here" at the end of that year. I just ran out of steam. It happens, especially when you hit age seventy-nine. Ti estimates that I'd worked about six and a half days a week for more than half a century—thanks, dear, for keeping track—and I felt as though I had given my all, with no regrets. Besides, I had had a few more health setbacks—broken shoulder, broken hip—so the prospect of a peaceful retirement in the home I shared with Dottie in Commander's shadow looked pretty damn inviting.

Alas, it was not to be, at least at the beginning.

Dottie and I enjoyed being there for the team but letting them run the show. Folks from next door would pop in to the house all the time (the passing parade in our never-dull home) wanting advice on this or that, but we were finally getting to slow down a bit.

Then the phone rang.

Dottie's daughter, Brenne, was riding her horse in Kentucky and fell off, unconscious. She'd had a heart attack at age forty-eight. It didn't look good. Dottie and Ti raced to the airport and arrived to find Brenne brain-dead. After a few excruciating days, they came home with her ashes. Devastating. It felt like a knockout sucker punch to the gut.

Brenne had one son, Pepper, who was fourteen. Instinctively, we Brennans did what we do: we circled the wagons. Dottie dove into raising Pepper along with his father, Alvin Baumer, the owner of Baumer Foods. Ti and I were right there as well, and so were my niece, Lauren Brennan Brower, and her husband, George Brower, and Susan and Ralph Brennan. They have children Pepper's age, and they scooped him up every chance they got just as Lynne and Claire Brennan and Georgia Trist had done for my children when I got divorced. If ever there was a kid raised by a village, it's Pepper. I am proud to say that he has turned into a fine young man with no shortage of personality and a true love for business. These days he's working with his father at Baumer Foods, maker of our favorite hot sauce, Crystal.

Ten months after Brenne's death, we were functioning, but barely. Dottie did her stiff upper lip thing, but has truly never been the same. We were coping somehow. It was the end of August 2005 when Ti called and said, "I didn't want to wake you up too early, but I need you to get packed and ready to leave town by two p.m."

"Today?"

"Yes, today. That storm, Katrina, took a turn last night and it's headed our way. I've got rooms for us up in Jackson, Mississippi."

Our city would never be the same.

As New Orleanians we don't focus on Katrina much. We just want to move forward. In fact, we were all so darn glad to get the tenth anniversary of the storm behind us. It was wonderful that the nation and the world wanted to check in and see how we were doing, but most of us didn't want to go through it again. Once was enough.

As Katrina approached, Dottie and I went to Shreveport, Louisiana, to visit a friend while Ti was in Jackson, and Lally was in Florida. After the storm, when it quickly became clear we weren't going home anytime soon, we all made our way to Houston to be near Alex.

I couldn't believe what I was seeing on TV. I was paralyzed. I watched Ti and Lally as they took over trying to find our employees who'd been scattered across the region. In 2005, businesses still only had home phone numbers for most employees, not cell phone numbers. Hard to imagine now. There were no home phones working in New Orleans and no one to answer them if there had been. The logistical nightmares were not to be believed. We lost over 1,800 citizens. Over 200,000 homes were flooded in the region. That's not counting any public buildings or infrastructure. It was biblical in scale.

The federal government was slow in coming to deal with the breached levees that had been built and maintained by federal engineers. But America, and even some folks from across the globe, came and helped. They came by the thousands to help rebuild, to clean out the muck, to save people and animals, or they took our residents into their homes and schools. It was extraordinary to watch. We could never have done it without you, America. We thank you, truly. We know what you did, and we will not forget it.

And what a town Houston was! I don't think ever in the history of our country has one major city been better to another one. My God, everyone in Houston did something. They showed up at the Astrodome to donate clothes and food and to take people into their homes, they wrote checks, they had fundraisers. I am still in awe.

In fact, even before the second hurricane, Rita, hit right on Katrina's heels, Alex was taking us all in, finding places for us and all our employees, who eventually figured out we'd be in Houston. They started contacting us with awful stories of lost homes and jobless families who still had to pay mortgages on their now-ruined homes, pay for somewhere else to stay, and look for jobs.

Amid the chaos, Alex asked Ti what the two of them could do to help. She said she wanted to help our people, meaning all the service industry workers of New Orleans. Alex quickly set up the Hospitality Workers Disaster Relief Fund with the help of the Greater Houston Foundation. The idea was to quickly give out grants of up to $3,000 to people trying to move back to New Orleans, and to have the red tape be minimal. Well, it worked. Alex got started so early that other friends around the country and plenty of people we didn't know threw fundraisers and just sent the money to Alex's fund. He raised and gave away over $1 million.

Wow. The fact that he led that effort in the midst of all that chaos still amazes me and makes me very proud.

The sad truth for us is that Hurricane Rita, which came along just three and a half weeks after Katrina, did Commander's in. If we had been able to go and have the roof fixed right after the first storm, the restaurant would have been OK. But just when we were allowed to go home, Rita struck. Now it was headed for Texas, so there we were again, on the highway looking for somewhere to go. Everyone went west, but we went east and were taken in by dear family friend Bruce McAlpin in Pensacola, Florida. I called his place the Pensacola Ritz. Bruce's home on Bayou Texar, with its beautiful view of the bays, looks like it's torn from the pages of *Architectural Digest*. Even my old friend Lee Bailey had nothing on Bruce when it came to cooking and entertaining. We were lavishly cared for. I didn't want to leave.

Eventually, we ended up back in Houston until we were finally allowed home. Like most New Orleanians, what we thought would be three nights away ended up being two months. And then we returned to a broken city. No electricity in most places. No streetlights or stoplights. No schools open. No refrigerators. We all had to throw them out. You don't even want to hear about that. No mail—for over a year. Just no mail. The obituaries seemed endless. Pages and pages every day. And Army and National Guard tanks and helicopters everywhere. Truly surreal.

The first restaurants to open, which included some of Dickie's and Ralph's, as well as the Swizzle Stick Bar, had to do so with only bottled water.

Commander's was in no shape to reopen. Rita had poured rain into the building since we hadn't been able to get back to fix the damage Katrina had inflicted. And then the mold set in. The long and short of it was that it took thirteen months and $6.5 million for us to reopen. Under the circumstances, with the entire restaurant having to be gutted down to the studs and a serious shortage of every kind of tradesman, that now seems remarkably fast. We were well insured, but it never seemed to be quite enough. We had to start work without complete construction plans and without knowing what it would eventually cost. Or more importantly, whether New Orleans would come back.

We were scared. We'd have been fools not to be. But we never even paused to consider not coming back. No way. Hell no. New Orleans is our town and she needed us as much as we needed her. Ti and Lally say that while we may hold the keys to Commander's, Commander's belongs to New Orleans.

During that period when we were closed for thirteen months, I kind of forgot everything and just did my best to not think about it. I can clearly remember riding my bike as a little girl, but it's very hard for me to remember much about what was happening after the storms. When I think back now on the Commander's reopening in September 2006, it was rather extraordinary. People came in droves. People were ready. They needed some fun in their lives, something happening that was good. It took us a long time to get back to where we'd been, but we did our best because the people needed their city to come back. And as one place after another reopened, the city began to function.

Ti assured me that Tory was a rock throughout this ordeal. He made do. We didn't have the right people at the time. He didn't always have the right supplies—the fish, crabs, crawfish that are the backbone of our menu. But he made do. Every day. The fish men were coming in the back door and saying, "This is all we have. This is all we have." Tory just stood up and made the thing move so smoothly, and that's when I really knew who he was. He stayed with us when he could have gone somewhere else, and he kept pulling his team together.

• • •

With those crises behind us, I was finally able to settle into a comfortable routine at home with Dottie. Since the mid-1980s we've been ensconced next to Commander's in a beautiful house that was a part of the deal when we bought the restaurant. It has high ceilings and gorgeous moldings and wood floors, and thanks to Dottie's style and talent, we are surrounded by lovely things. She went all out in every room except the kitchen, where she said, "Paint it white and lock the door." She knows how to cook but no longer wants to. The room service from Commander's next door is grand. Better still, we send the dirty dishes back.

Our life is not unlike the European way of living above the shop. We have the joy of staying connected to Commander's without the stress of being in charge. What a luxury. The day in, day out is a joy and never dull with the cast of characters that are running around. Lally and Ti and Brad and Pepper are in and out daily, filling me in on the restaurants and their lives. Alex and his wife, Robin, come often, and now my grandchildren, Addie and Lexie, are old enough to come on their own. And Dottie's grandchildren too—Brooke, Ashley, and Tyler. How I treasure them. Add to that Dottie's special beau, Mo, and all my nieces and nephews and extended family and their children, and well, it's everything I could hope for. One day it's Lindsey, Lauren's daughter, stopping by. The next it's

ROOM SERVICE FIT FOR QUEENS

Chef Tory McPhail has the unique—and perhaps ulcer-inducing—task of making sure Ella and Dottie are fed to their liking when they order their nightly meals from the Commander's kitchen. Here's how his team pulls it off:

"The ladies can have anything that they want, but more often than not, they just want really good cooking. Simple stuff, too. I'll pick up the telephone on the sideline when we're slam-packed busy in the kitchen. We may have hundreds of people on the reservations, and one of the ladies will call up and say, 'You know, Tory, I just want a really good redfish po' boy.' And I'm like, OK, they don't want steak or foie gras or caviar or fresh flounder. You know they don't want béarnaise. They just said, 'No, we want seared redfish. Grab your freshest bread. We want Creole tomatoes, we want arugula, we want tartar sauce made with fresh lemons and pickled okra. Do the best fish po' boy you can possibly do.'

"'Yes, ma'am, absolutely.'

So when Ella calls, the world stops spinning, and I tell the sous chef in the middle of service, 'Look, I need two redfish po' boys for Ella and Dottie Brennan.' They say, 'Yes, chef,' and they're on it. They stop what they're doing and tend to the redfish, and when it comes out, it's perfectly seasoned. It's perfectly seared. We gather the rest of the ingredients, and we slice the fresh tomatoes. We season those on both sides. The salad is dressed with fresh arugula. We add the nice mayonnaise to the top of it and paint the bread like you would paint Mom's house. There are no dry little bits where you didn't get around the windows of the house. You go all the way to the edge, perfectly painted so every single bite is exactly perfect.

"So when the ladies get even a simple dish like a seared redfish po' boy, you want them to say, 'It' the best fish po' boy I've ever had in my life.' Same philosophy for a peanut butter and jelly sandwich."

Georgia Trist with grandkids Sophie and Georgia. And the next it's great-neph-
ews Thomas and Geordie coming to pick my brain about business. I revel in
every one of our young tribe.

But I especially revel in Dottie. She takes such good care of me and we have
so much fun together. She treats me like a queen. She has so much of Adelaide's
style and strength, and a generosity and joie de vivre all her own. We laugh, God
we laugh—mostly at ourselves. Dottie is as selfless as they come. Generous to a
fault. And wise. She is the most progressive, least judgmental, kindest person I
know. She is always there for all of us. I admire her more than she'll ever know.
Nah—she probably knows, that's how close we are. We are siblings, though, so
teasing comes with the territory. The kids say we're like a sitcom with all the
one-liners flying back and forth.

When I retired, I was fascinated with television at first. Over the years I'd
heard people talking about sitcoms and game shows and things like that, but I
was never able to watch them because I was seldom at home. And if I was home,
I was being a mom. Well, I started watching TV, got over it very quickly and went
back to reading books. How glorious to read all day, all I want! Some days are
interrupted only by Dottie or my sweet Maria bringing me coffee just the way I
like it. Only coffee and chicory for this gal.

My calendar has quiet built into it at least three days a week. I like quiet. I
want to read, be here by myself. I told Ti, "Mark your calendar for when you
want to sleep. Plan it and do it." Regardless of our schedules, Ti insists on looking in on me at least once a day. She comes in and says, "I can't stay, but I just
want to look at you . . . " and then she's out the door. I finally said, "Why are you
doing this to me? You come in and you leave." She said, "I want to look at you.
Once I see you and you're OK, then I'm gone. I don't have to worry about you."
So she takes a look every day. And if I pass inspection, she's gone.

A few years ago I fell and broke my hip. Now, you know they say that is the
beginning of the end for old ladies, so that's what I thought: time's up. Never
thought I'd live this long anyway. Ti says I haven't done anything to deserve the
good overall health that I have enjoyed. Funny thing is, I didn't die. I was ready
to, I really was. I don't know how to explain that. Dottie and I used to say, "We
can't die now, we need to stick around and see how all this turns out." Well,

LIKE TWO PEAS IN A PALACE

The baby of the six Brennan siblings has long been Ella's best friend, confidant and good-natured caretaker. Here, Dottie reveals some scenes from a "marriage":

"When Ella and I moved in together, I decided that she could not do her hair properly. And she knew that she couldn't do it properly, so she said, 'Well, you do it.' And so, I started doing her hair. Every morning before we went over to the restaurant, she would come into my bathroom and sit down, and I would do her hair and her makeup. And we would get her some clothes to put on and send her on her merry way. And you know, that was just supposed to be for like a week or for special occasions, but as it turned out, I still do it every day!

"I guess people are curious about our relationship because there's a big difference in our age. But there has never ever been a rivalry, and I have always wanted to help her and please her, and she does the same thing for me. I would never ever say or do anything to hurt her. And I am sure that she feels the same way. Consequently, we really don't fight. We can disagree, but we do it as friends."

it's turned out rather well. I'm ready to go whenever it's time, but I just haven't found the exit.

Even though we had round-the-clock nurses a couple of times, I just kept getting better. I finally decided that if I wasn't going to die, I'd better start living again. So I did. I even ventured out to see what my nephew Ralph has done with the beautifully revamped Brennan's on Royal Street. And it's been fun. We're all going to die, but I don't think about it in a fearful way. Maybe that's my Catholic upbringing or just the comforting thought that I will get to be with all the people I love one day.

Or maybe it's just that I've had a damn good time!

13

'Lucky, Lucky Me'

**"LIFE IS JUST A BOWL OF CHERRIES, SO LIVE
AND LAUGH AT IT ALL."**

—LYRICS BY LEW BROWN

On those rare occasions in my childhood when Daddy and Nellie would fuss about something, perhaps his racetrack outings or her stinginess with a pie slice, he'd gently mock her with a sigh and murmur, "Poor, poor me." The more trivial the topic, the deeper the sigh.

I believe it was his way of saying, "Well, if that is all we have to worry about, we're pretty darn fortunate, aren't we?" Now, in the twilight of my life, as I look back on decades and decades and decades of incomparable experiences, I've taken to murmuring my own phrase: "Lucky, lucky me."

I've said this to myself so many times because I truly believe I'm the luckiest woman in the world. I mean that in every way you can imagine. I'm in my home, surrounded by family who take care of me, and I still have longtime friends with whom I can clink glasses and mull over current events. People who no longer see me in the restaurant every day may wonder, "Are you a recluse?" Recluse?

There's a passing parade in my house—and it's catered! Just look at the cooks' shoes lined up outside my back door.

Mind you, I'm not discounting the hours and energy that I've invested in nurturing a family, pursuing a career and helping others better their own lives. Those things are the concrete core of my life, and a source of great pride and satisfaction. My goals were to build a business and take care of my family. I worked at it all my life and achieved that.

Rather, I'm talking about the fortuitous circumstances in which I conducted my life: being born into *this* loving and resourceful family, which happened to steer me into *this* stimulating and rewarding profession in *this* endlessly fascinating city in *this* particularly fertile culinary era in America. I could not have asked for a better launching pad and a richer environment in which to thrive. And the rewards continue to wash over me every time I see a family member or employee or fellow citizen achieve more than they thought possible.

So I say, "Lucky, lucky me."

Now, I would like to end this saga with my views on topics that are dearest to me and offer my hopes for the future. Having hung in there this long, I guess I've learned a thing or two, and I feel pretty good about tomorrow (cue up "What a Wonderful World," please).

MY FAMILY

People give me credit for a lot of things, but one of the things that I am most proud of is how Ti, Lally and Alex have become restaurateurs. They know the business inside and out. They started very young, fell in love with it, and they are still learning to this day. They won't quit—I promise you they couldn't even if they wanted to. I couldn't be more proud of them. Seeing them grow up and fall in love with the same things that I love is rather spectacular. I get tears in my eyes when I look at them.

I know Ti has her dreams. She always wanted to be a writer, but she gave that up when she came into the business. And I know that she mainly did that to take care of me. I know Alex in Houston is hoping his children will go into the business, but you never know. You can't predict that. You just have to say to them that the opportunity is there. I don't think it has to be drudgery like it was for us in the beginning. We didn't have a choice. We didn't have a business, so we had to build one. But once you get it built, you can have a very decent life if you have partners that work together.

We have a lot of young women in our family, and I'm gratified to see some of them entering the hospitality business. It's a place where a woman can have a lot of control and find room to grow, as Ti and Lally have shown. I recall talking to my great-niece Katherine, who was preparing to work at Brennan's on Royal Street after her father, Ralph, and a partner bought the place out of bankruptcy and revamped it. She was nervous and asked me what I thought. I said, "I think you're perfect, and I really mean that. You have the right background. So just be yourself and have confidence in yourself. If you weren't able to do the job, I

TAKE-CHARGE WOMEN

Ella's influence on young women entering the hospitality business has been incalculable, says Lally, who was mentored by her aunt:

"All the young women who have worked with Aunt Ella have stayed connected. They always ask, 'How's she doing? Can we see her? Can we come by?' They feel that way because one of Aunt Ella's missions in life is to make sure that a young woman can take care of herself and not have to rely on somebody else. My generation's ladies grew up not always thinking that way. I found myself smack-dab in that place at an early age, but no way would Aunt Ella let me stay there.

"I've had so many conversations with her, sitting in her office, about the importance of continuing to grow, of reading, of figuring out life. Not just to sit back and let it pass you by. She'd say, 'Let's go, let's figure out what happened and why and how to get to the next place.' She pushed me a lot, and I'm so thankful for it. I've been exposed to things I never would have been exposed to. It's not the path I thought my life was going to take, but I'm kinda glad I took this fork in the road."

wouldn't let you." Now she's been there more than a year, and I hear she is doing a fine job.

Coming up, I never viewed myself or my career through the lens of feminism, but I was one of the very, very few female managers in the hospitality business until things started opening up a bit in the 1990s. (I later learned that a Madame Begue had run a restaurant on Decatur Street in the mid to late 1800s, so I tip my hat to a fellow local pioneer.) I couldn't have been more fortunate being in a family business and being my own boss. I didn't know what the hell I was doing when I started, but they let me learn on the job. I think it worked out pretty well.

Still, there were times . . .

All my life the men in my family would say, "Get so-and-so on the phone." I'd shoot back: "Why the hell don't *you* do it? Are your fingers broken?" and ignore them. That's why I advised Ti to never learn how to type or take dictation, because she might end up doing those tasks for somebody the rest of her life. Ha! Today she runs her own show. I wish she'd been around in 1955 to help me deal with those damn bankers.

Have I achieved all the success that I'd hoped for? Basically, yes. I haven't reached for goals that were not achievable. There were opportunities that I didn't take advantage of that maybe I should have, but I don't regret it. I'm a very satisfied person day to day.

I tell all of the next generation of Brennans that they really have to put themselves into a position where they can take care of themselves. You never know what's going to happen in the world, especially with jobs, so if you can get your own business, at least you can control what you're doing while other stuff is going on. So I would like them to be in business for themselves. My granddaughters can go to Brennan's of Houston if that's what they want to do, and Dottie's children can come to Commander's if they like. If they choose to do something different, they have to be prepared to take care of themselves. They're young enough now that that message has to be put across to them. They're not old enough to know that's what they have to do.

The most important things I want are for them to be good citizens and good parents, to lead a decent life and accept their responsibility to the community.

MY PROFESSION

The world changes so much. Even ridiculously simple things change. But somehow, down in my deepest feelings, I think that people will always want to go out and have dinner with friends—enjoy the conversation and the food and the wine. (Oh, the wine! One of the most civilized things that we have left on this earth.) It's an ultra-privilege. I just don't see anything happening that would want to make people take a pill for nourishment instead of dining. At least for the next fifty years or so.

The future of hospitality engages my mind all the time. There have been so many changes on every front. We've had change in the past, but nothing like this. People are now talking about how we should handle salaries and wages. I don't remember the public ever getting involved in that before. It's not that you have any secrets, but people now talk openly about how much you pay and whom you hired and why you hired them. That's very different from what it used to be, and most of the time I think it's for the better.

I hope the role of restaurateur doesn't change a hell of a lot. To me it means hospitality, and hospitality is at the root of our business. To be successful you have to really love and care for people. If you don't want to be around them, if you're a loner, then don't go into this business. And you have to accept that it's not a nine-to-five job, it's a way of life. It's demanding, but so wonderful. If you have to work for a living, the restaurant biz is a delightful way to do it.

When it comes to food, it's a different world out there—what you serve, how it's prepared, what's good for you. They came out with this thing the other day that said processed meat gives you cancer. That may be true, but God . . . the next thing you know it's going to be celery. I hadn't had eggs in years because they said it was bad, but now I do. I am so damn glad! I *love* eggs, as you already know. Could eat them every day. And now the food police have put them back on the approved list. I wanted to hug Julia Child years ago when "they" were warning us not to eat butter, or eggs, or red wine, and on and on. Julia said in the middle of all that in her inimitable style, "There's nothing wrong with a little butter." God love her. My point isn't that everything is wrong, it's that it's happening so fast. How do you work all those changes into your everyday life? Was it right yesterday? Is it right today? Just constant change.

There are things on the menu today that thirty or forty years ago you'd never have dreamt of serving. Today it may be organ meats—I call them innards. I saw *The New York Times* recently wrote about chicken feet. Awful-looking dish, but now they're doing it all over the place.

You just have to be willing to say, "OK, let's try that," and make the leap (within reason). I thought I had eaten eggs every way a person could, and then a couple years ago our chef, Tory, comes up with the five-hour egg. After trying version after version, he cooked an egg for 5 hours in the immersion cooker at 141 degrees. Not $4\frac{1}{2}$ hours at 143 degrees. Nope—5 hours at 141 degrees. All I can tell you is it comes out with the consistency of flan and an intense egg flavor. Heaven. Then he serves it different ways, sometimes with mushroom and leeks—I love that one. By God, he can cook. Lucky, lucky me.

I think there's a lot more to explore in food. Every time I eat an ethnic cuisine I've never had, I get so excited and I think, "What can we learn from this?" I see the culinary world going more toward a global cuisine cooked locally. I think the cuisines of China and Asia and the Pacific Islands are just now coming to our attention. People all over the globe are getting ideas and expressing and exporting them.

Of course, unfettered creativity can take you down some strange paths. Molecular cuisine, for instance. In my opinion, when practiced in a restaurant it's absurd. It's absolutely to the point of being funny, it's so bad. Now, if they want to explore different tastes and different products they want people to eat, that's all right in the laboratory. But that shouldn't happen in a dining room. I think people go into a dining room to eat a great meal with great friends and enjoy themselves. I think this experimentation, like you're in a laboratory, is ridiculous.

I'll never forget the time that Ti took me and Dottie to a very famous place that was known for its experimental cooking. "This is a very modern restaurant, very different—and don't you dare laugh," Ti said. They came out with this foie gras in a test tube that you had to suck out of the container. Now, I love foie gras, but this presentation just turned me off like crazy. I had no idea what to do. It seemed so silly. Ti kept saying, "No, no, no, don't touch it. Our waiter is going to tell you how to eat it. Don't touch it."

"OK, so how do you do it? How do you suck foie gras out of a tube? And *why*, for God's sake?"

I was trying to be on good behavior but we all just collapsed in hysterics. Check, please . . .

I think it's unbelievable what these people are willing and wanting to do. But it's not ready for the public. Don't put it out there. *You* may think it's ready for the public, but the public isn't ready for it.

What the public will always be ready for is food cooked by talented people who are well grounded in the basics. I wish I had done a culinary school for New Orleans, but now Ti, Dickie and his brother-in-law, George Brower, are trying to do it with their New Orleans Culinary and Hospitality Institute, which is just getting off the ground as of this writing. I think that New Orleans should be the culinary and hospitality capital of America, just the way Detroit is—or was— with automobiles. That's what I want. Everyone in the business ought to know about the magic we have here and how they can build on it for the future. Learn what we have done, what is possible to do and what more needs to be done.

MY CITY

Most people eat to live, but in New Orleans we live to eat. It's a town where you get up in the morning and check your lunch plans right away. Then at lunch the first thing you ask is, "Where are you going to dinner tonight? Who are you going to dinner with?" At dinner you say, "Do you have any plans for tomorrow? No? Well let's go to lunch." And repeat. New Orleanians' lives revolve around who they'll be eating with, where they'll be eating and what they'll be having. That's what the city is about—and what makes my profession so challenging and rewarding.

Needless to say, I was made for this place, and this place was made for me. Lucky, lucky me. It's a city where the people simply enjoy living. They work hard, they do everything they can to nurture solid families. New Orleans is a family city. I can take you all over this town, and you will see families gathering and doing things together. No matter how much or how little money you have, you eat well because everybody goes fishing and crabbing and crawfishing, and that leads to great feasts in the backyard, usually accompanied by musicians. And the greatest cooks in the world are to be found working every day in the home kitchens of New Orleans—that's who our city's chefs compete against, not each other! I think my fellow citizens have the best life in the world.

And it's getting better, especially after Katrina. New Orleans is growing as a high-tech center. I don't know a thing about technology, but I know its impact on the economy here is very real. Our hospitals are growing and doing very well. We're breaking ground on more hotels. Our restaurant scene is so incredibly vibrant, with hundreds more places operating now than before Katrina. We've recently redone some of our old theaters, and that's boosted the cultural scene. We're attracting young, creative and ambitious entrepreneurs to move here. All of this makes our economy more diverse and stable and less dependent on the energy and tourism industries.

Still, there are some things that make me mad about this city, especially how we've let down some of those family standards. Too many families don't have a situation where the mother and father teach their kids the rules, the rules, the rules. When I was growing up, every family taught proper behavior, and I promise you, you did *not* break the rules. If you broke them at school, your parents would get called away from their jobs to deal with it—and there would be consequences for the offender. Today I don't see that nearly as much. I see too many neglected children, and children without a purpose.

I think certain people have become very selfish—interested only in themselves and the hell with everyone else. I know quite a few. So many of our politicians are mean and nasty, and we've lost the "civil" part of civilization. Some of this ugliness has been going on for a long time, especially in politics. But when it got down to governing, it used to be that you had faith that a leader would emerge. That faith has been shaken for me.

Our school system is getting better, but it's still not as great as it should be. We're late on this, but I'm excited that things are happening.

We need to do something about poverty in this city. Things are good for many, but not for the guy who's down, down, down. And poverty contributes to crime, which remains a headache for all.

So yes, there are many things we need to keep working on, but I can't imagine living anywhere else in the world. I see other towns and I think, "Boy, there ain't going to be a jazz band marching down *this* street." And it's so sad because music brings joy to life and to the community. It excites people and breaks the rules. But lucky, lucky me, we have the best music right here. In my backyard. I've got to tell you, I don't want a restaurant where a jazz band can't come marching through.

AFTERWORD

Saloon in the Sky

"THE MEMORY OF THINGS GONE IS IMPORTANT TO A JAZZ MUSICIAN."
—LOUIS ARMSTRONG

My brother Owen loved the word "saloon." In his mind, it was a great gathering place for interesting people who were just enjoying themselves, and that's what he had in mind when he ran the Old Absinthe House on Bourbon Street. So when five of our family members and friends died in that short span between the mid-1950s and early 1960s, we got to talking about how, when I die, I'm going to go to the "Saloon in the Sky." Because I know that's where Owen and Adelaide are going to be.

(When I see Owen I'm going to give him a great big hug. Then I'm going to punch him in the gut for leaving me with that mess. Adelaide most certainly will make an entrance according to her own schedule.)

My brothers John and Dick will be there, and Mom and Daddy and Brenne, and I'll see John's wife, Claire, now that she's there. There will be people with magic in their hands, like Leona Nichols. And only the people I love get in. Looking forward to swapping stories again with Charlie Gresham and Ralph Alexis and Lindy Boggs. And a bunch of others. You know who you are.

So if there's a place to be, that's where they'll be. We'll meet in the Saloon in the Sky and have a marvelous time. The idea just caught on and now I get teased about it a lot.

What's it feel like? It's a great, wonderful bar—a combination of what the Old Absinthe House used to be, Café Lafitte and '21' in New York. Not too fancy, but very comfortable. Open all the time. There'll be good conversation and, of course, music. "Fats" Pichon is on the piano playing "How Deep Is the Ocean." Judy Garland is singing "Happy Days are Here Again." And I've always said if Louis Armstrong and Ella Fitzgerald aren't there, I'm not going. There are a lot of musicians I love, but Louie gets to me in a special way. I hope he won't mind playing "Do You Know What It Means to Miss New Orleans?" one more time, with Ella chiming in. Or maybe a thousand more times . . .

Drinks just flow. The cocktail before dinner will have to be a Sazerac—absinthe, rye and cognac with bitters and sugar. We'll have a couple of them. In the Saloon in the Sky there are no hangovers.

There will be food—New Orleans food. Eggs and sautéed bananas for sure. Maybe Jamie Shannon is riding his motorcycle in and out of the kitchen, waving to Paul Prudhomme. I love the great restaurants of Paris and New York, but it's different here. And with that food, there will be some great wines of course. Château Margaux and Pontet-Canet were always my favorite Bordeaux. And some Burgundies, both red and white. I really love great wine, and we'll be well stocked.

We'll need after-dinner drinks too. Truth of the matter is, when it gets late in the evening, I'll have a stinger or two. I can't drink 'em today but I sure love 'em. John taught me to drink them—white crème de menthe and brandy. I think everybody in the Navy was drinking them at that time, and now he'll join me in another round. Or two. Wow, what a lovely drink for after dinner.

And for your information, I'm not sitting on a stool telling people what to do. I'm just having a good time. There's no BOD—Brennan On Duty. In the Saloon in the Sky, nobody works. You just enjoy.

Ella Brennan in her home (photo courtesy of Jerry Siegel).